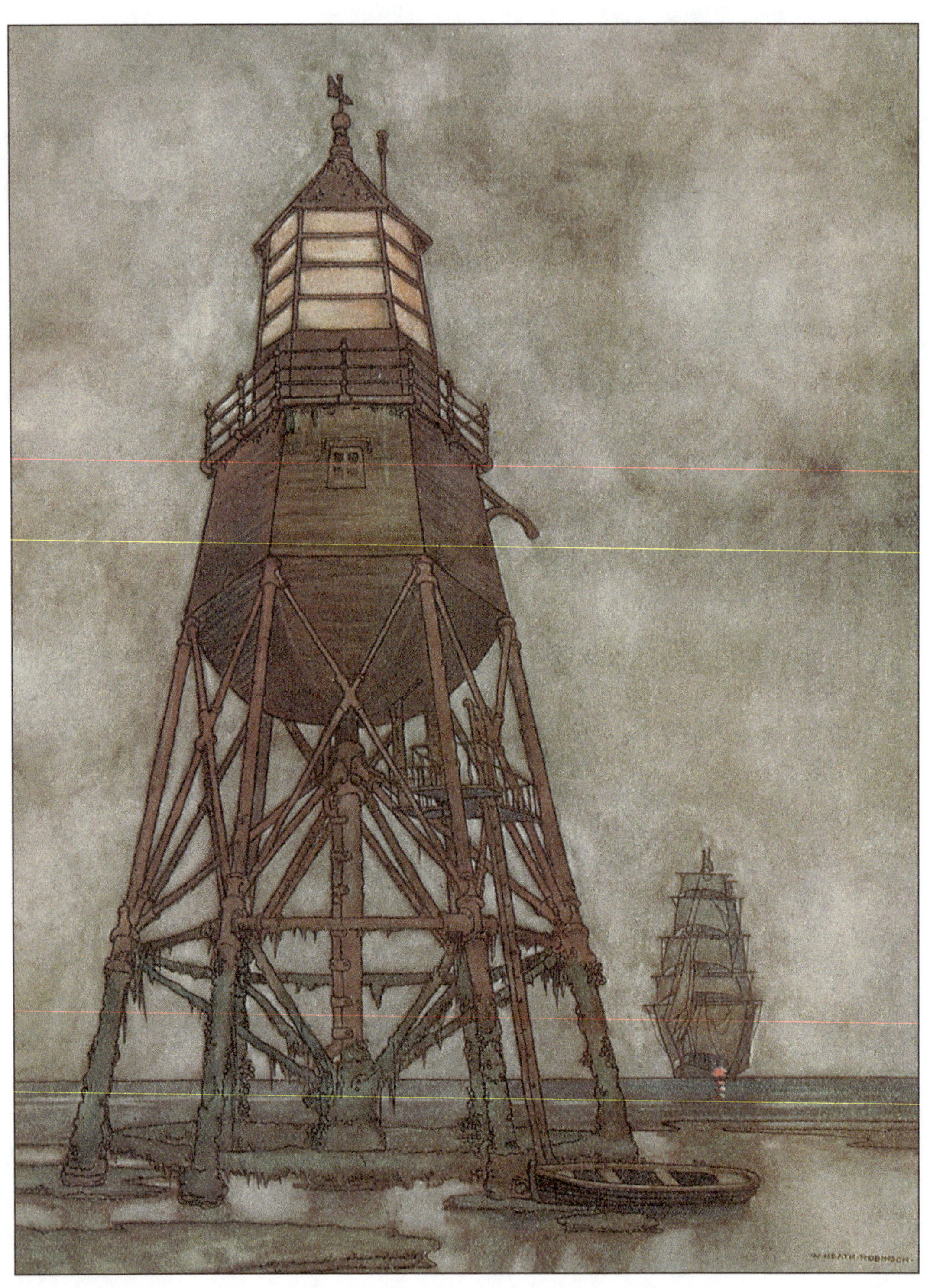

The coastwise lights of England

A Song of the English, 1909

Golden Age Illustrations of
W. Heath Robinson

Selected and Edited by Jeff A. Menges

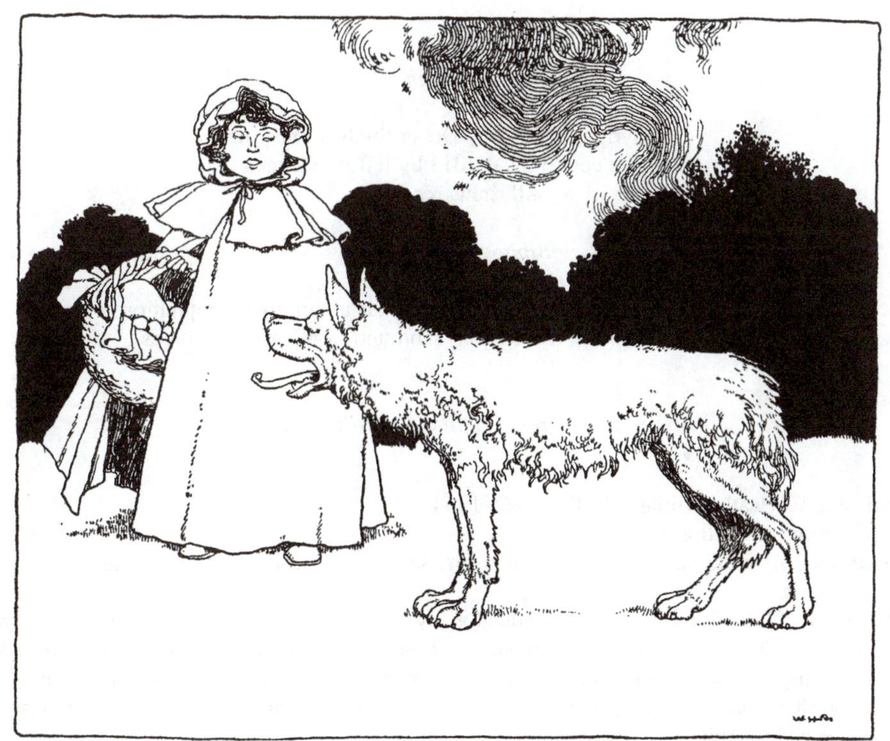

Dover Publications, Inc., Mineola, New York

Copyright

Bibliographical Note

This Dover edition, first published in 2013, is an original compilation of W. Heath Robinson illustrations reprinted from various sources.

Library of Congress Cataloging-in-Publication Data

Robinson, W. Heath (William Heath), 1872–1944.
[Illustrations. Selections]
Golden age illustrations of W. Heath Robinson / selected and edited by Jeff A. Menges.
pages cm
Summary: "Edited and with an Introduction by an expert on Golden Age illustrators, this anthology is the first full-scale treatment of Robinson's early output. More than 100 Art Nouveau-inspired illustrations feature images from fairy tales, children's literature, and the works of Shakespeare, Kipling, and Poe, many in full glorious color."— Provided by publisher.
Includes bibliographical references.
ISBN-13: 978-0-486-49793-8 (pbk.)
ISBN-10: 0-486-49793-3
1. Robinson, W. Heath (William Heath), 1872–1944.—Themes, motives. I. Menges, Jeff A., editor of compilation. II. Title.
NC978.5.R63A4 2013
741.6092—dc23

2013016055

Printed in Canada
49793304 2025
www.doverpublications.com

Contents

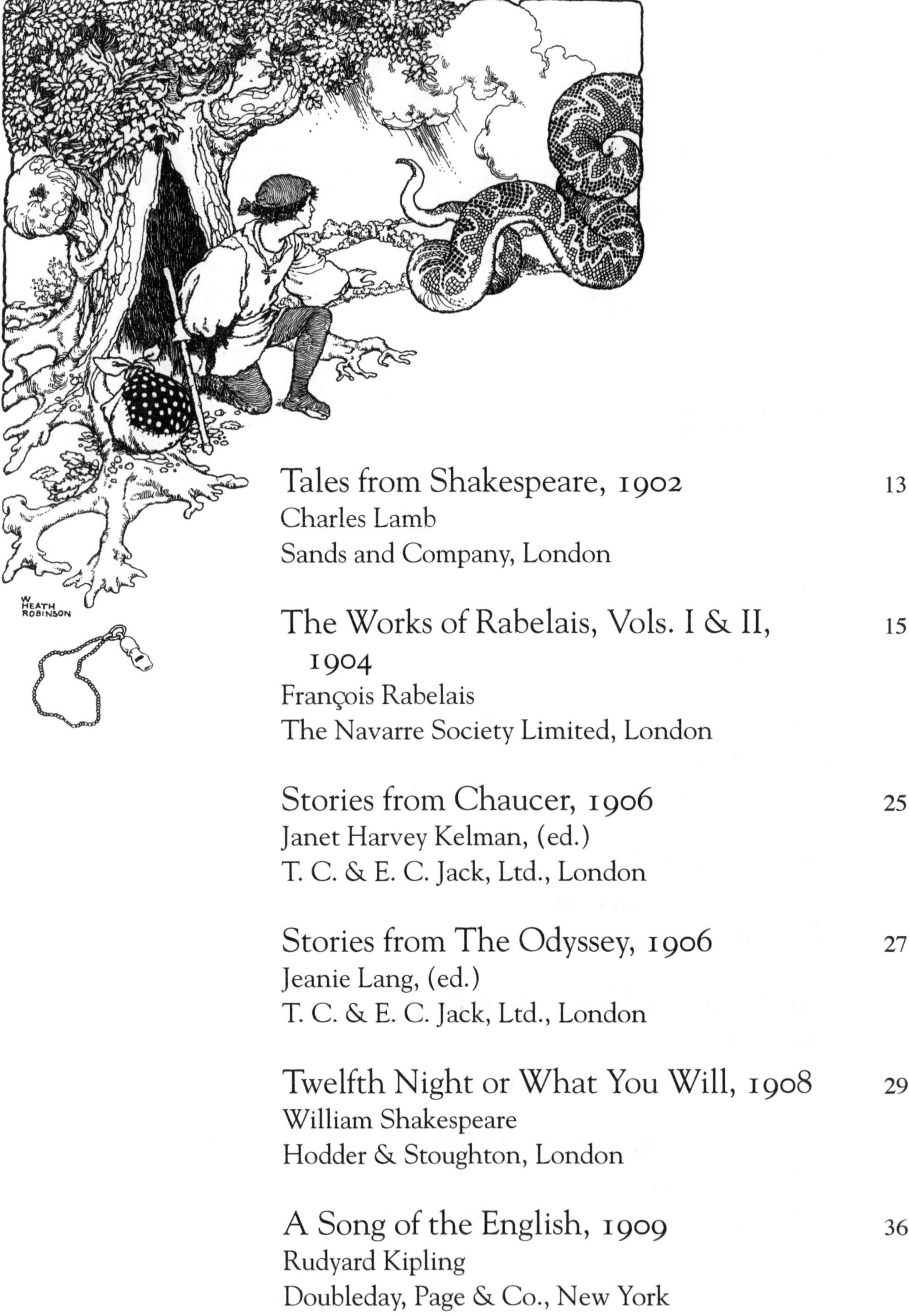
W HEATH ROBINSON

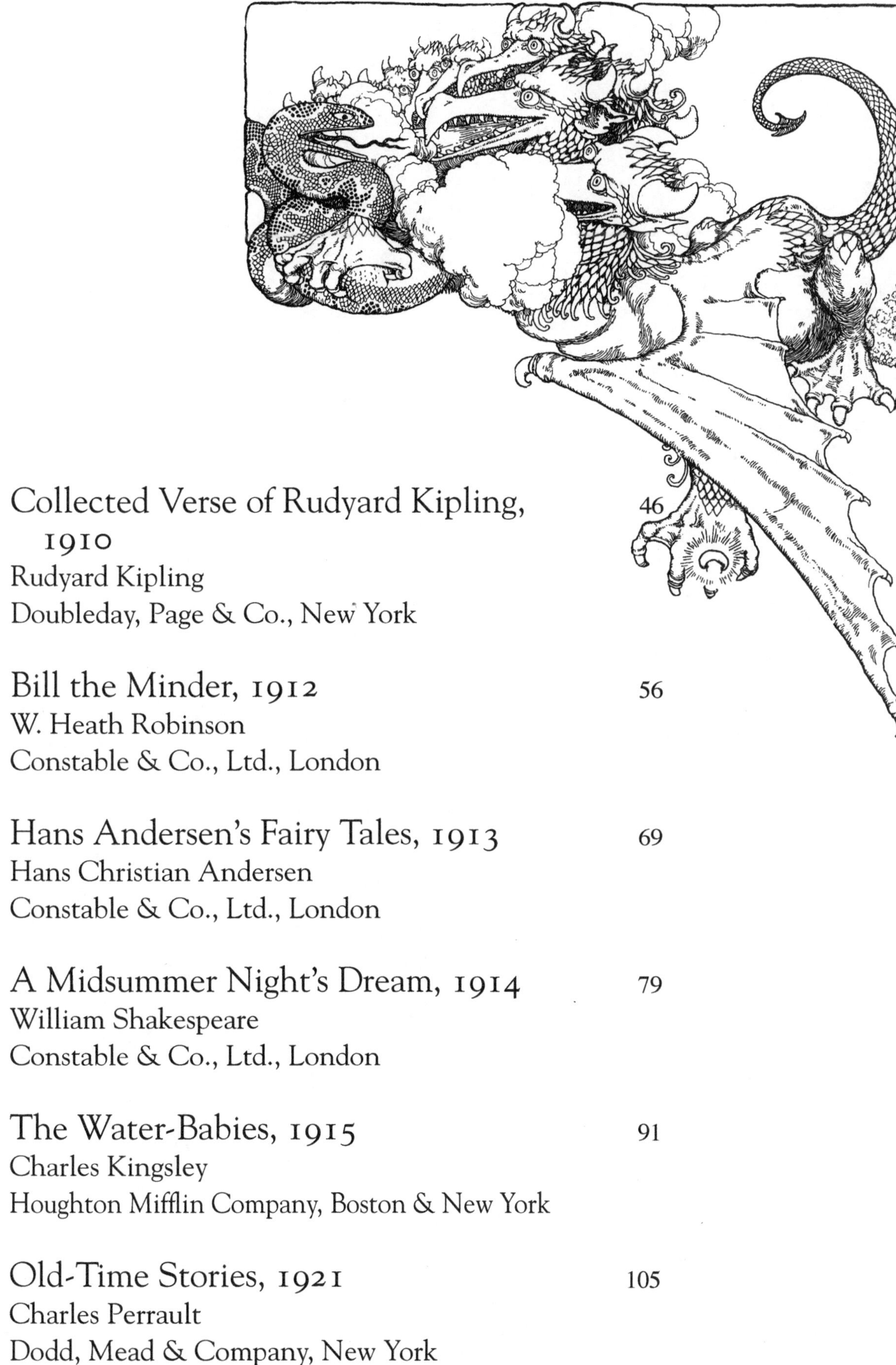

Introduction

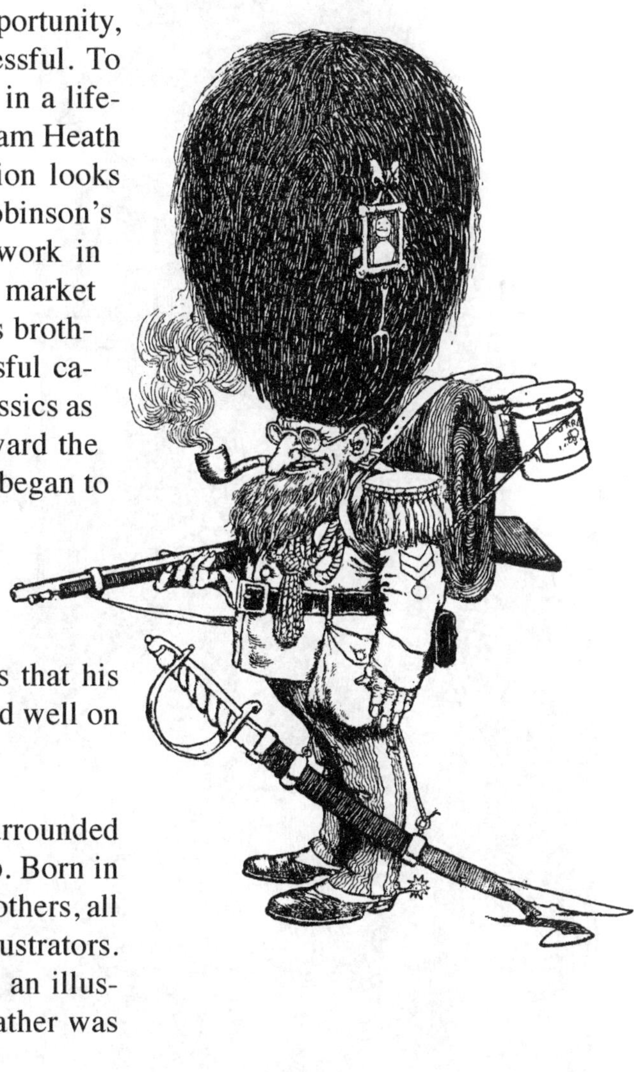

It takes a combination of talent, opportunity, and timing for an artist to be successful. To achieve this success more than once in a lifetime is highly improbable—yet William Heath Robinson did just that. This collection looks at the earlier stage in W. Heath Robinson's career in illustration, primarily his work in books. When the illustrated book market was booming, Robinson followed his brothers Thomas and Charles into successful careers in illustration by working on classics as well as a few books of his own. Toward the 1920s, when the needs of publishers began to change, his humor and clever cartooning were still much in demand. These became the dominant form of artistic expression during his later career. This volume, however, shows that his more traditional illustrations can stand well on their own.

William Heath Robinson was surrounded by creative individuals as he grew up. Born in 1872, he was the youngest of three brothers, all of whom would become successful illustrators. Their father, Thomas Robinson, was an illustrator and engraver, and their grandfather was an engraver as well. William Heath (Heath was his mother's maiden name) spent some time at the Islington School of Art and at the Royal Academy, and hoped to take a slightly different creative path. In fact, he attempted to support himself as a landscape painter. After a year it became evident that if he wanted to sustain himself, he would have a better chance following his brothers into illustration. By 1897 he was off to a good start, getting line work in four different books of children's stories. The quality and design of his earliest work took on a number of different looks as he continued to search for his own style.

By 1900, the Art Nouveau style had made a greater influence on him than the engravings of a generation before. His imagery began to take on a fullness and a more pol-

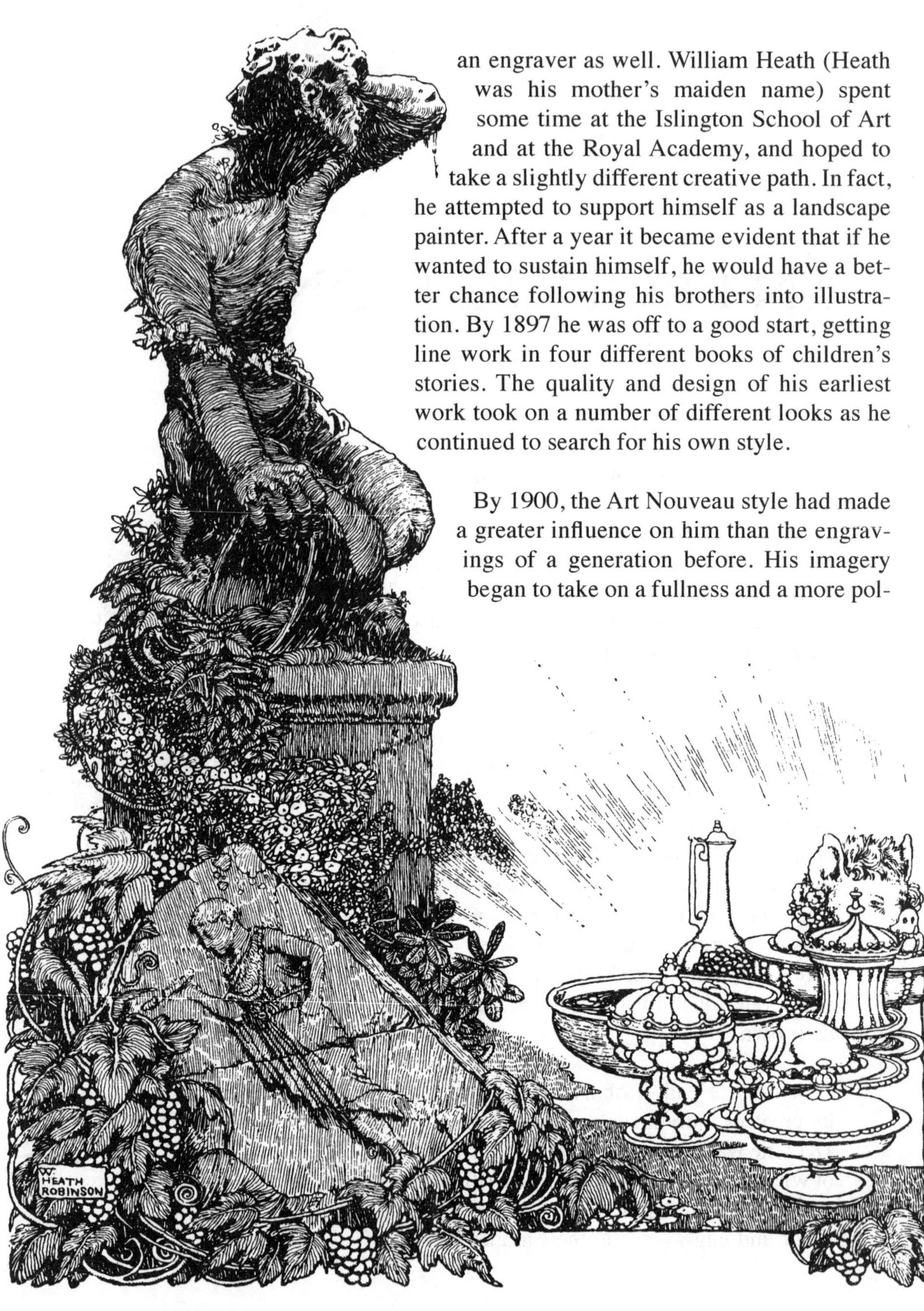

ished appearance. The work of Aubrey Beardsley was an early influence on Robinson. Like Beardsley, Robinson also made very effective usage of large solid areas, which often complemented other images filled with incredible complexities of line work. Broad areas of clean white extended an image of sea, sky, or a clean wall; whereas solid blacks might appear as an inky pool or the deep shadows of a lush forest. That same year, Robinson produced more than one hundred ink drawings for *The Poems of Edgar Allan Poe*. He followed that project with a self-authored book in 1902—*The Adventures of Uncle Lubin*. *Uncle Lubin* showed a facet of W. Heath Robinson's talent not always seen in work such as *The Poems of Edgar Allan Poe:* his ability to portray humor. The humor and fantasy depicted in *The Adventures of Uncle Lubin* sparked something that Robinson would revisit throughout the rest of his career. A 1904 edition of a two-volume set of *Rabelais* (with a staggering 250 drawings) continues to show this humorous approach to caricatures and situations.

However, in a crushing turn of events, the large, well-received edition of *Rabelais* that should have bolstered Robinson's career instead became a financial nightmare for him. The publisher declared bankruptcy before Robinson had been paid for months

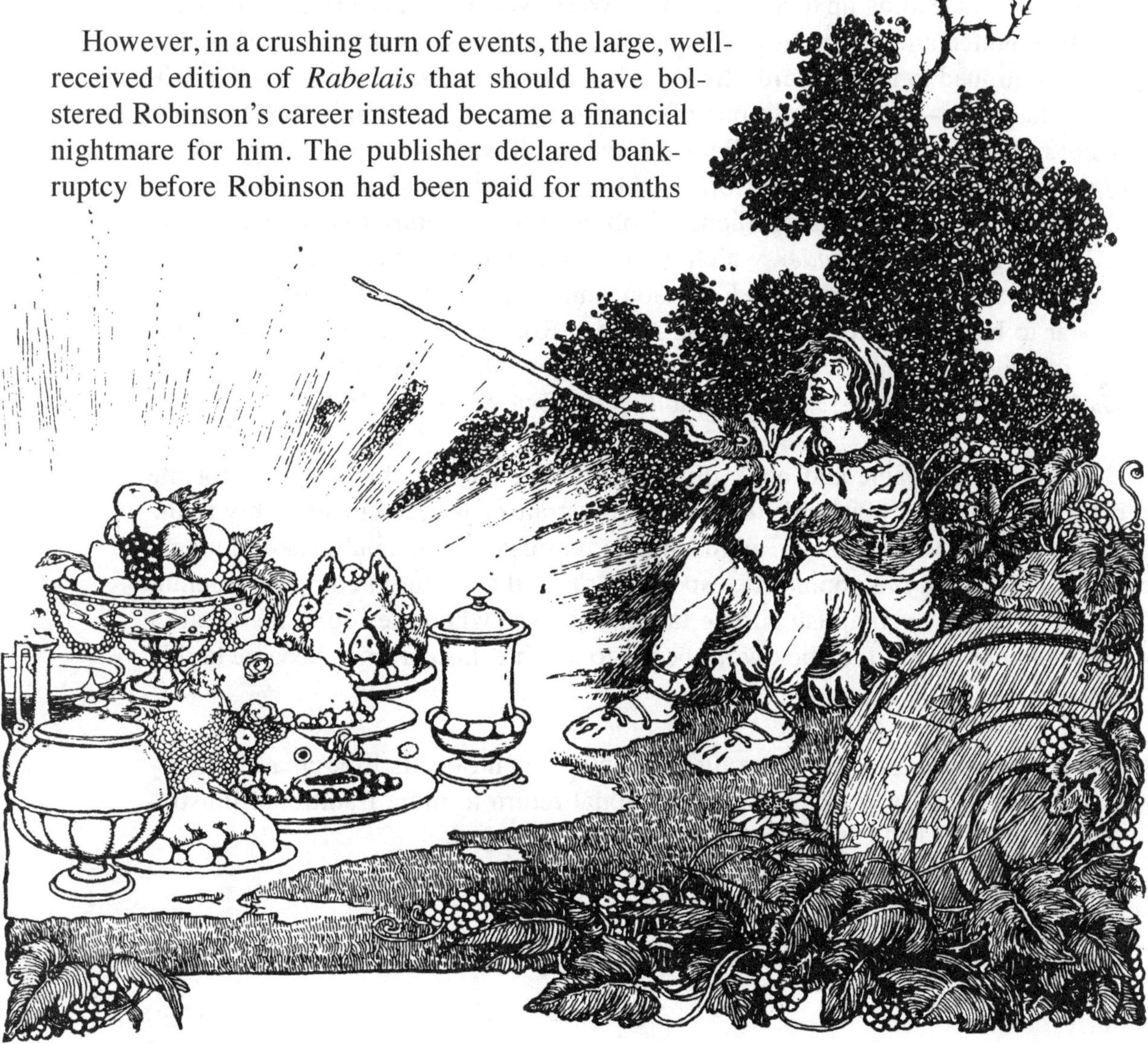

and months of work. Needing to secure income quickly, Robinson found work with weekly magazines that showcased his humorous work, which greatly boosted his career.

In the middle of the century's first decade—as color printing began to take hold in both book and magazine publishing, Robinson once again had to adjust his style to remain resilient in the changing industry. After a few early explorations with a variety of books and periodicals, Robinson got his first large "gift book" assignment: to illustrate Shakespeare's *Twelfth Night* in 1908. The book's first edition featured forty tipped-in color plates. While his sense of humor was largely put aside for this assignment, his love for landscape work was allowed to flourish.

In the years leading up to and including World War I, William Heath Robinson can be counted among the best of the Golden Age book illustrators. Robinson's work continued to lean toward titles that had a more mature audience—like that of Shakespeare—with his editions of *Twelfth Night* in 1908 and *A Midsummer Night's Dream* in 1912. Two brilliant volumes of illustrations for Kipling, *A Song of the English* in 1909 and *The Collected Verse of Rudyard Kipling* in 1910, were also geared toward a mature audience. Robinson would return to his own writing in 1912 with *Bill the Minder,* which directly led to more juvenile-themed work. The book was a true success for Robinson, and the publishers of children's books appear to have noticed. After *Bill the Minder,* Robinson completed assignments that included *Andersen's Fairy Tales* in 1913, an edition of Charles Kingsley's *The Water-Babies* in 1915, and Perrault's *Old-Time Stories* in 1921.

Although magazine and book illustration remained his chief support for the rest of his career, Robinson's focus as an illustrator changed considerably in the 1920s. During World War I, Robinson's humorous cartoons, published in magazines, grew wildly in popularity, especially those that featured complex machinery designed to accomplish simple tasks. This was where he found his greatest achievement, and as the book work began to decline, his cartoons became highly coveted.

Robinson continued to be productive until the end of his life, creating many books of humorous work, with an occasional return to more traditional illustration. He died in 1944 at the age of 72.

JEFF A. MENGES
December 2012

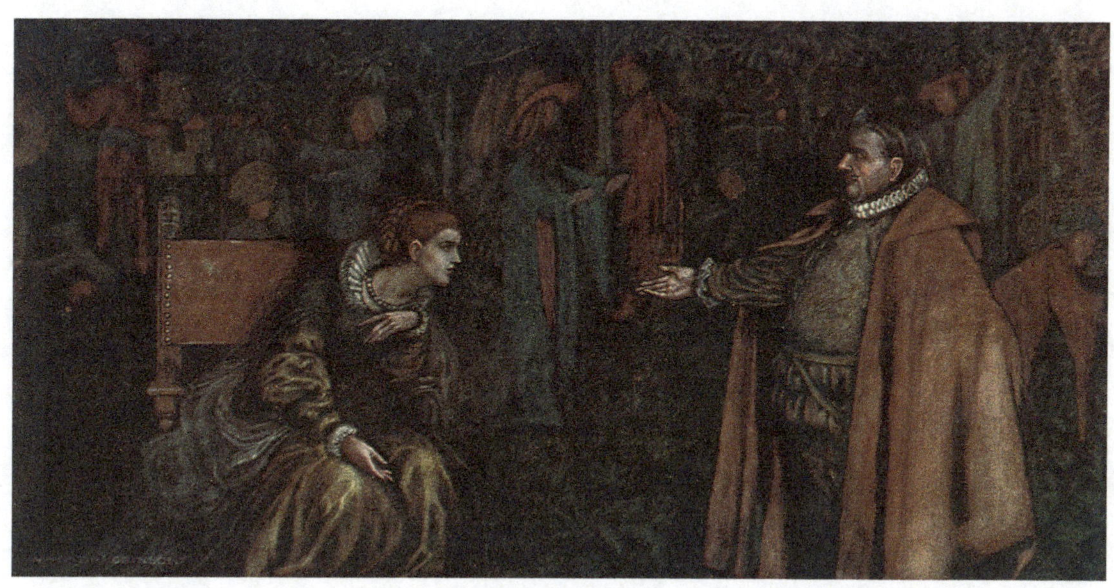

Act I. Scene V.
Sir Toby. Give me faith, say I

Twelfth Night or What You Will, 1908

Frontmatter Illustrations

The Plates

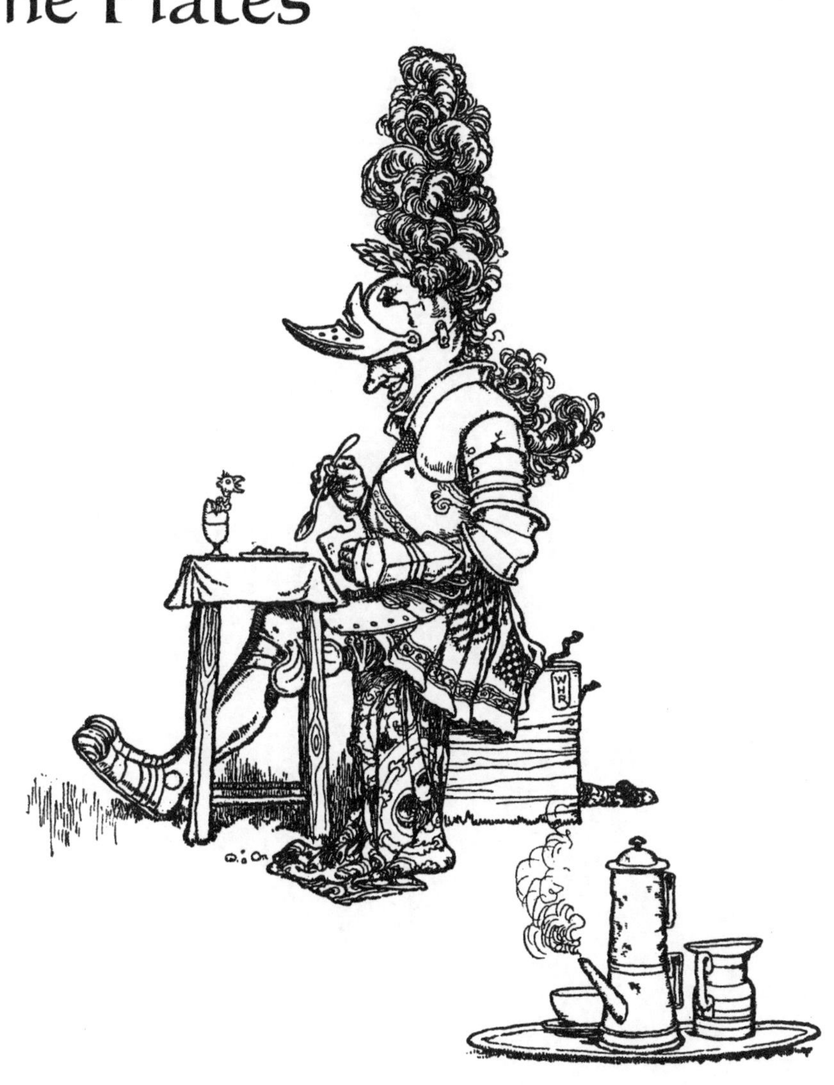

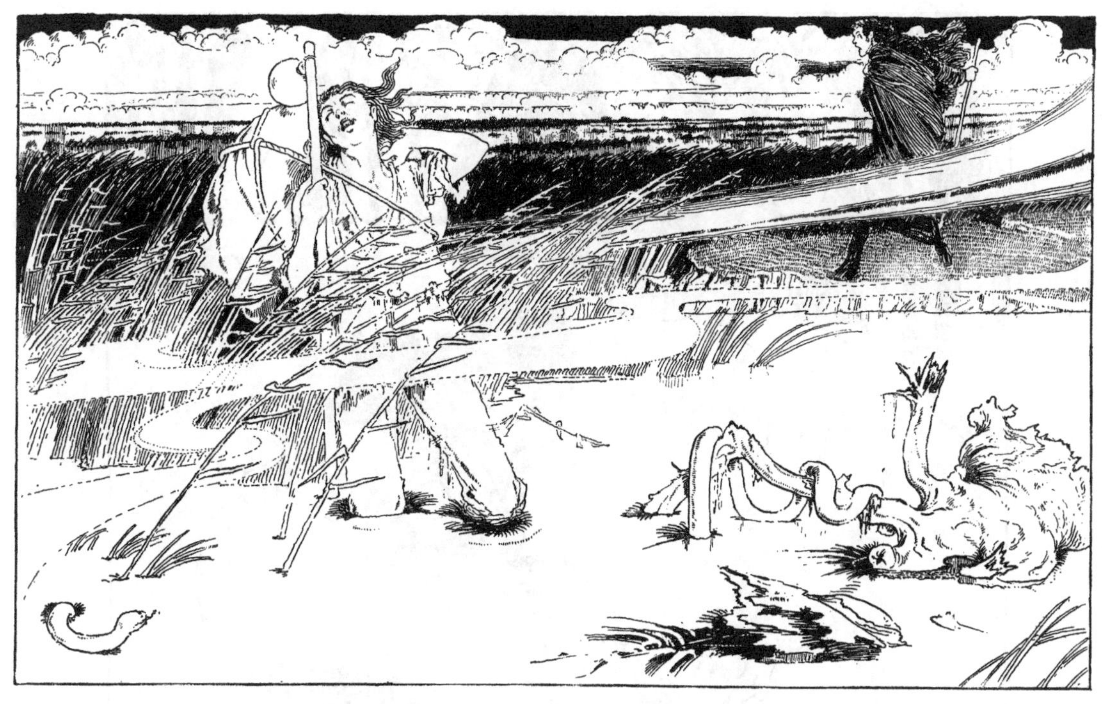

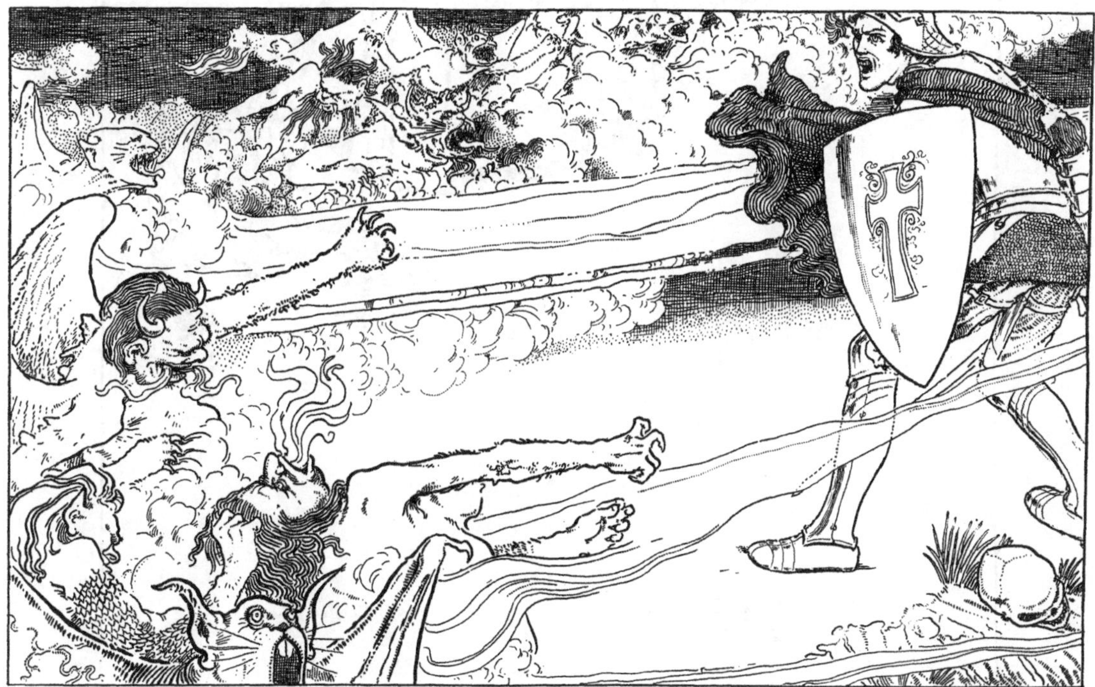

Top. Wherefore Christian was left to tumble in the slough of despond alone
Bottom. So they gave back, and came no further

THE PILGRIM'S PROGRESS, 1897

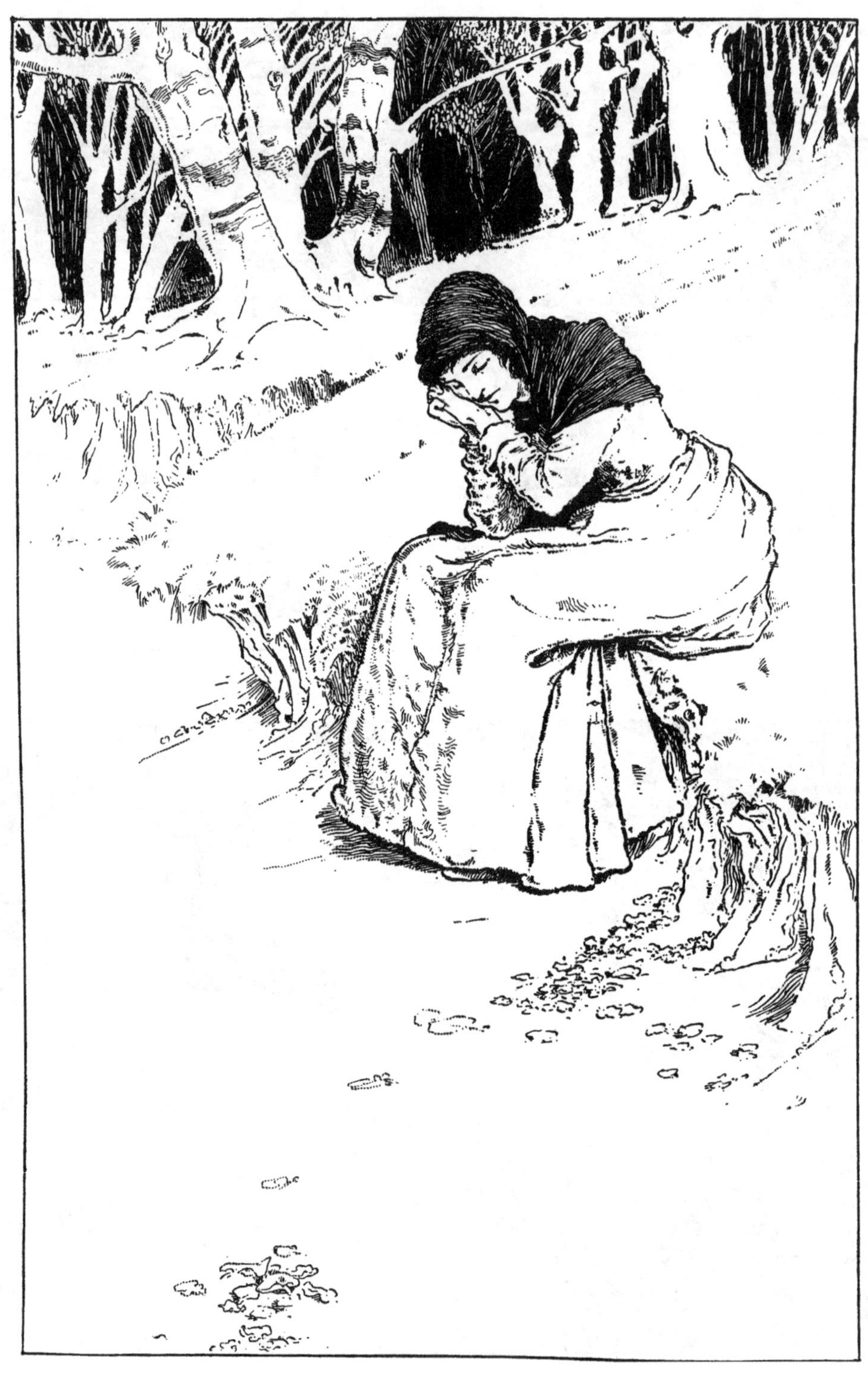

"I was a-dreamed that I sat all alone in a solitary place"

The Pilgrim's Progress, 1897

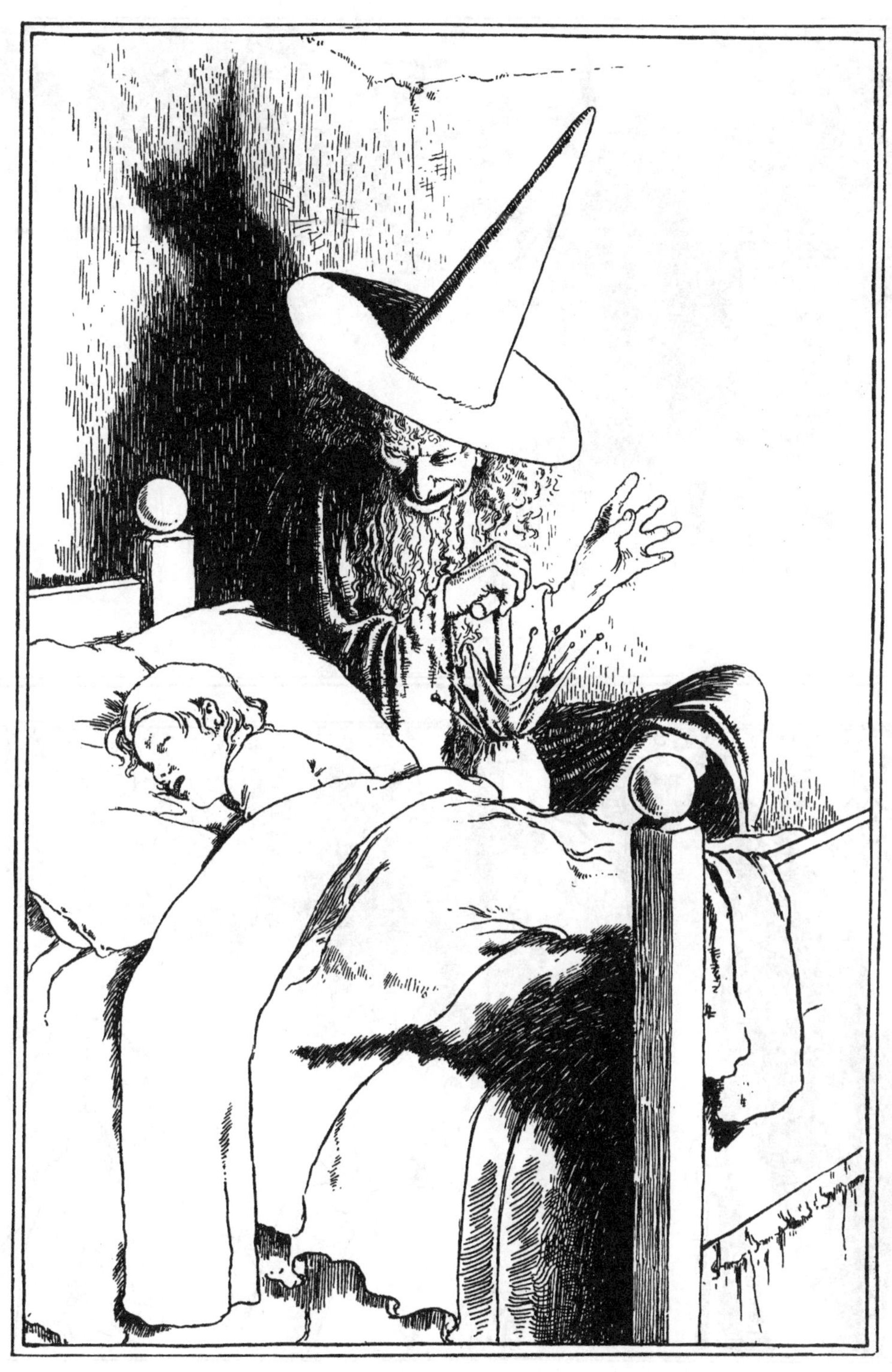

The Dustman

DANISH FAIRY TALES AND LEGENDS, 1897

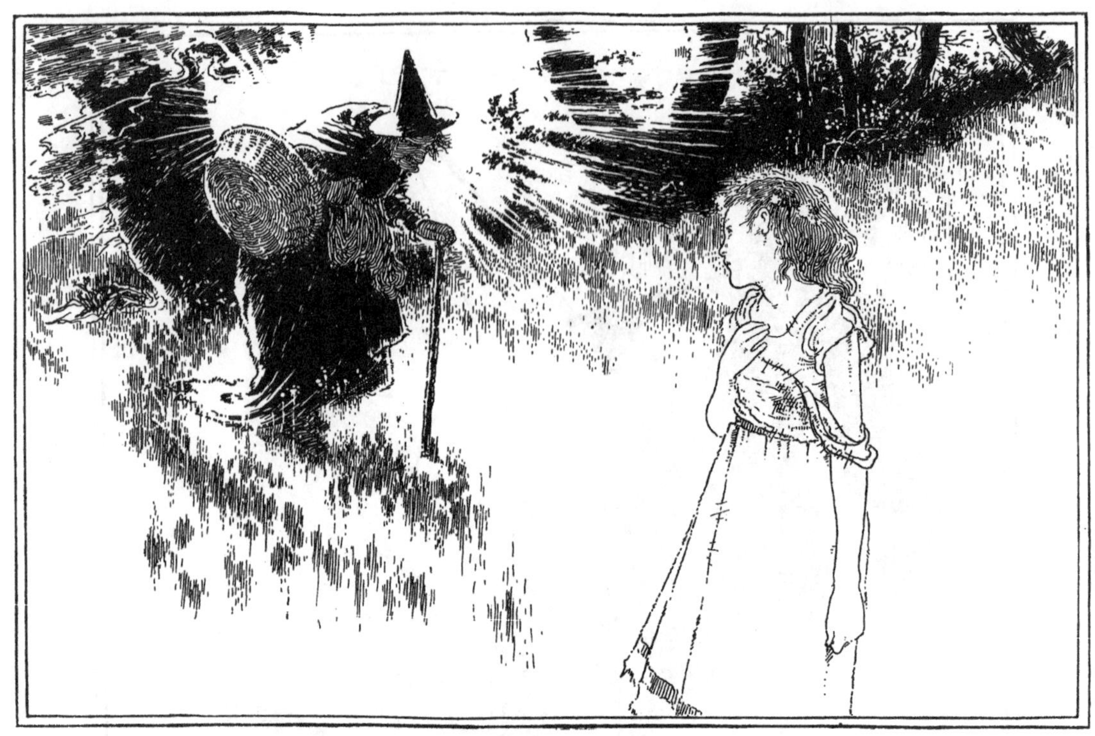

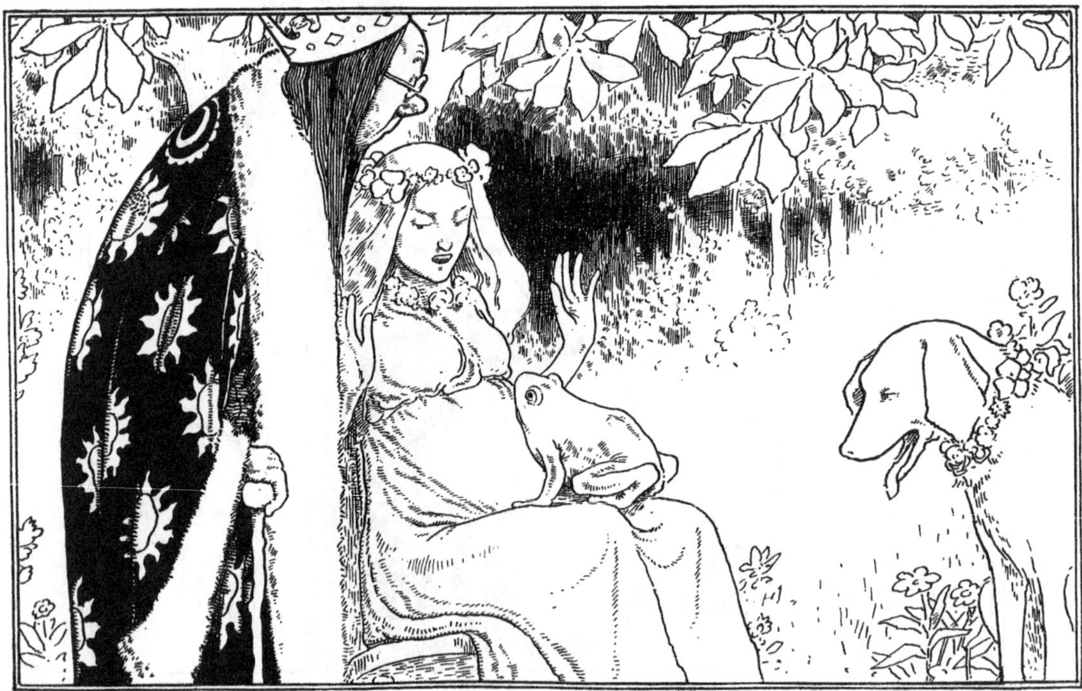

Top. She walked on a little farther and met an old woman with a basket full of berries
Bottom. . . . all at once he made a little side-long jump into the lap of the Princess

DANISH FAIRY TALES AND LEGENDS, 1897

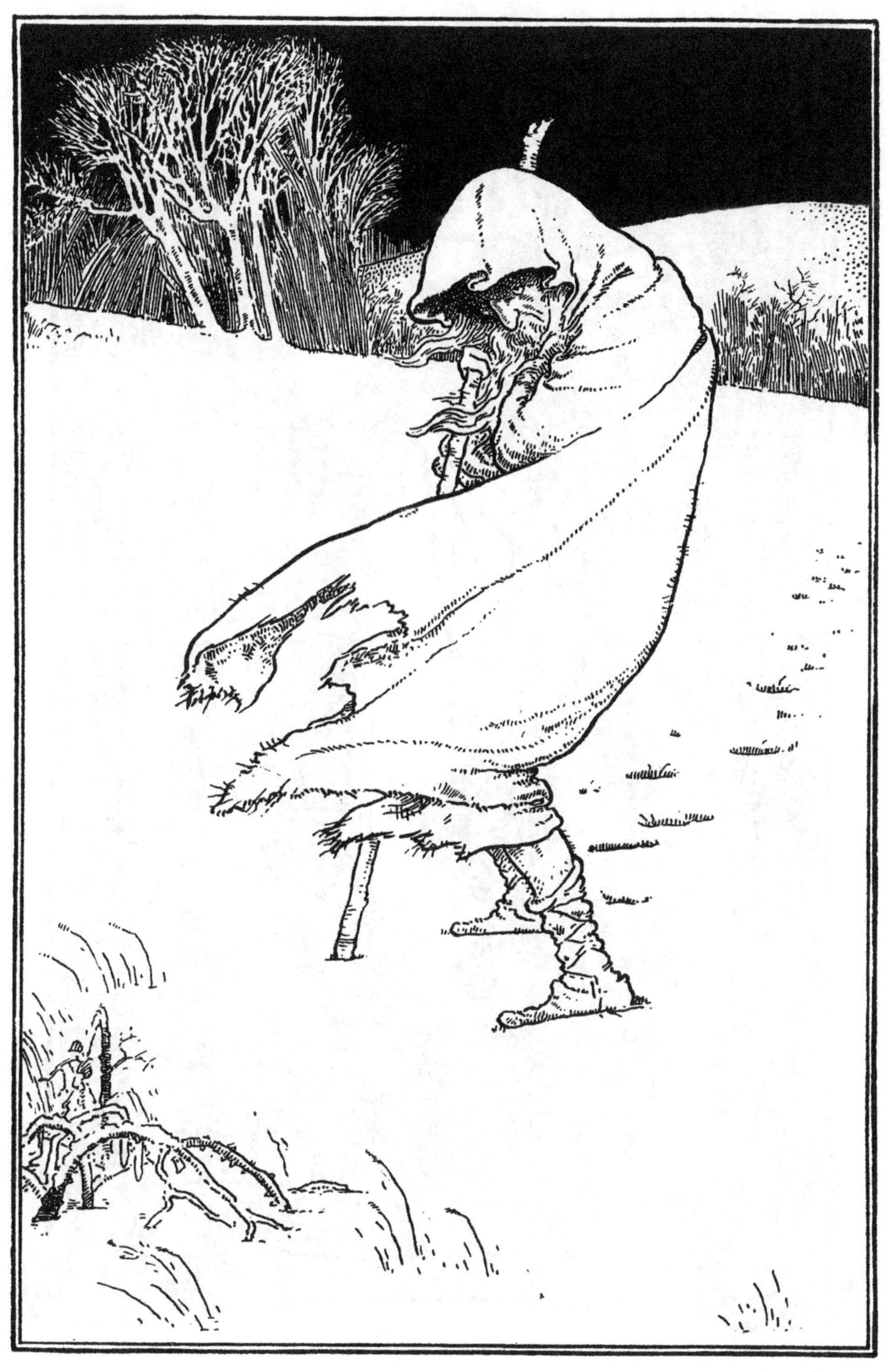

. . . and the wind blew keen and cutting into the wanderer's face

Danish Fairy Tales and Legends, 1897

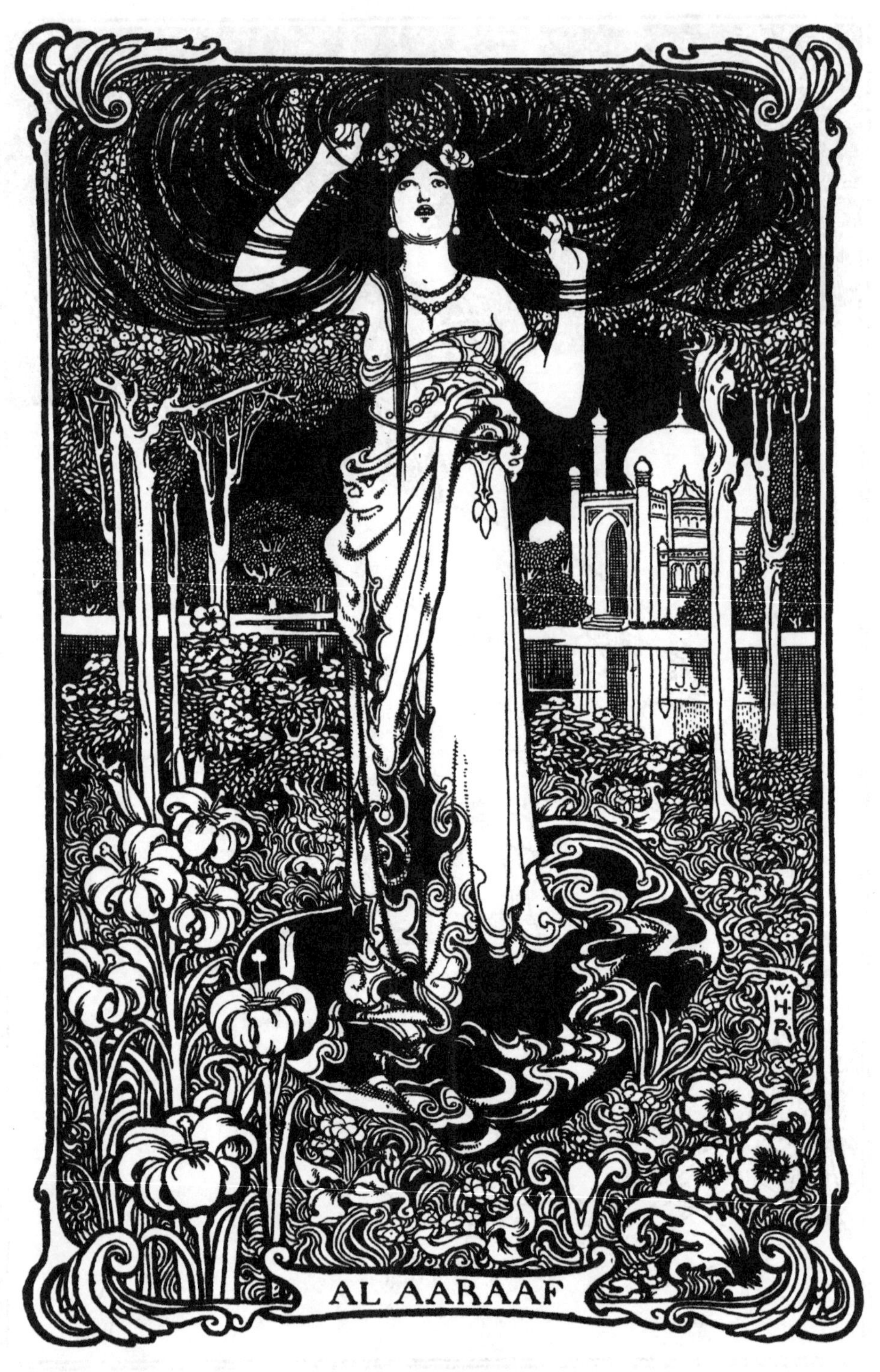

Al Aaraaf

The Poems of Edgar Allan Poe, 1900

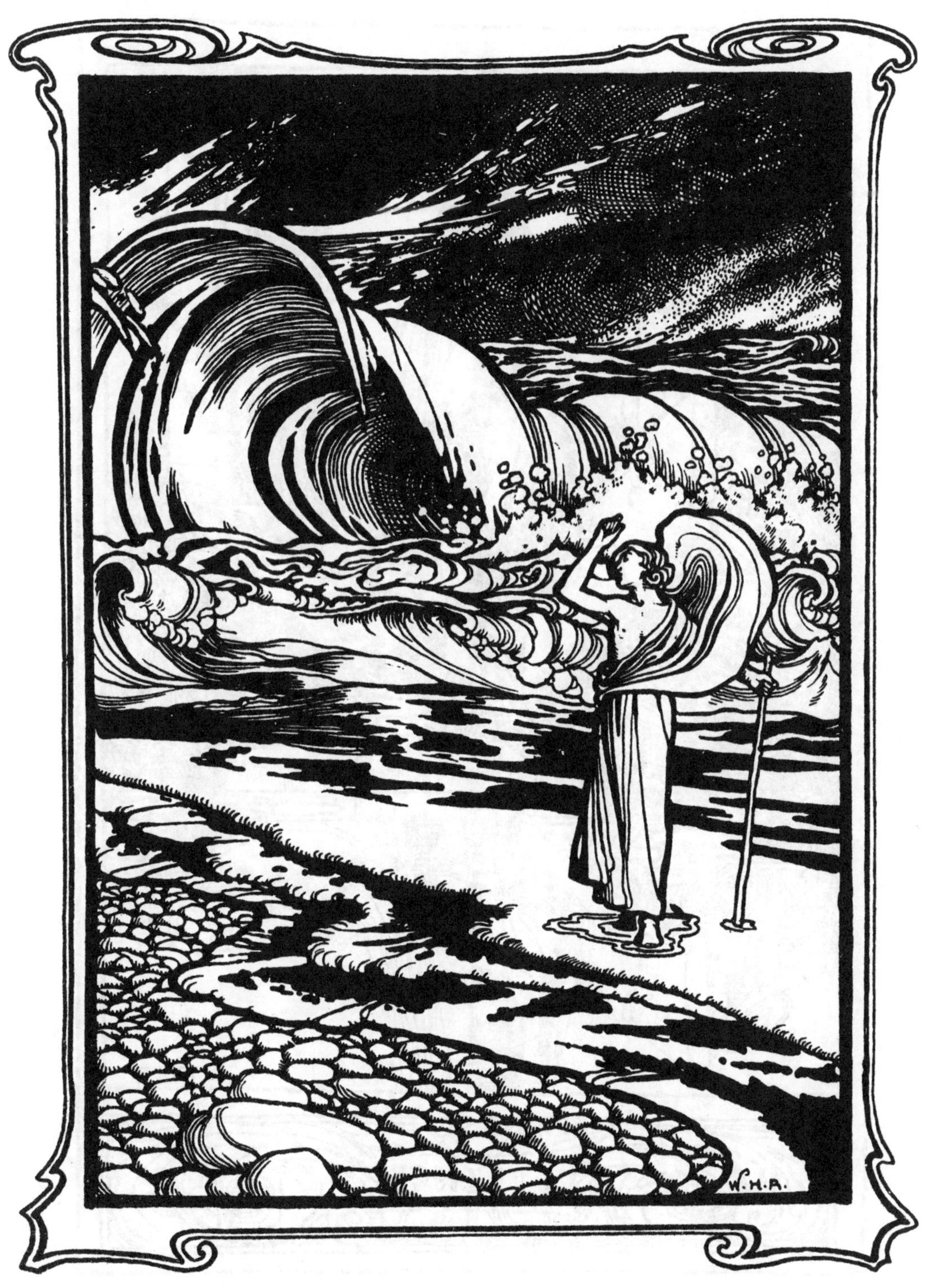

A Dream within a Dream

The Poems of Edgar Allan Poe, 1900

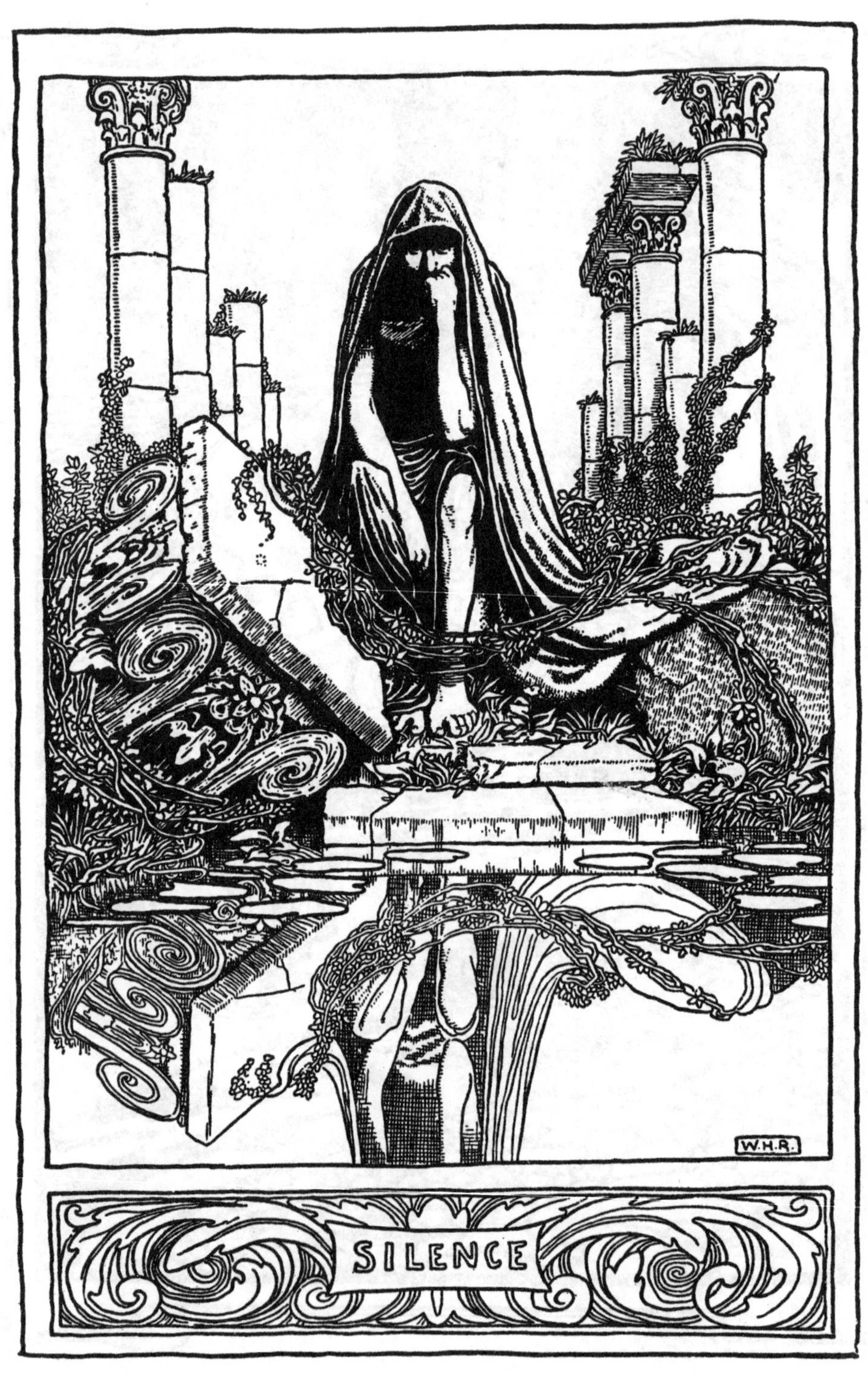

Silence

The Poems of Edgar Allan Poe, 1900

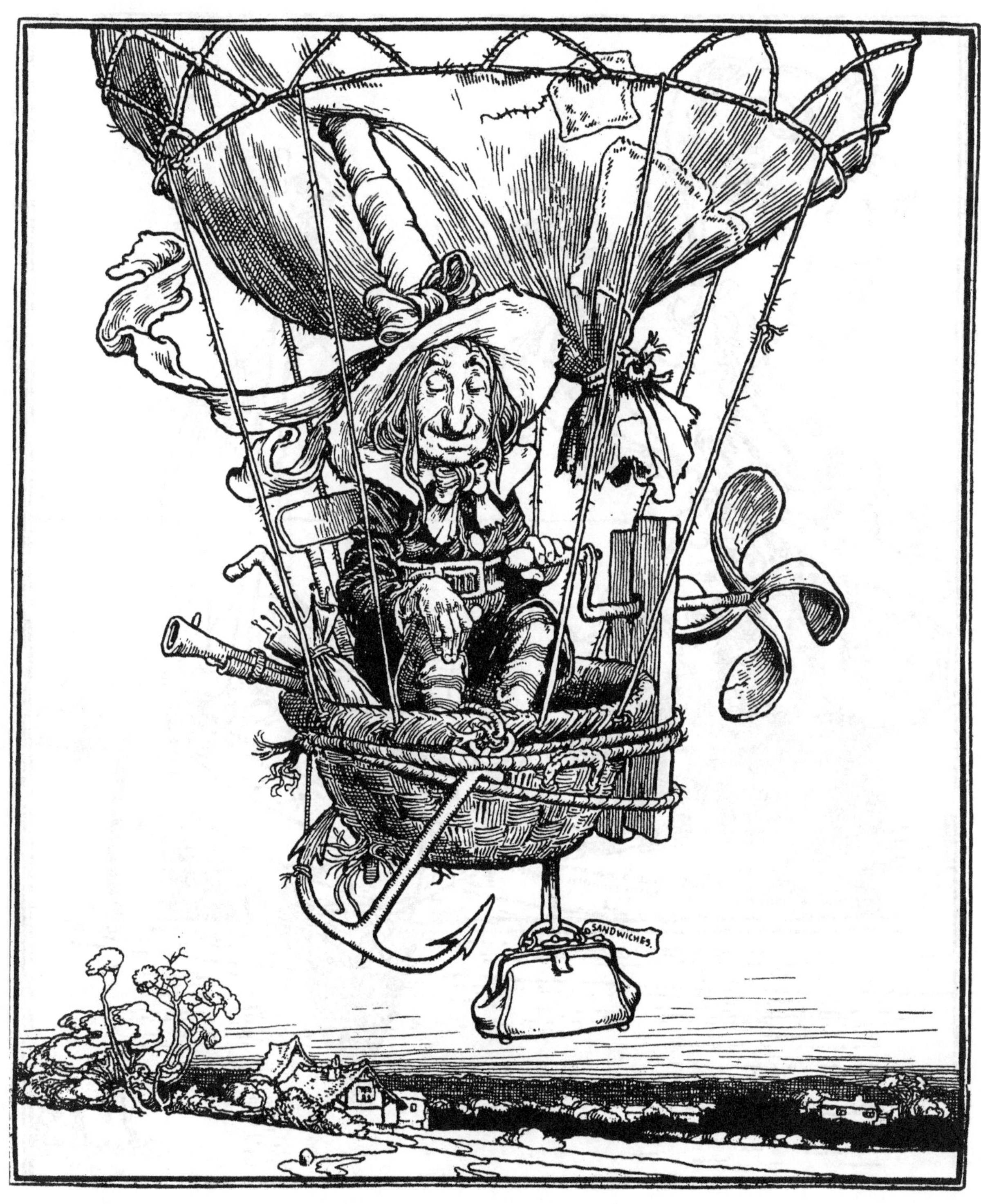

The Air-Ship

The Adventures of Uncle Lubin, 1902

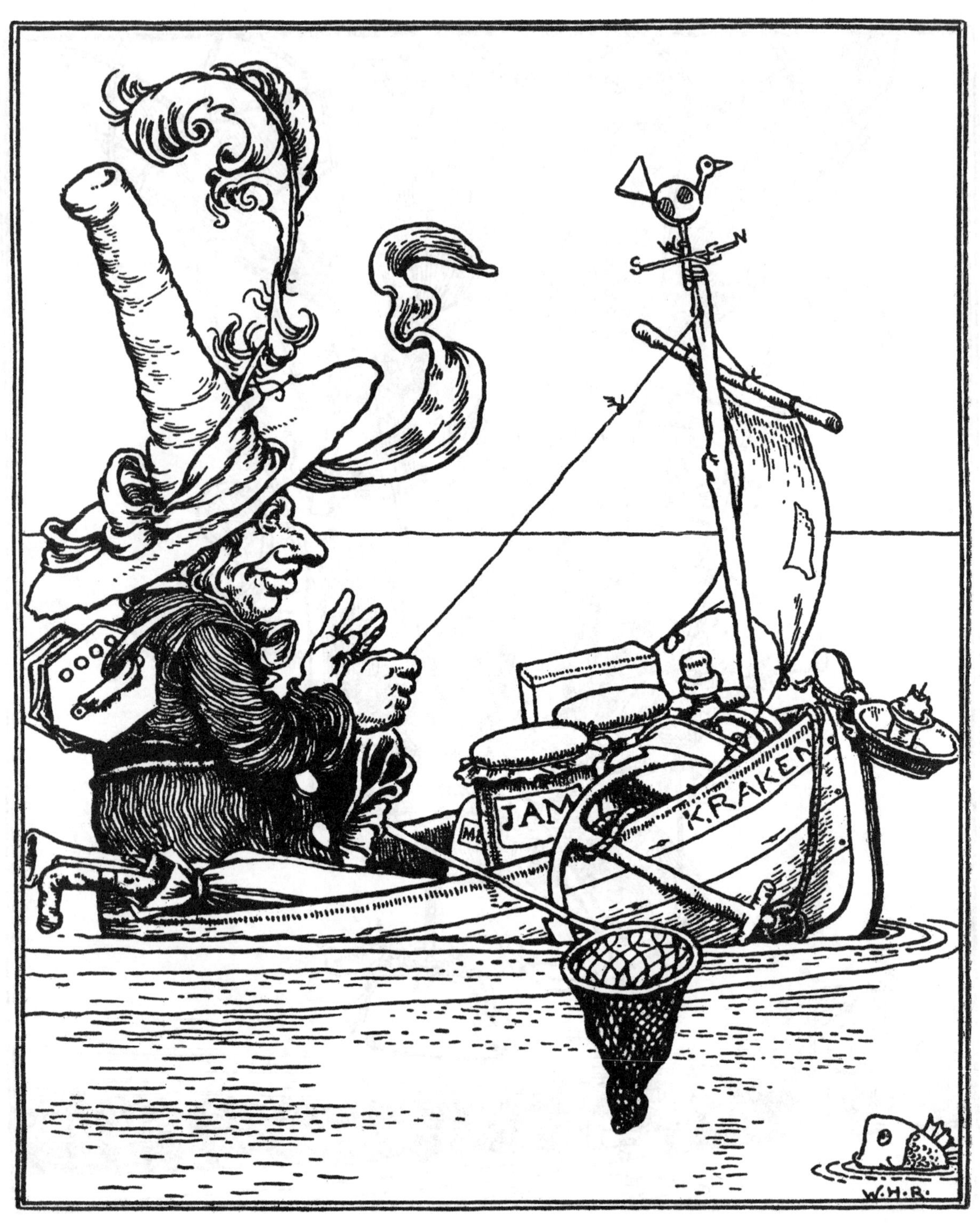

Vammadopper

The Adventures of Uncle Lubin, 1902

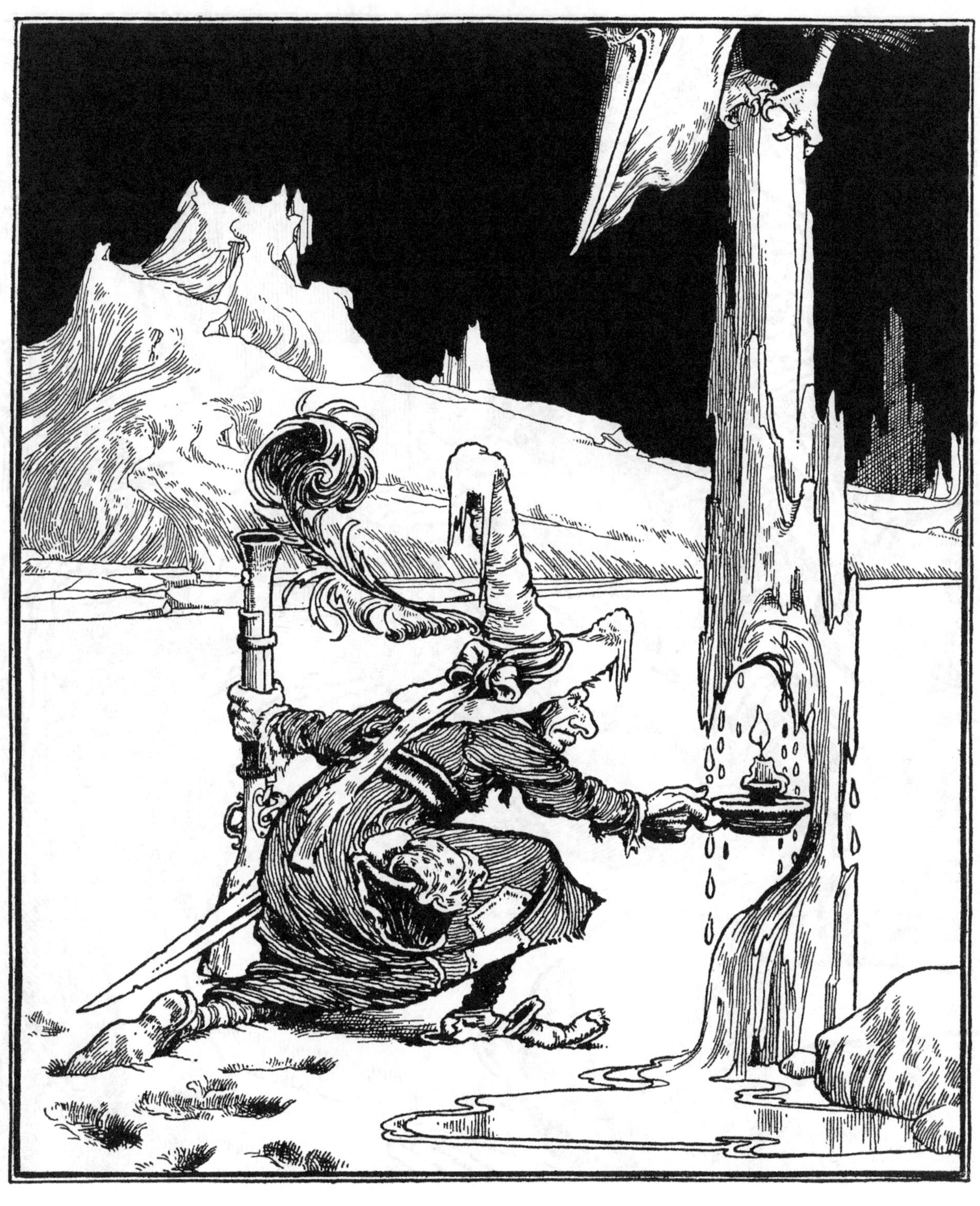

The Candle and the Iceberg

The Adventures of Uncle Lubin, 1902

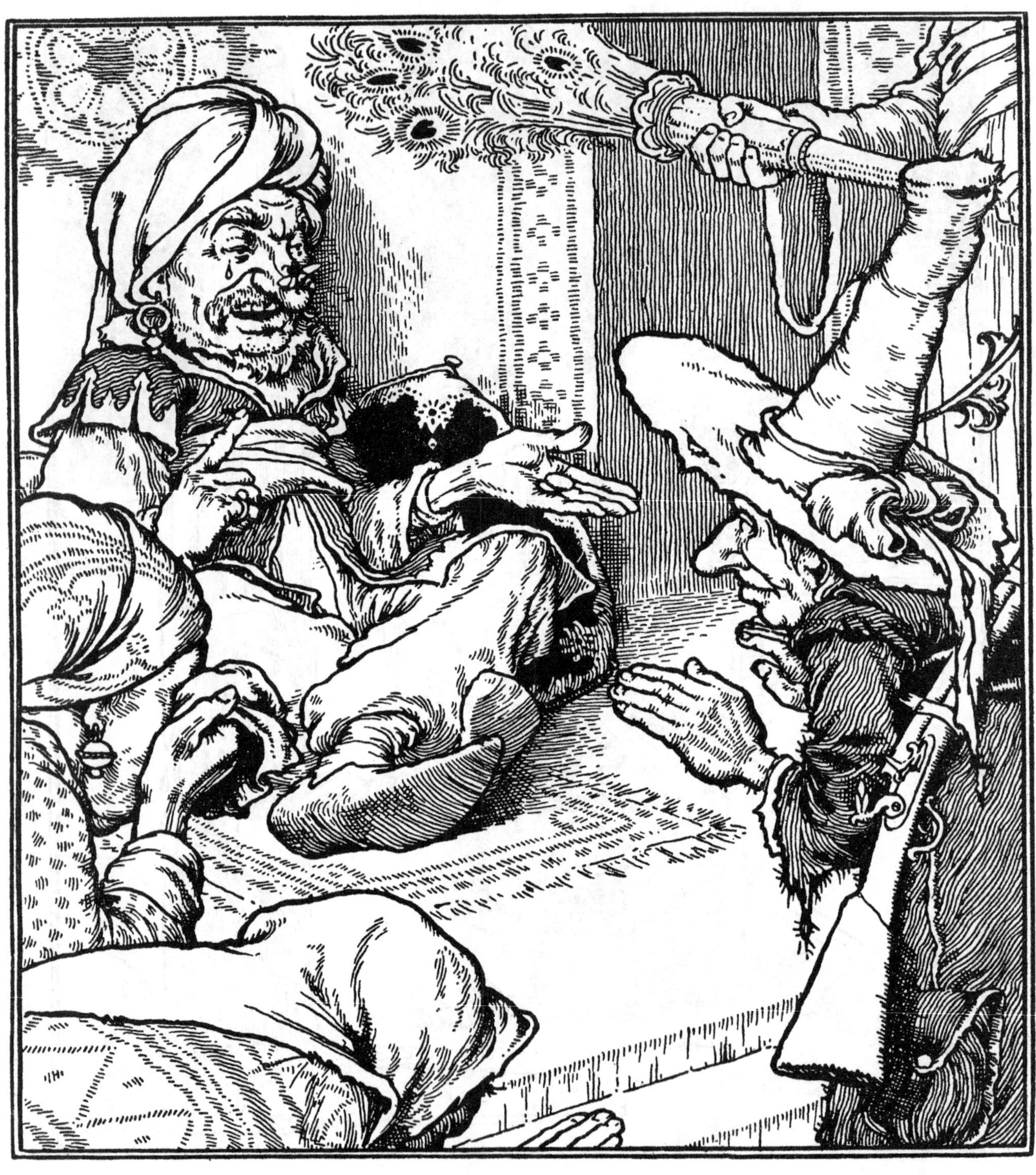

The Rajah

The Adventures of Uncle Lubin, 1902

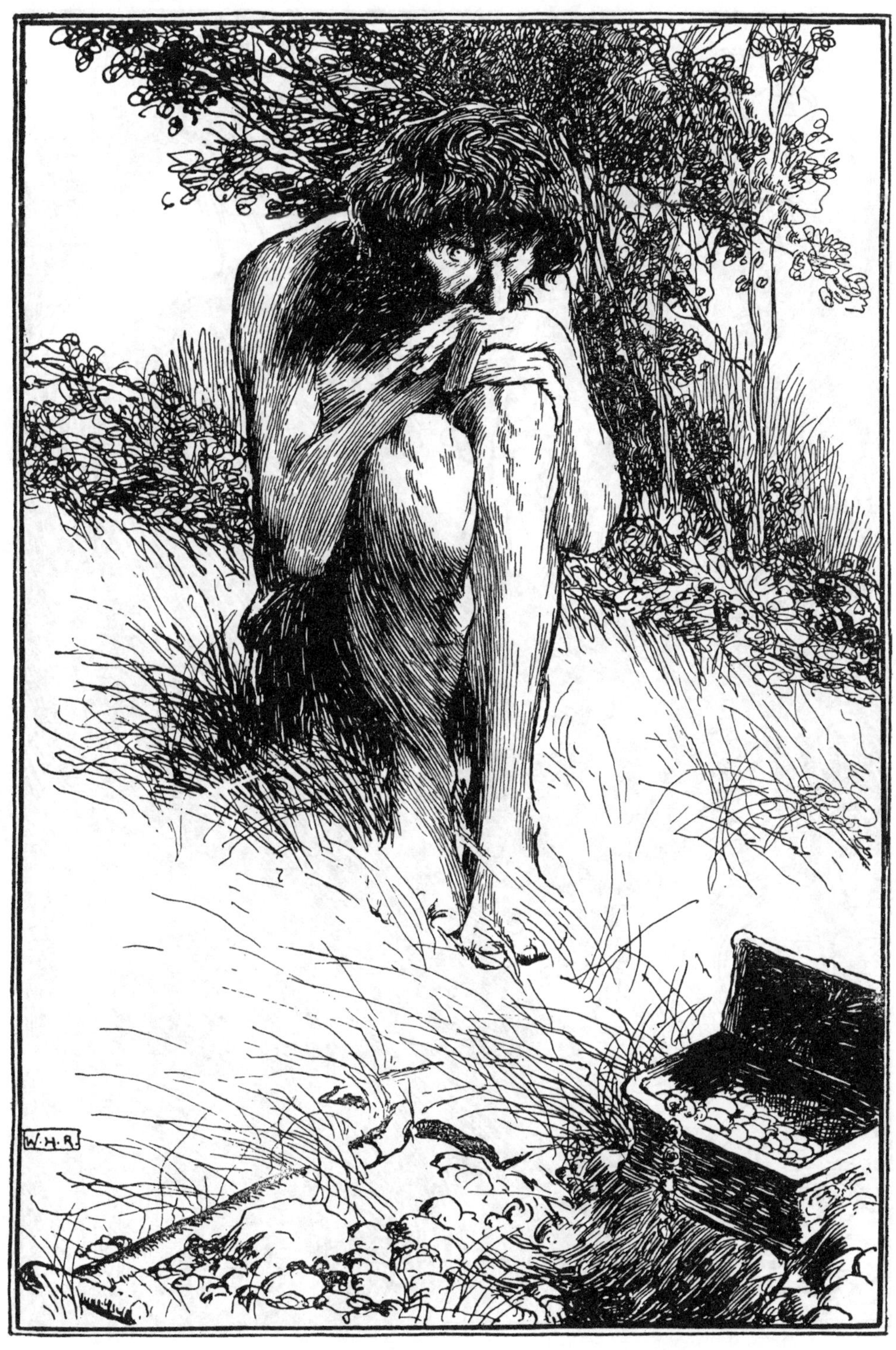

The sight of gold was poisonous to his eyes

TALES FROM SHAKESPEARE, 1902

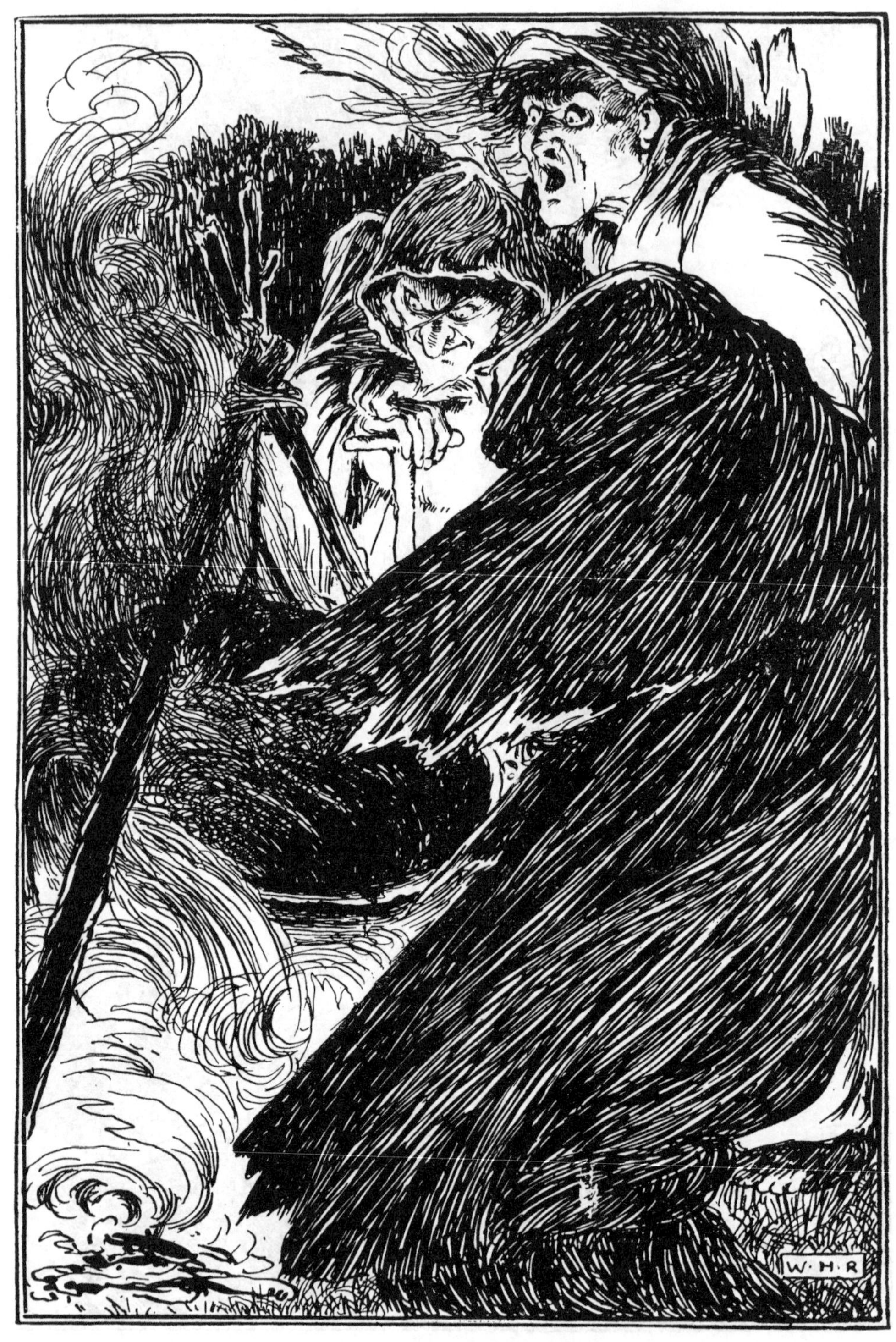

Engaged in preparing their dreadful charms

Tales from Shakespeare, 1902

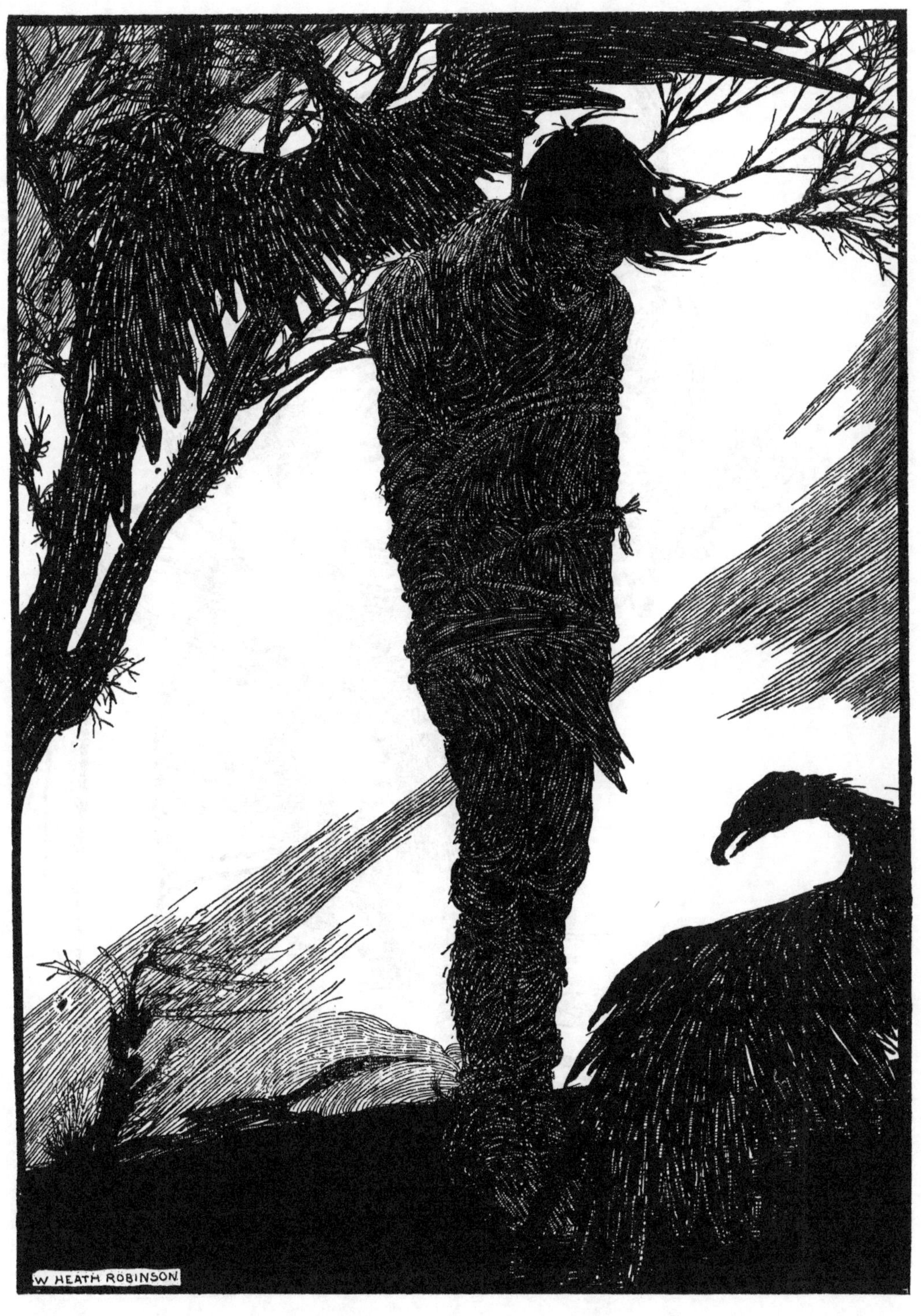

Exceeding odious and hateful to thieves and robbers

THE WORKS OF RABELAIS, 1904

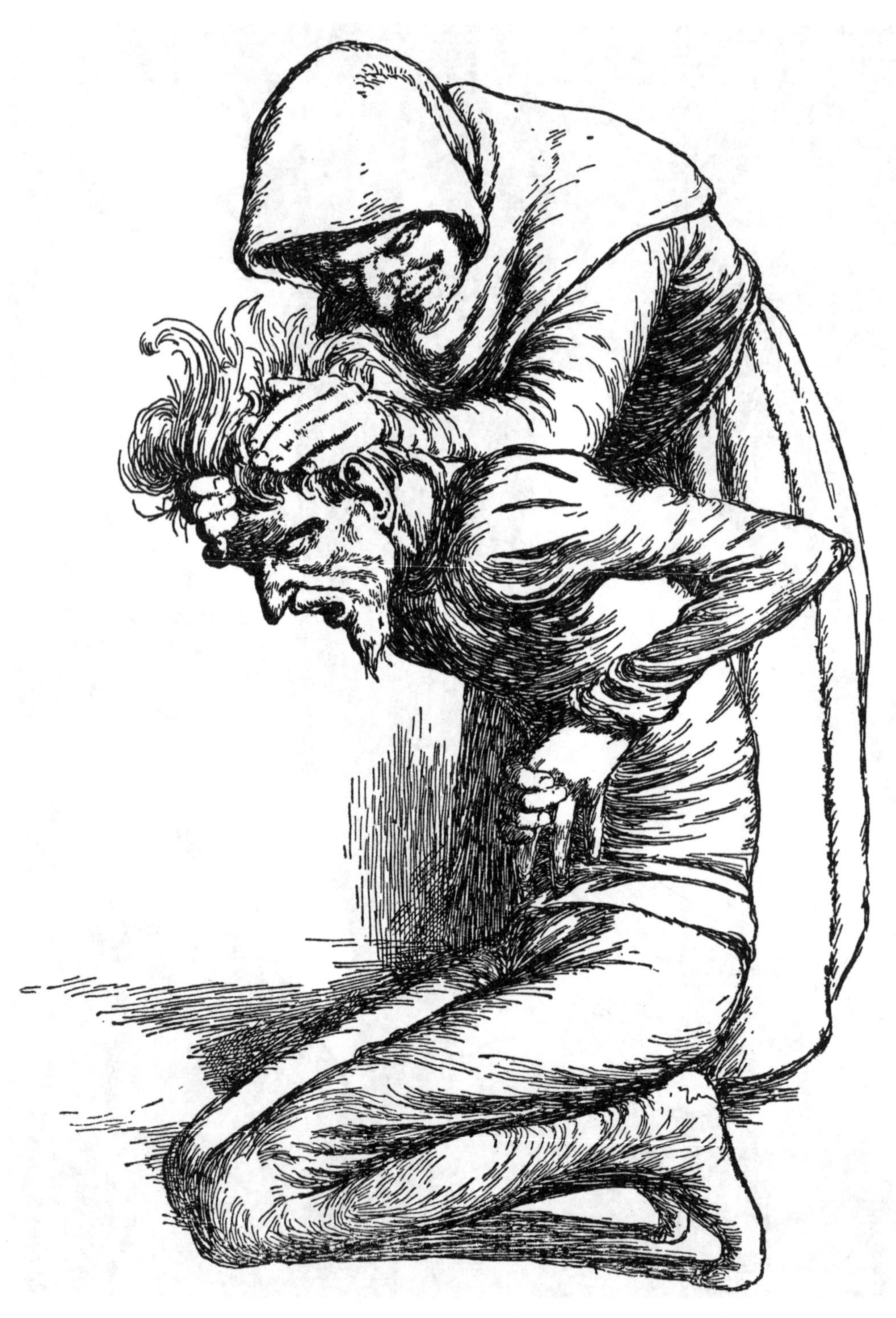

I sink, I sink, hah, my father, my uncle, my all

The Works of Rabelais, 1904

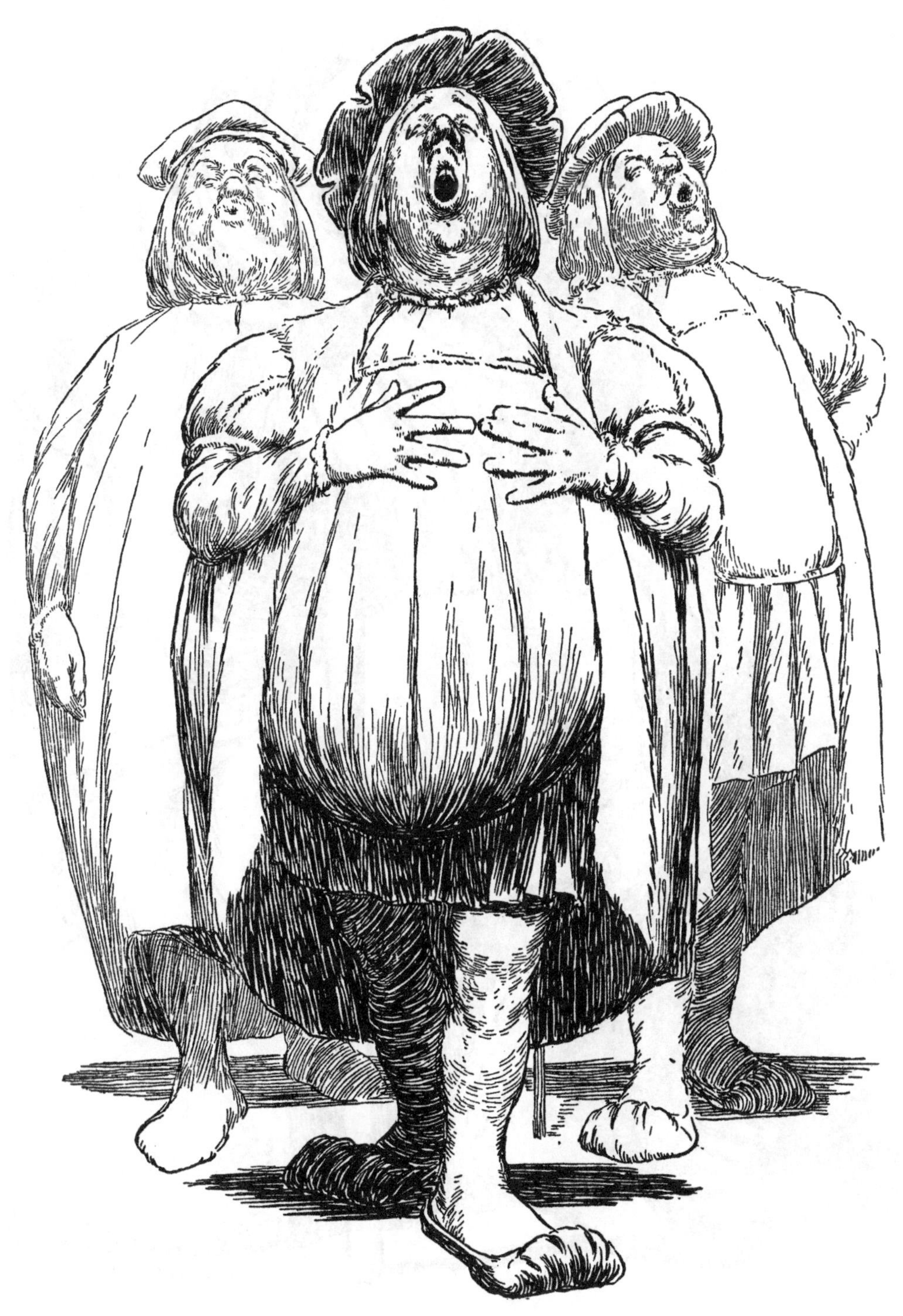

They live on nothing but wind

The Works of Rabelais, 1904

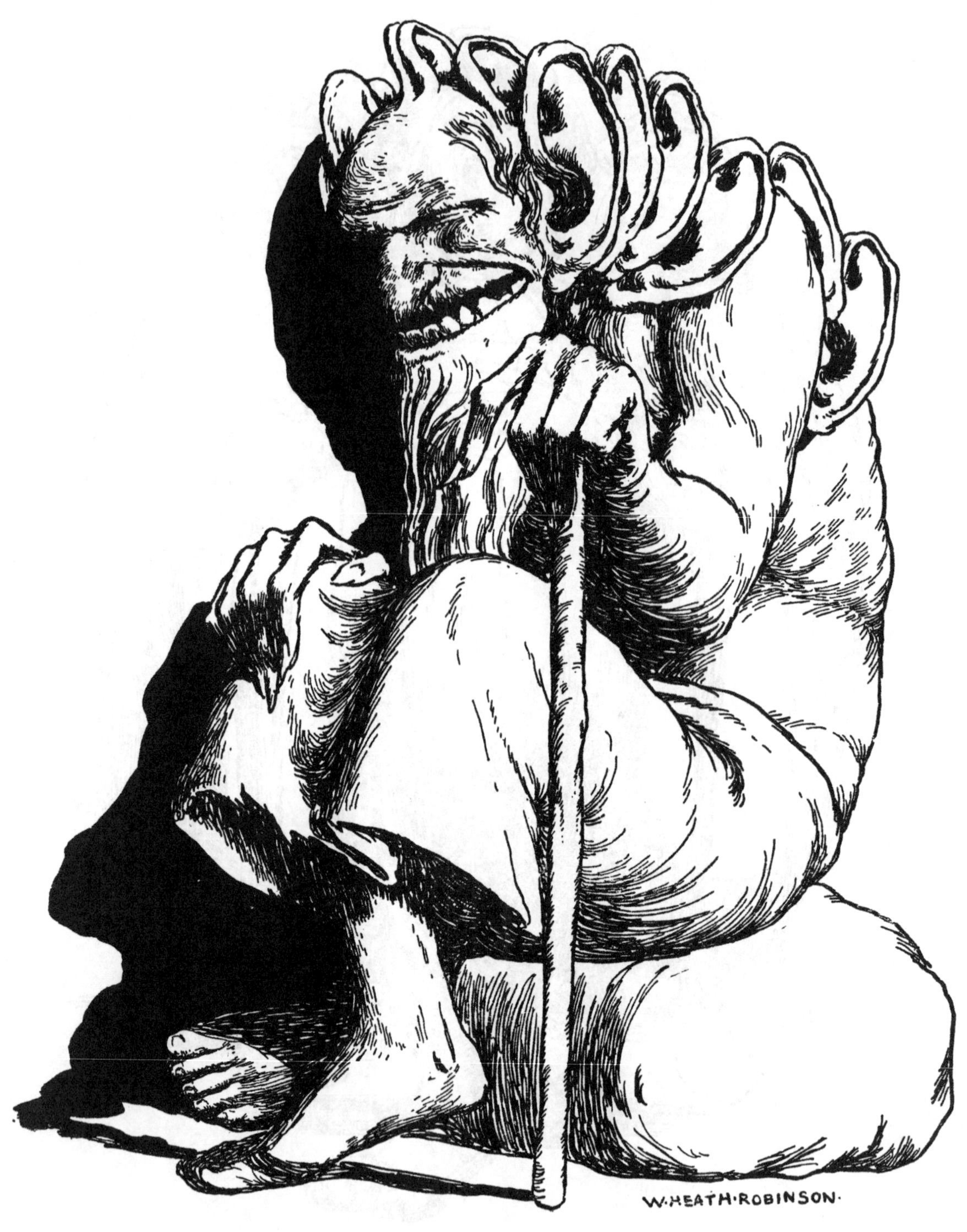

Hear-say

The Works of Rabelais, 1904

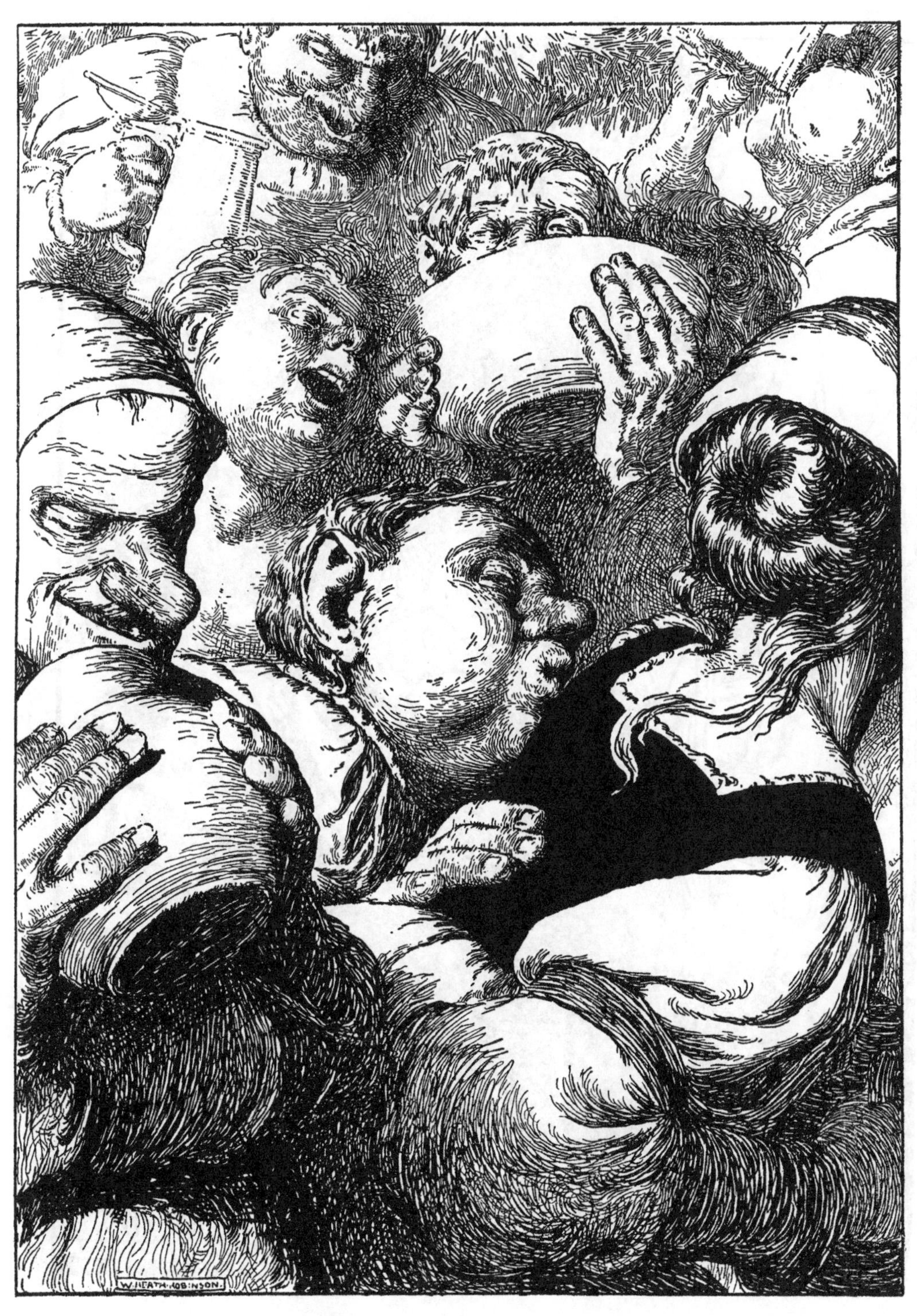

Ring, draw, reach, fill and mixe

The Works of Rabelais, 1904

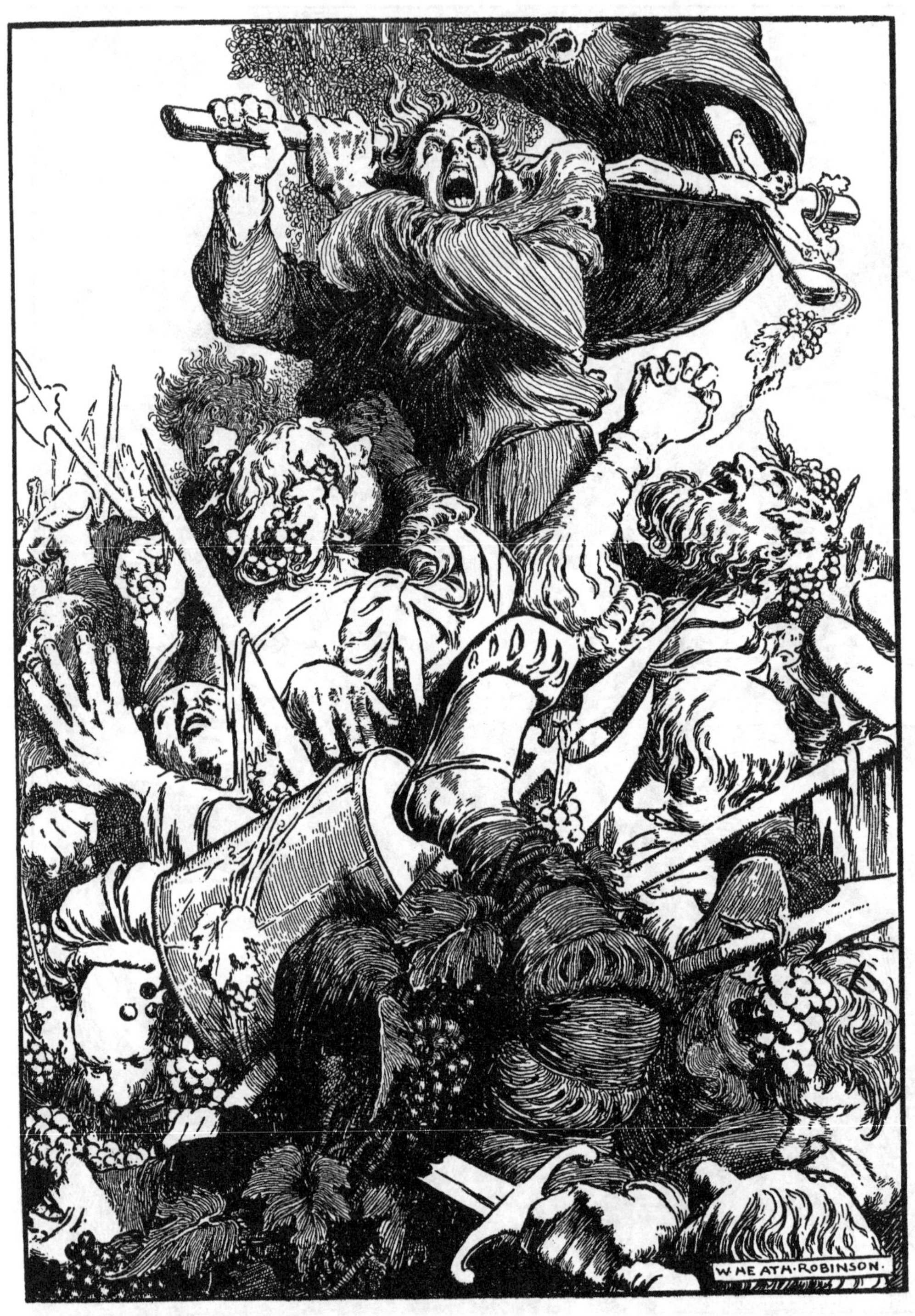

They fell down before him like hay before a mower

The Works of Rabelais, 1904

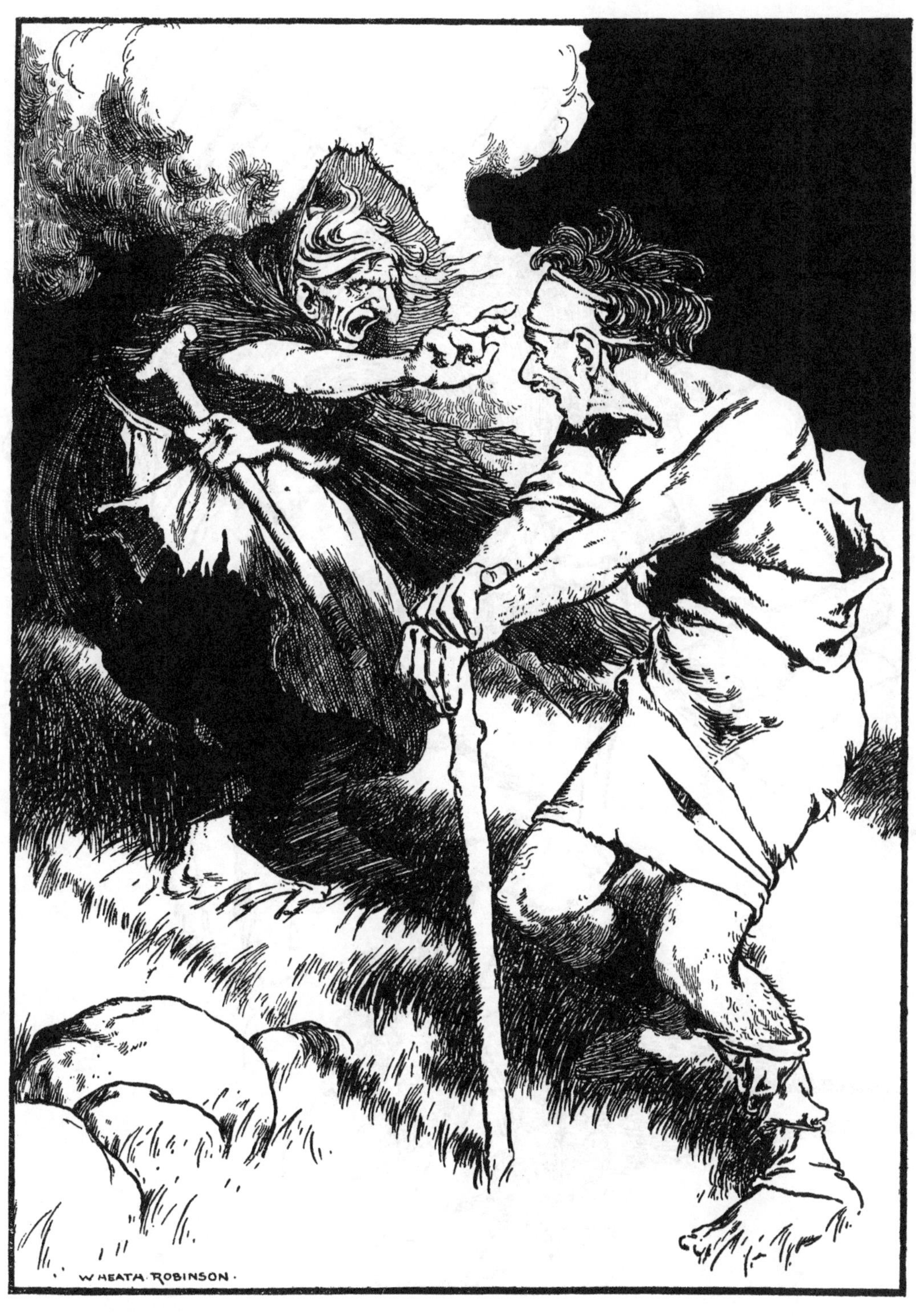

Was foretold by an old Lourpidon hag, that his kingdome should be restored to him at the coming of the Cocklicranes

The Works of Rabelais, 1904

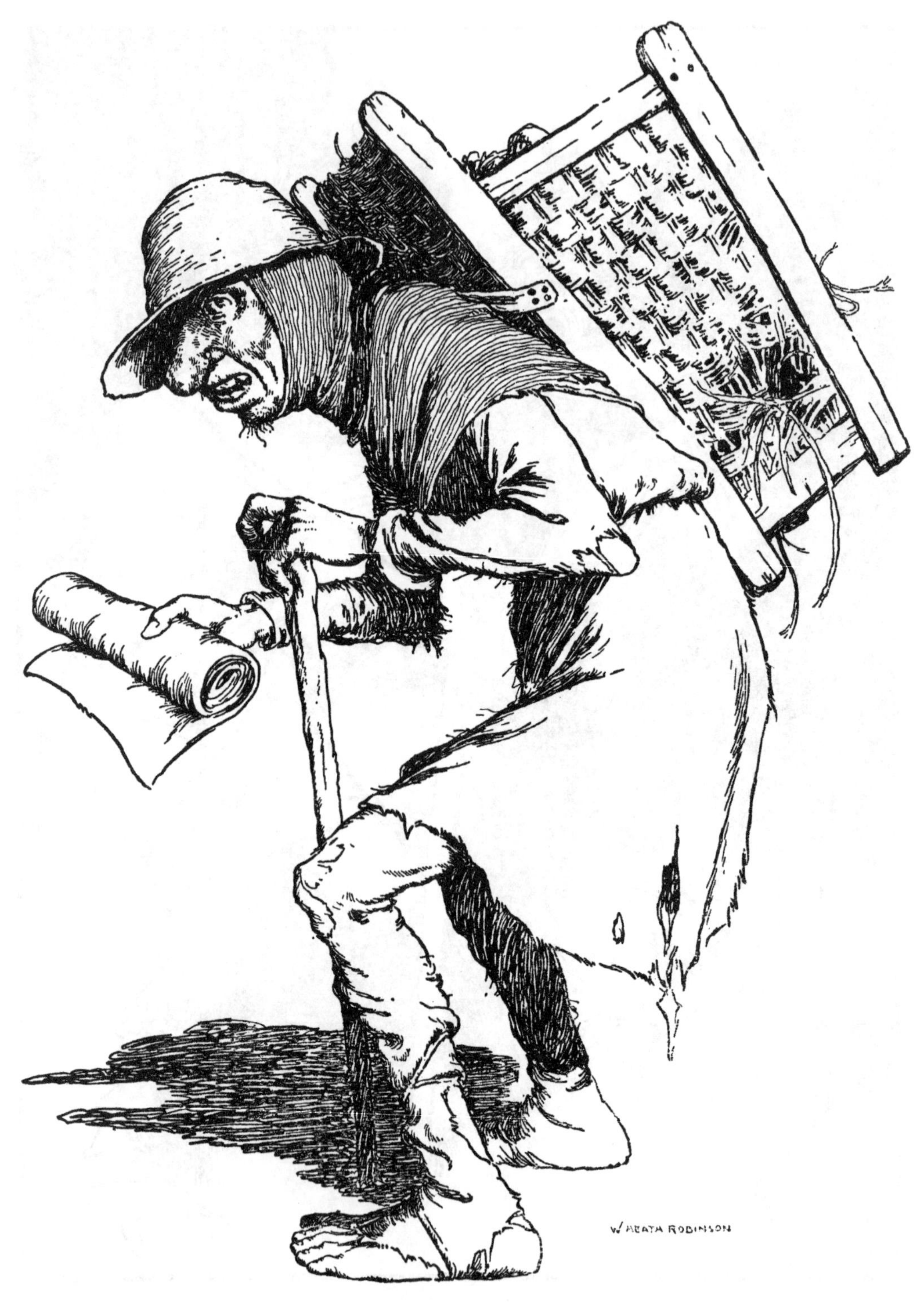

To the best beloved of the faire women

The Works of Rabelais, 1904

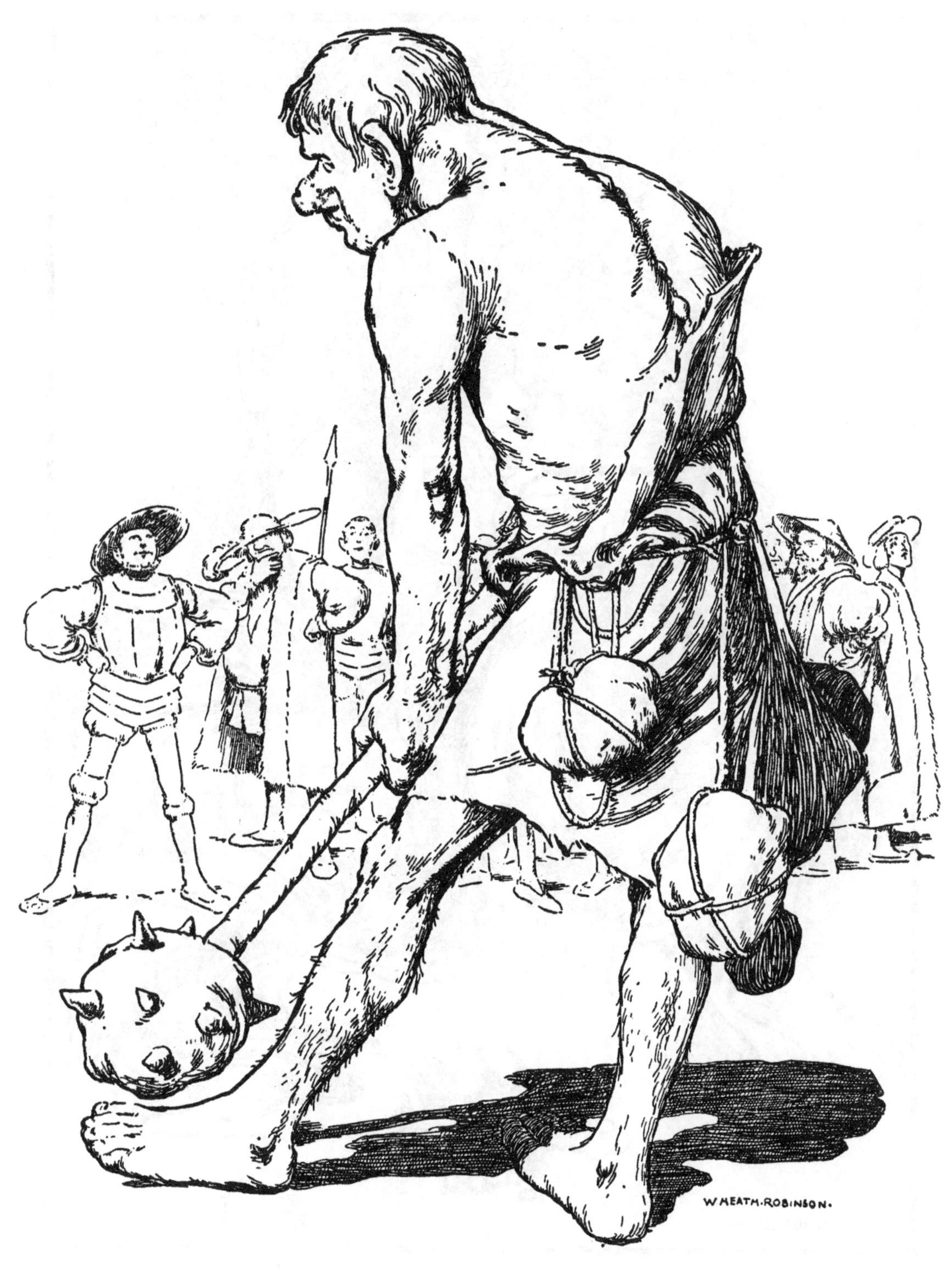

Loupgarou

The Works of Rabelais, 1904

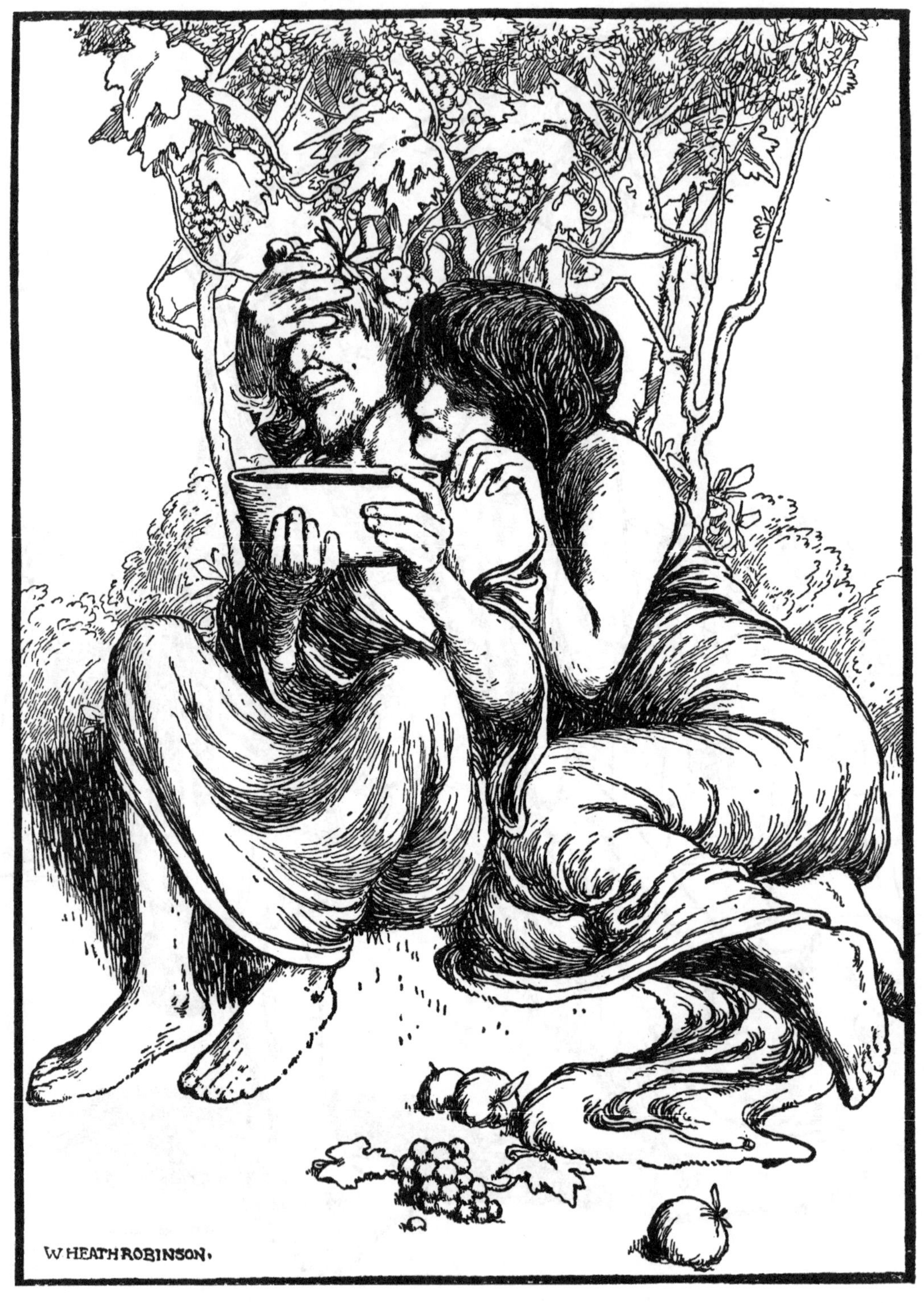

Never was man more glad than I was then

The Works of Rabelais, 1904

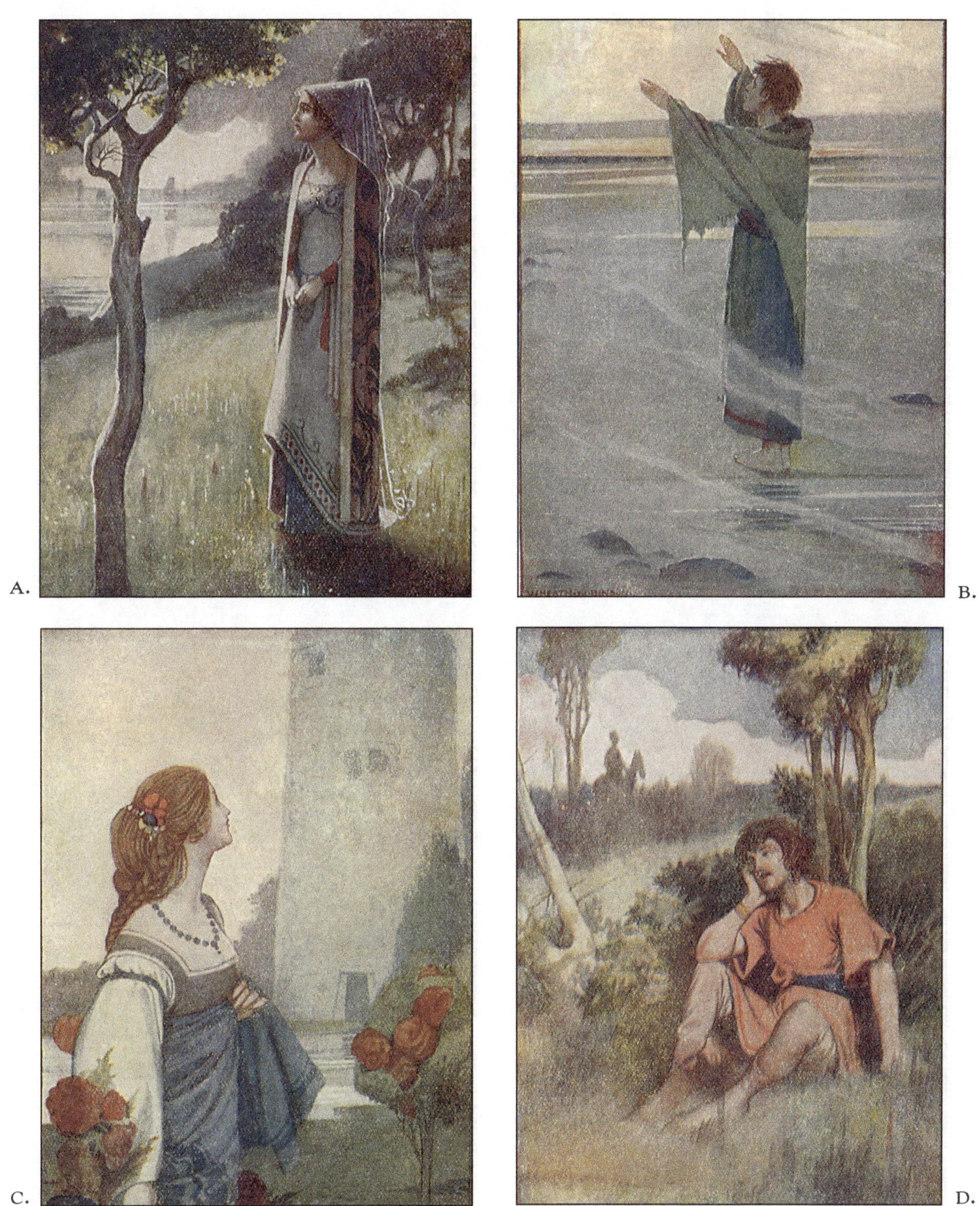

A. Alas! of all the ships I see, is there never one that will bring home my lord
B. He saw the magician standing on the shore
C. She thought of the two young princes who were prisoners there
D. Palamon lay beside a pool of water

Stories from Chaucer, 1906

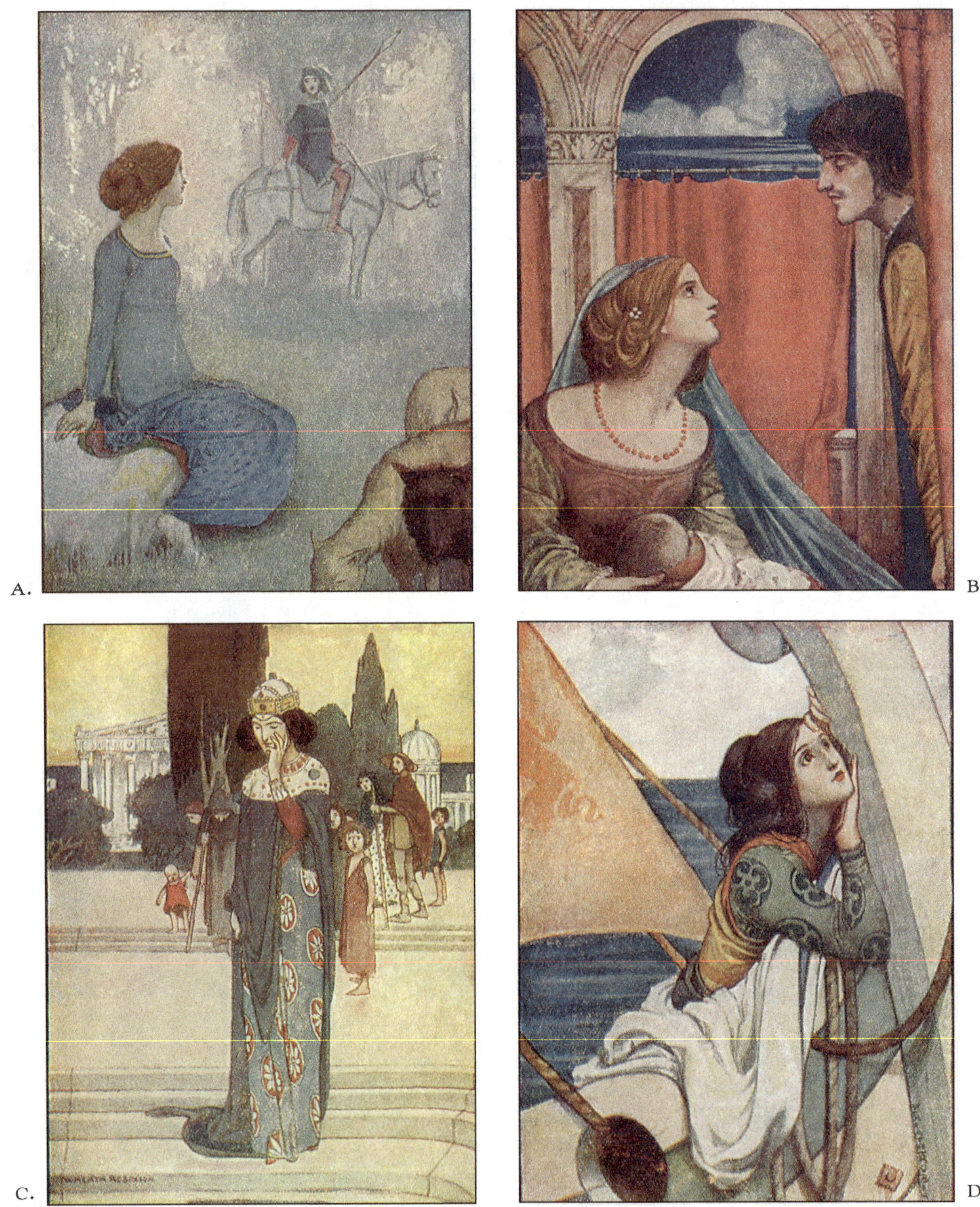

A. She rose to curtsy to him
B. Lord Walter came into the room
C. To them she seemed a martyr
D. When her boy lay asleep she knelt at the prow

Stories from Chaucer, 1906

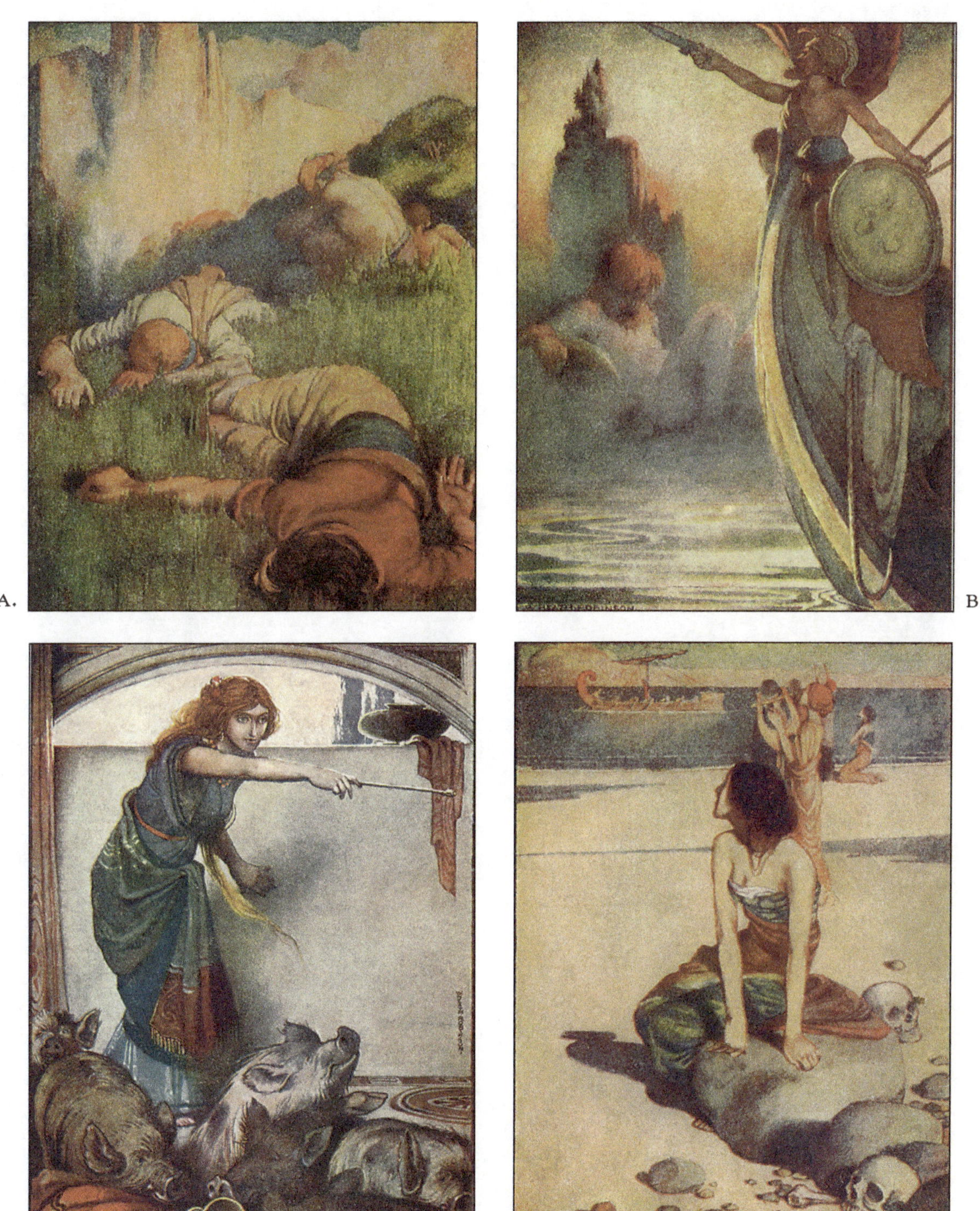

A. And dream idle, happy day-dreams that never ended

B. "Nevermore wilt thou have thy sight," mocked Odysseus

C. In one moment they were turned into swine

D. In the meadows where the Sirens sat were the bones of the men they had slain

STORIES FROM THE ODYSSEY, 1906

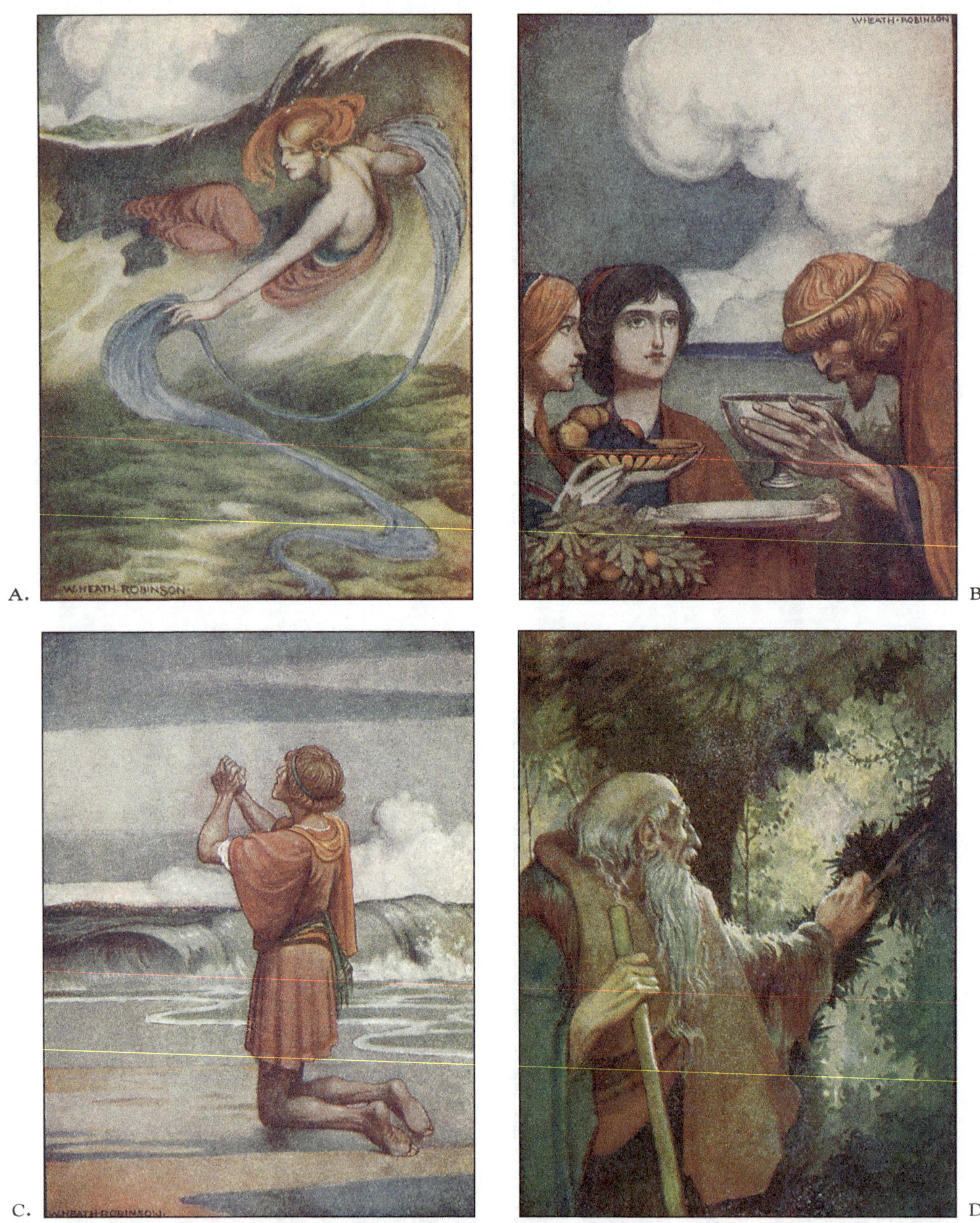

A. The nymph rose from the sea and bore the veil away
B. Nausicaa and her maidens brought him food and wine
C. Telemachus knelt where the grey water broke on the sand
D. Odysseus looked down at the woods and the sea

STORIES FROM THE ODYSSEY, 1906

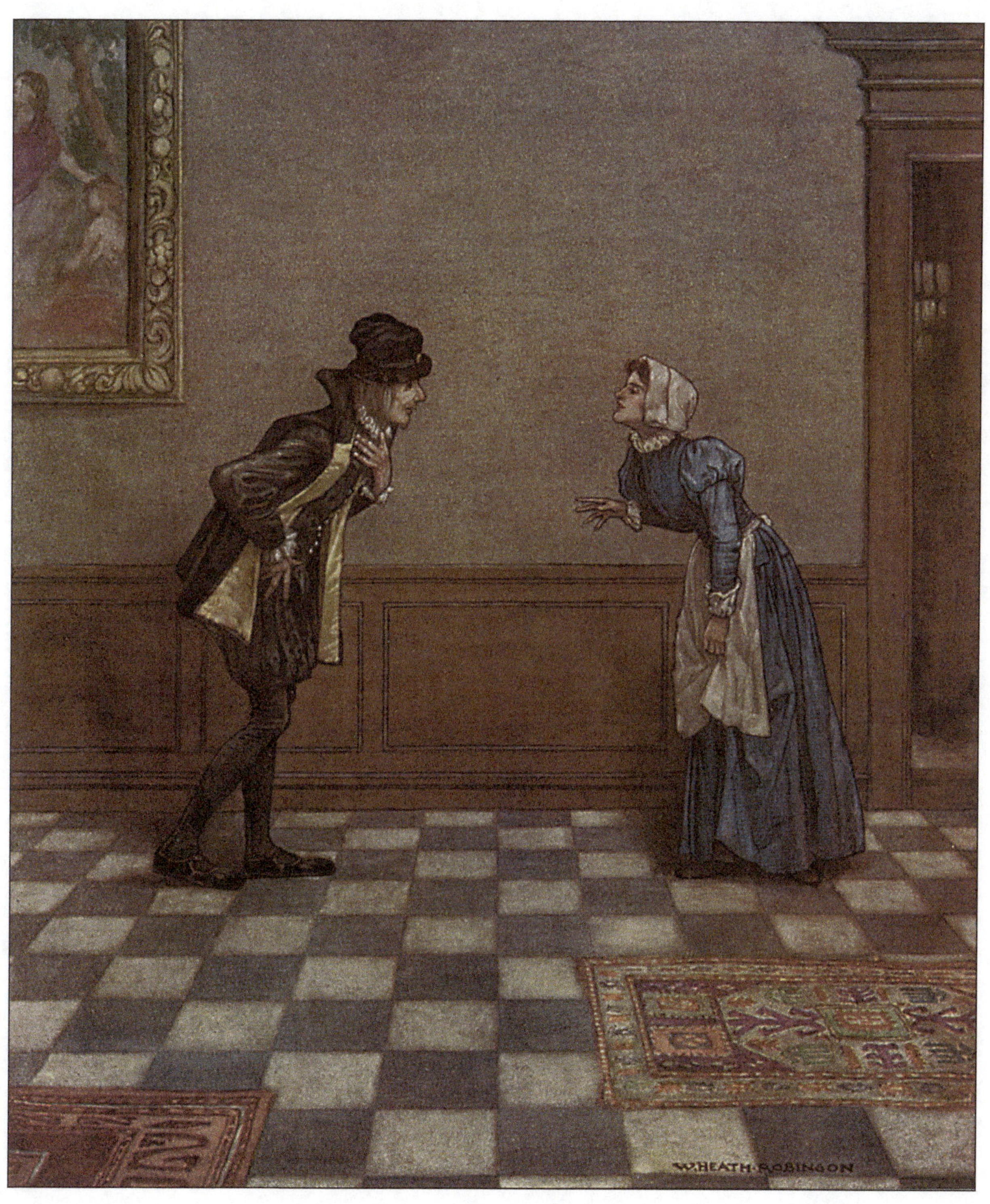

Act I. Scene III.
Maria. My name is Mary, sir

Twelfth Night or What You Will, 1908

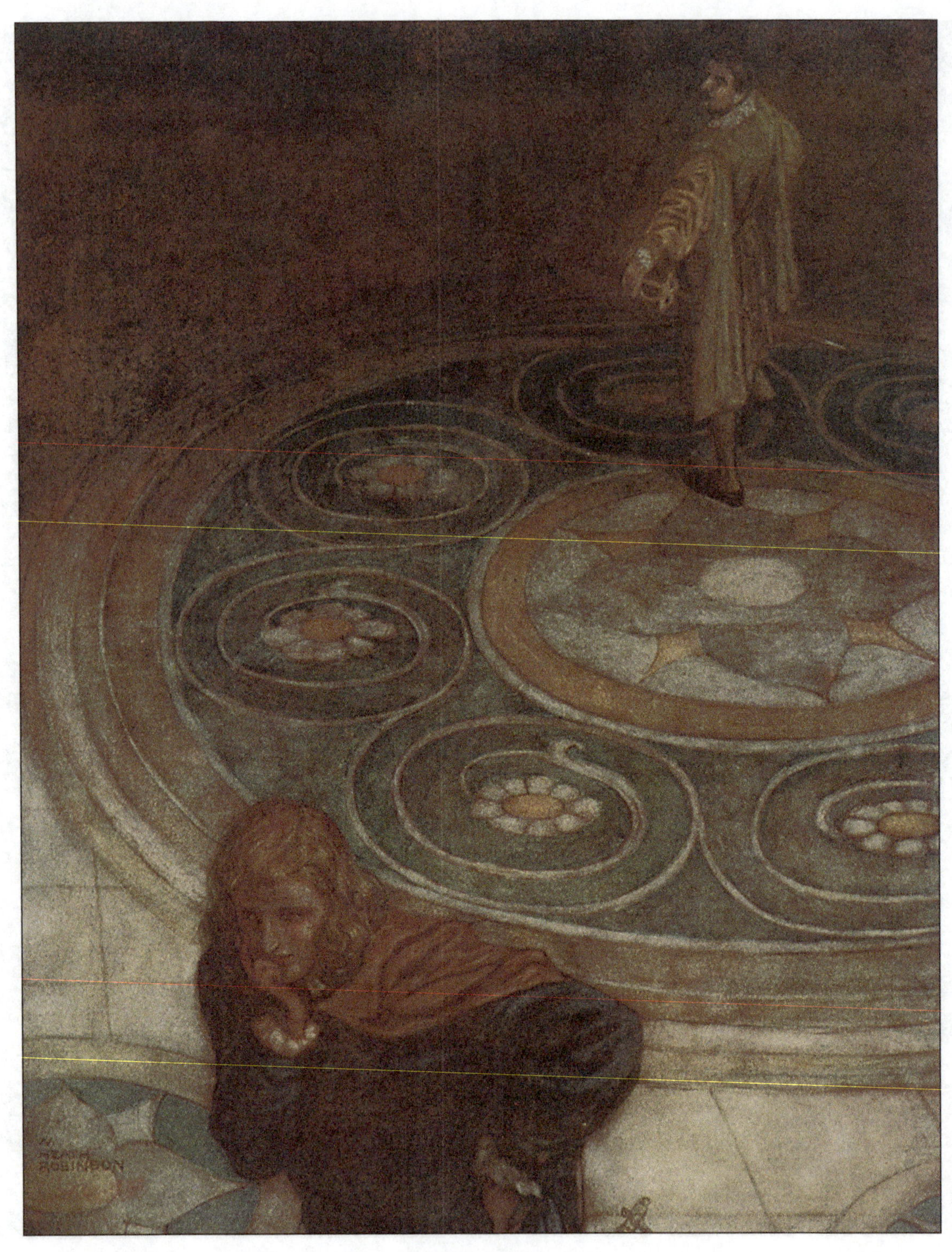

Act I. Scene IV.
Viola. Yet, a barful strife!
Whoe'er I woo, myself would be his wife

Twelfth Night or What You Will, 1908

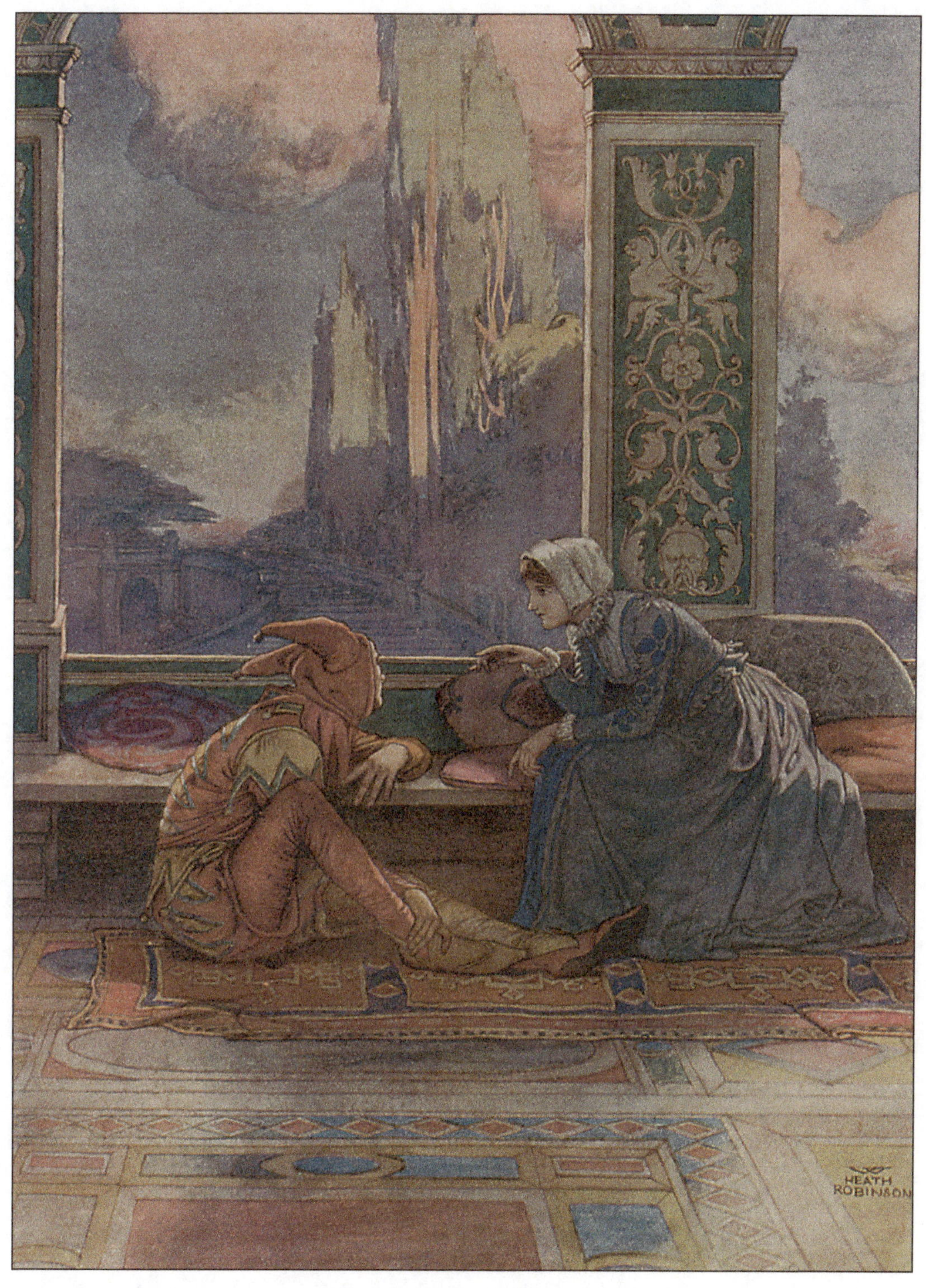

Act I. Scene V.
MARIA. Yet you will be hanged for being
so long absent

TWELFTH NIGHT OR WHAT YOU WILL, 1908

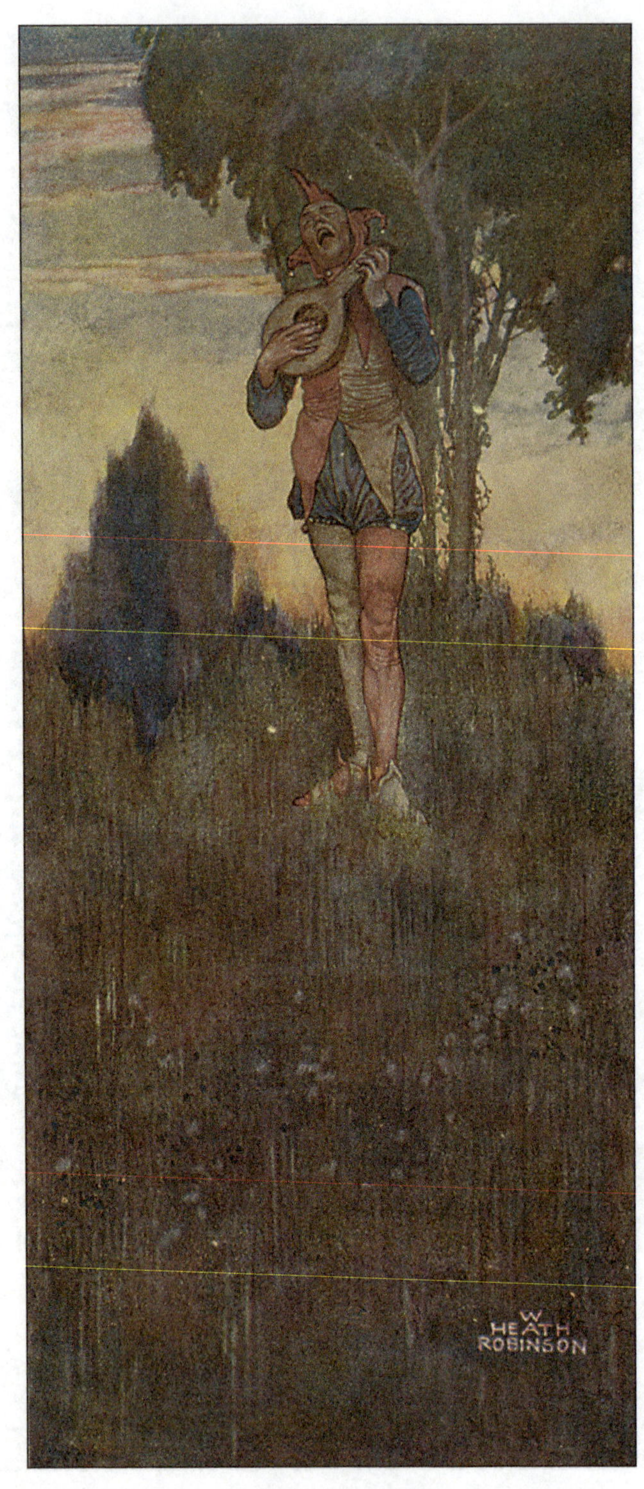

Act II. Scene III.
Clown (sings). That can sing both high and low

Twelfth Night or What You Will, 1908

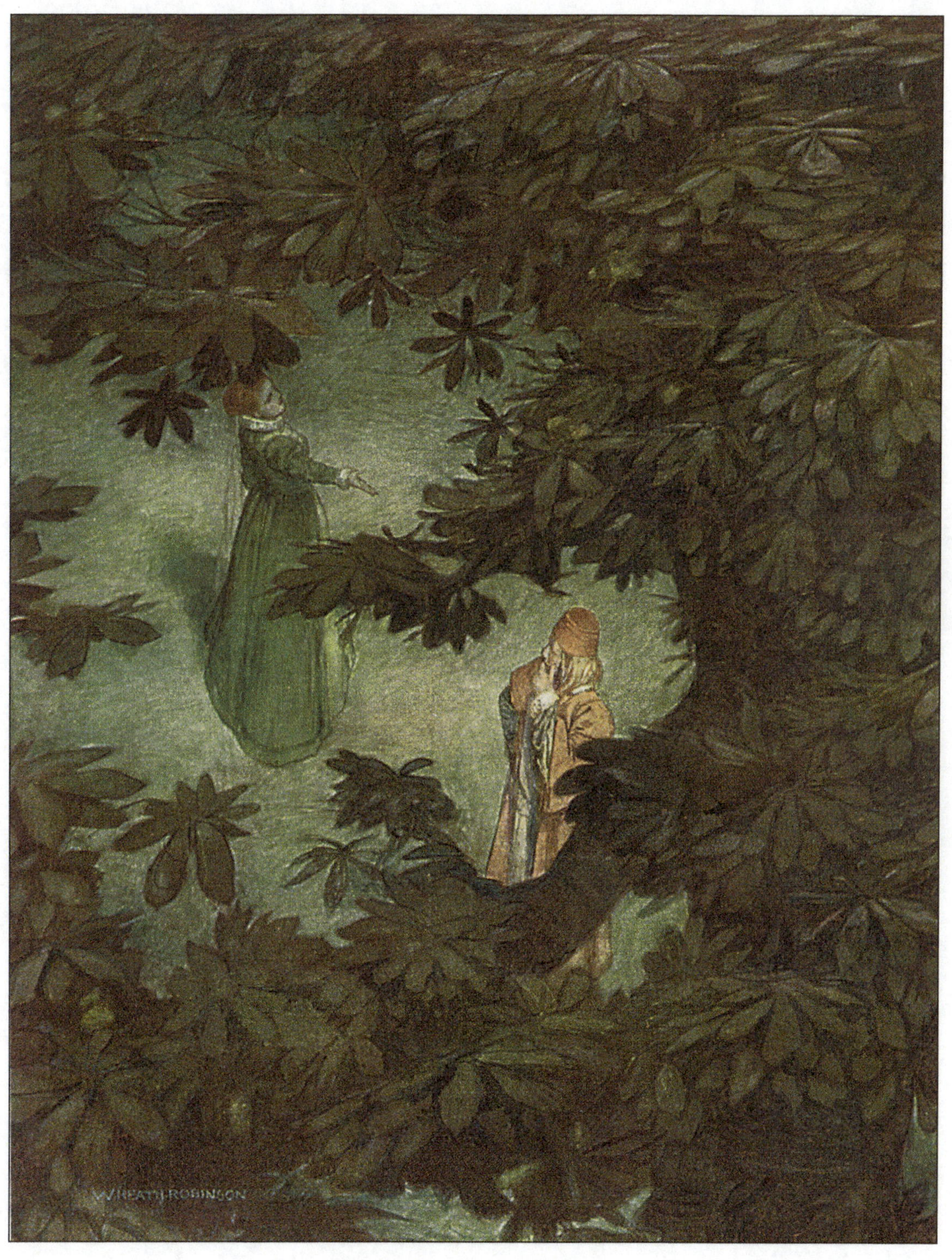

Act III. Scene IV.
Olivia. Well, come again to-morrow; fare thee well

Twelfth Night or What You Will, 1908

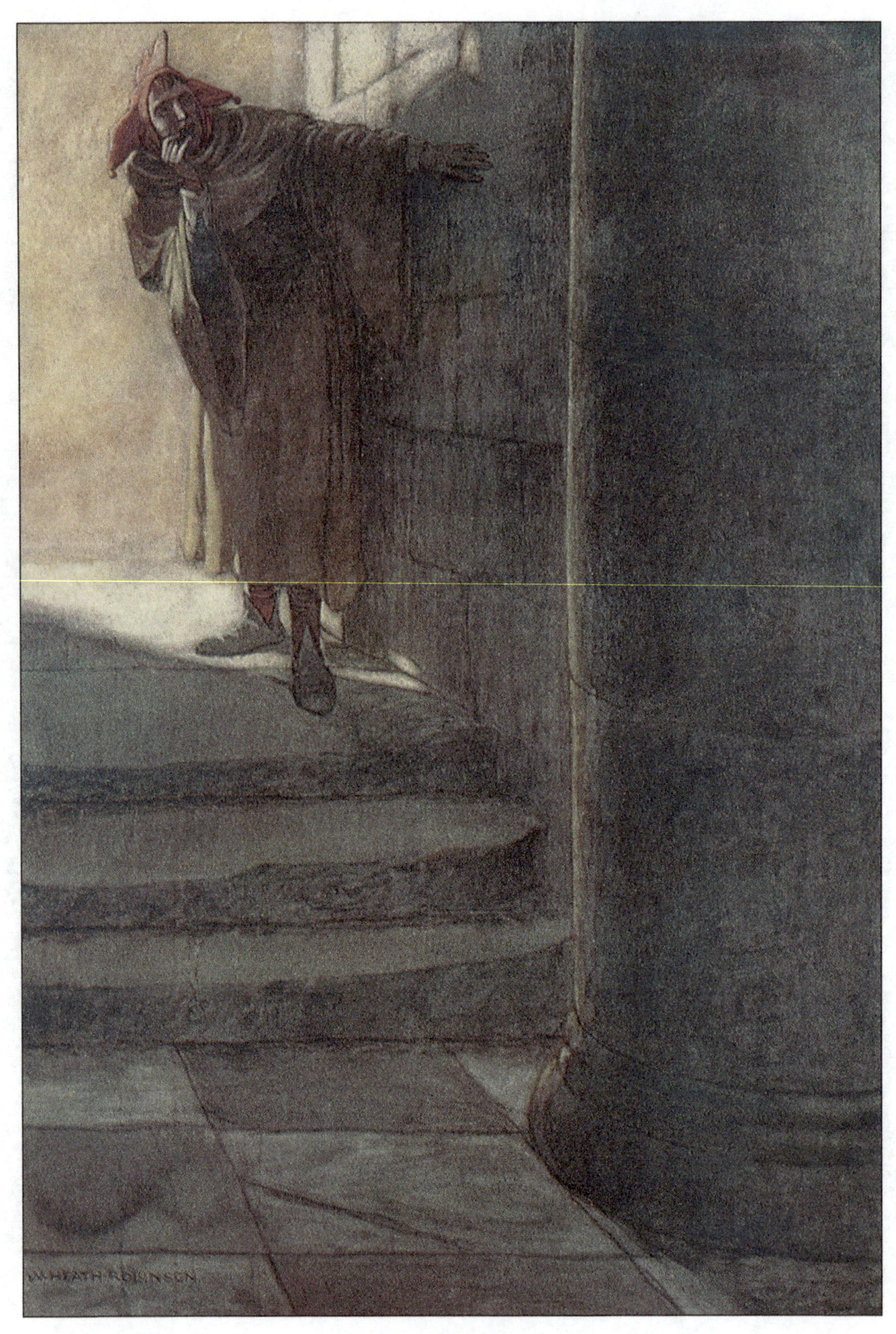

Act IV. Scene II.
Clown. Sayest thou that house is dark?

Twelfth Night or What You Will, 1908

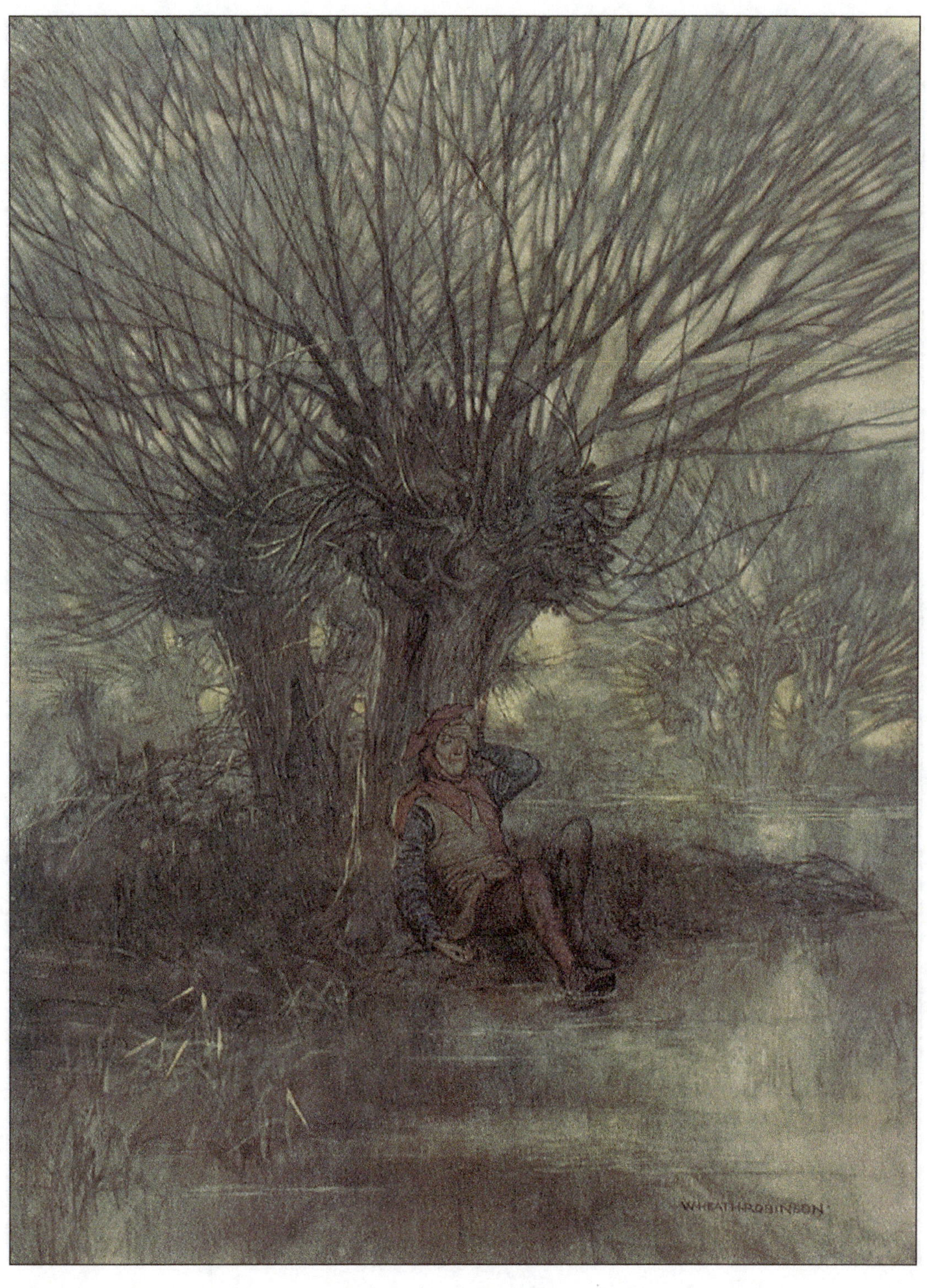

Act V. Scene I.
CLOWN (sings). With toss-pots still had drunken heads

TWELFTH NIGHT OR WHAT YOU WILL, 1908

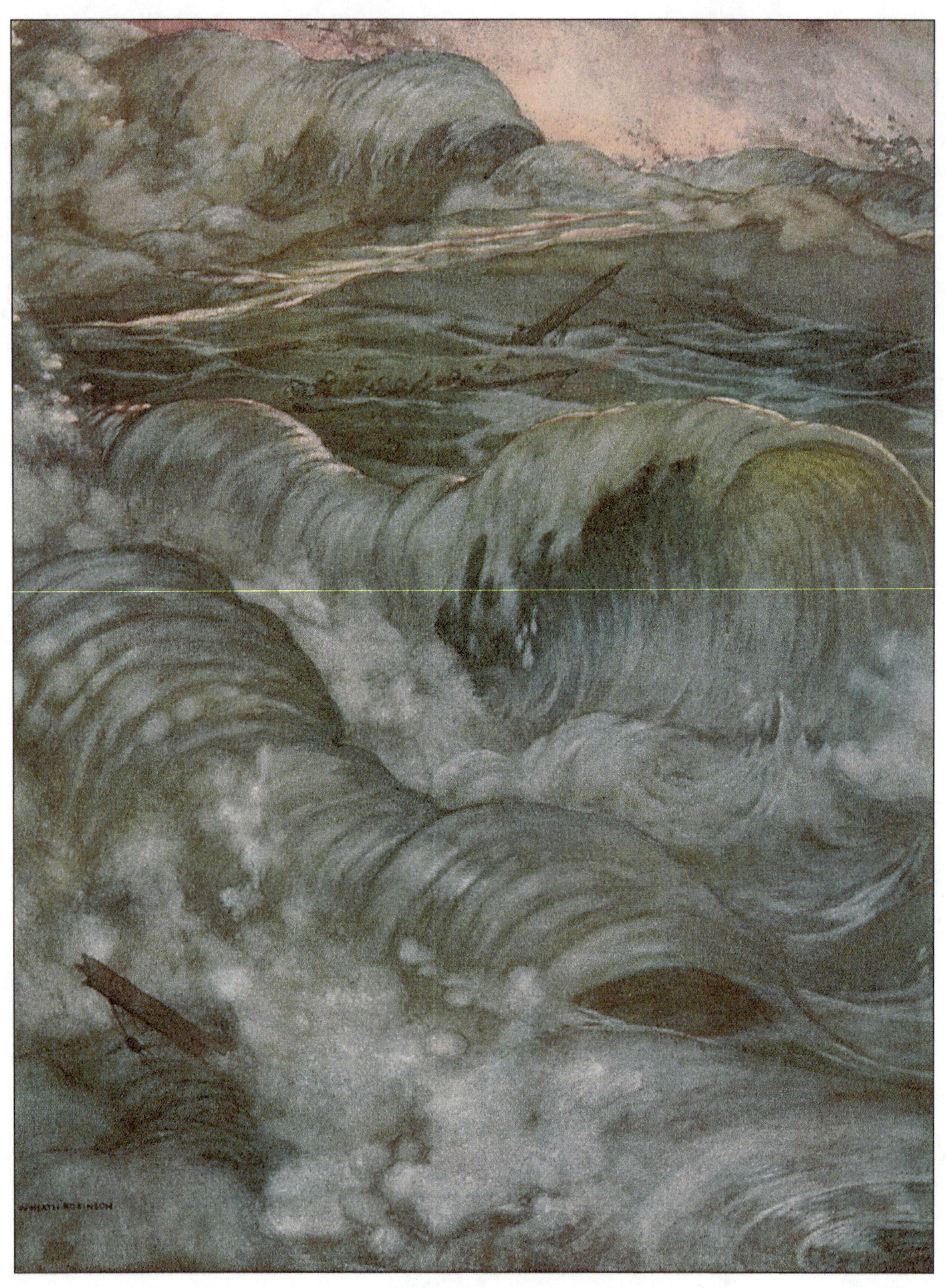

The swinging, smoking seas

A Song of the English, 1909

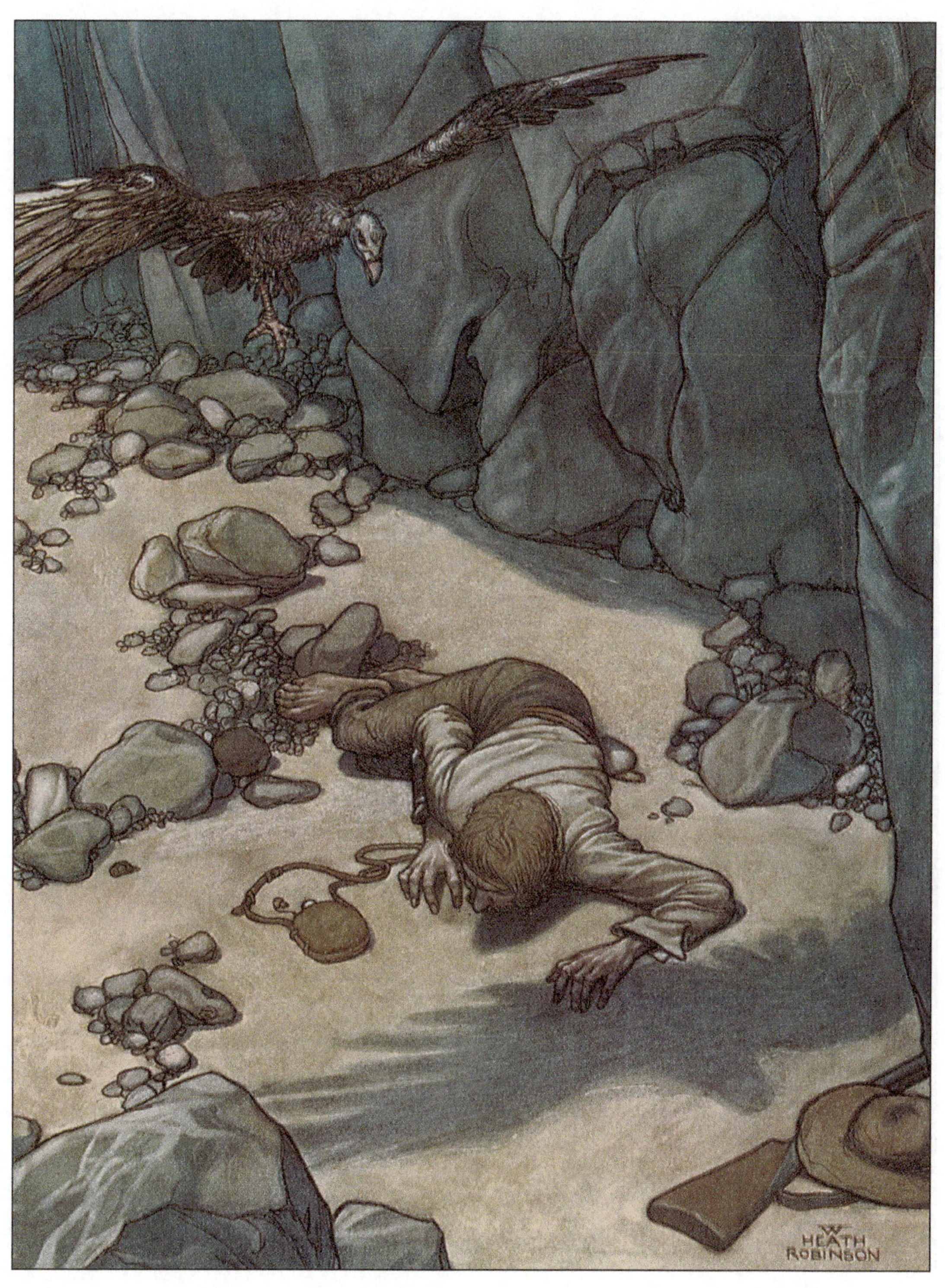

Then the last water dried

A Song of the English, 1909

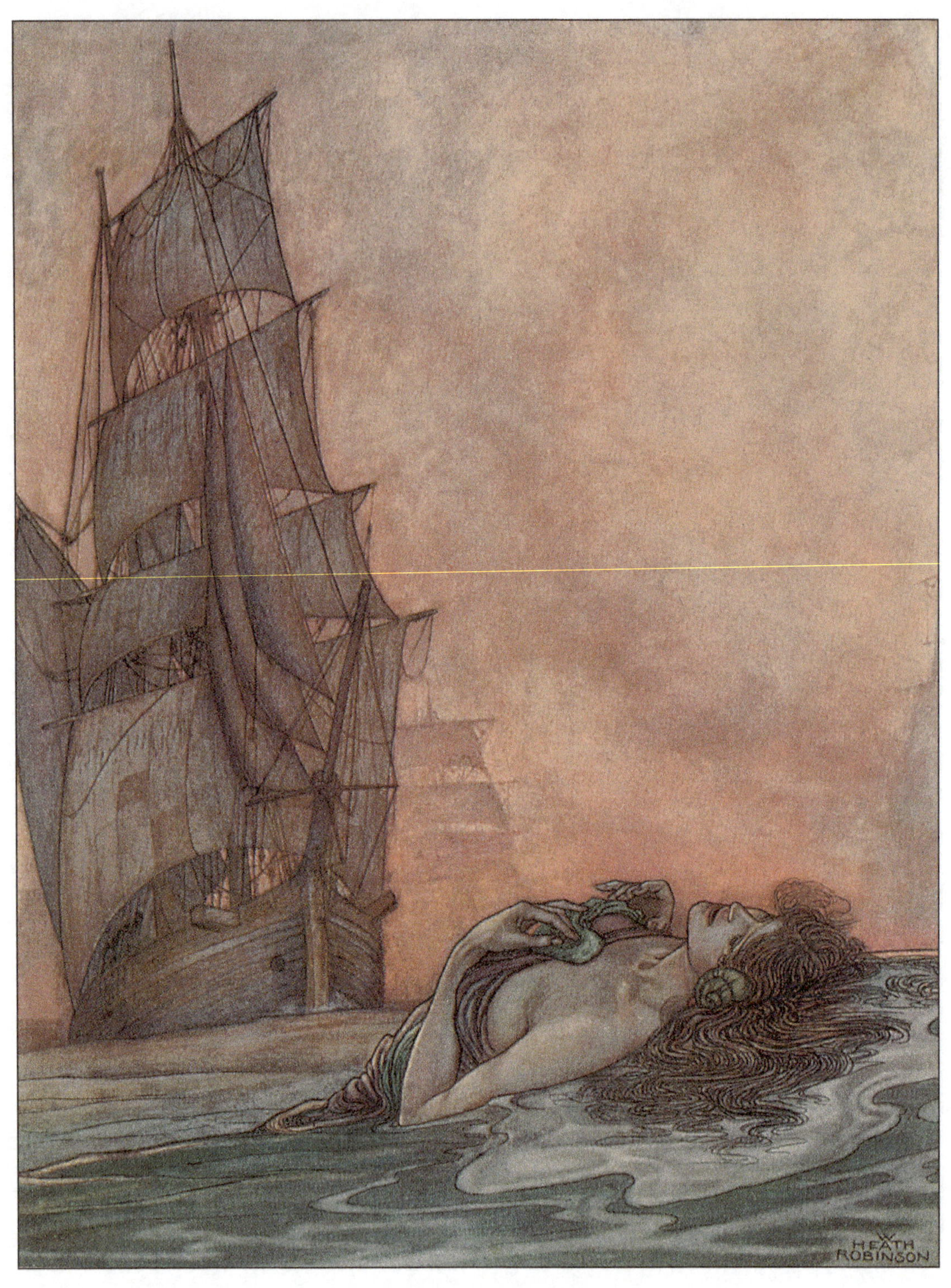

And she calls us, still unfed

A Song of the English, 1909

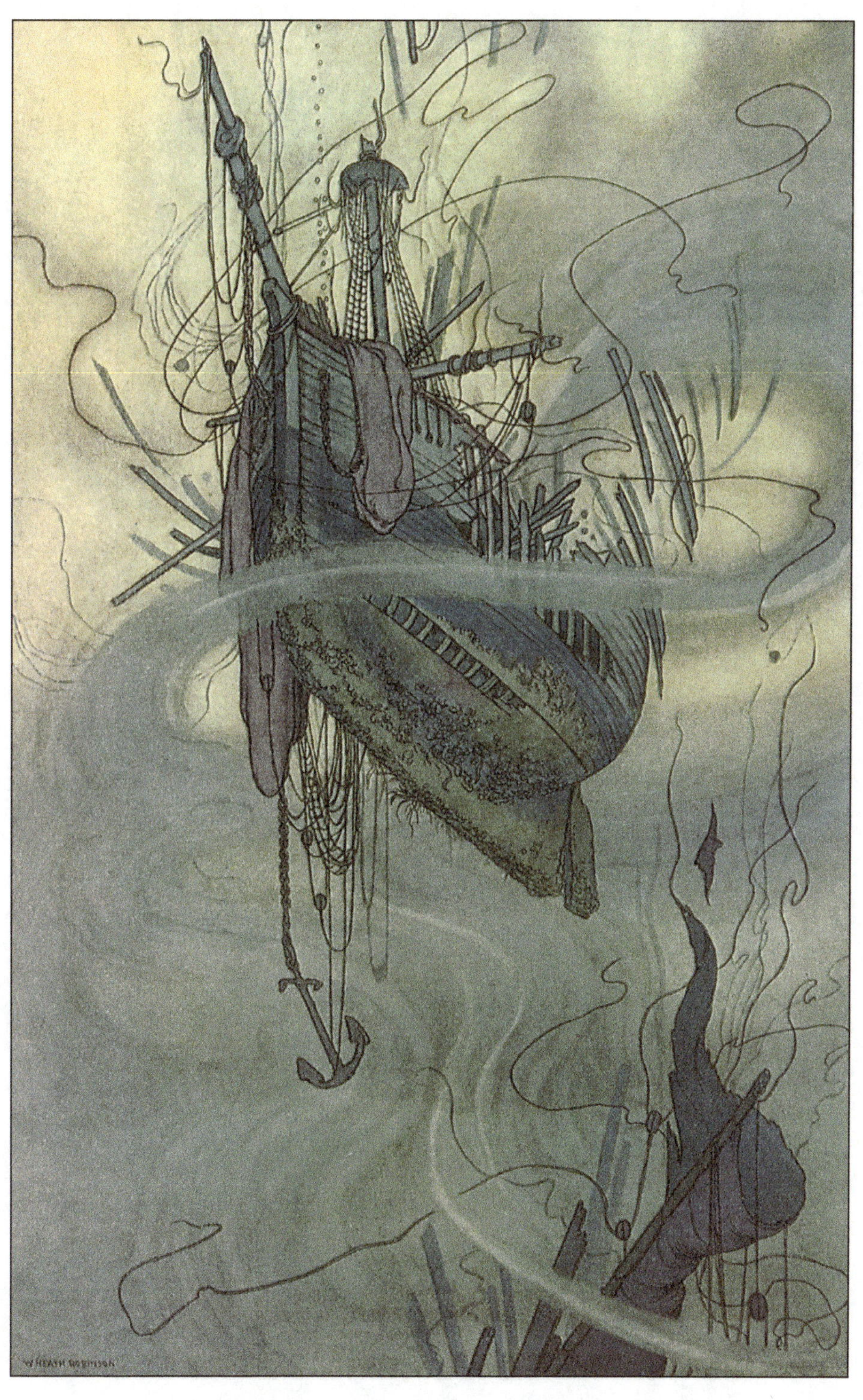

The wrecks dissolve above us

A Song of the English, 1909

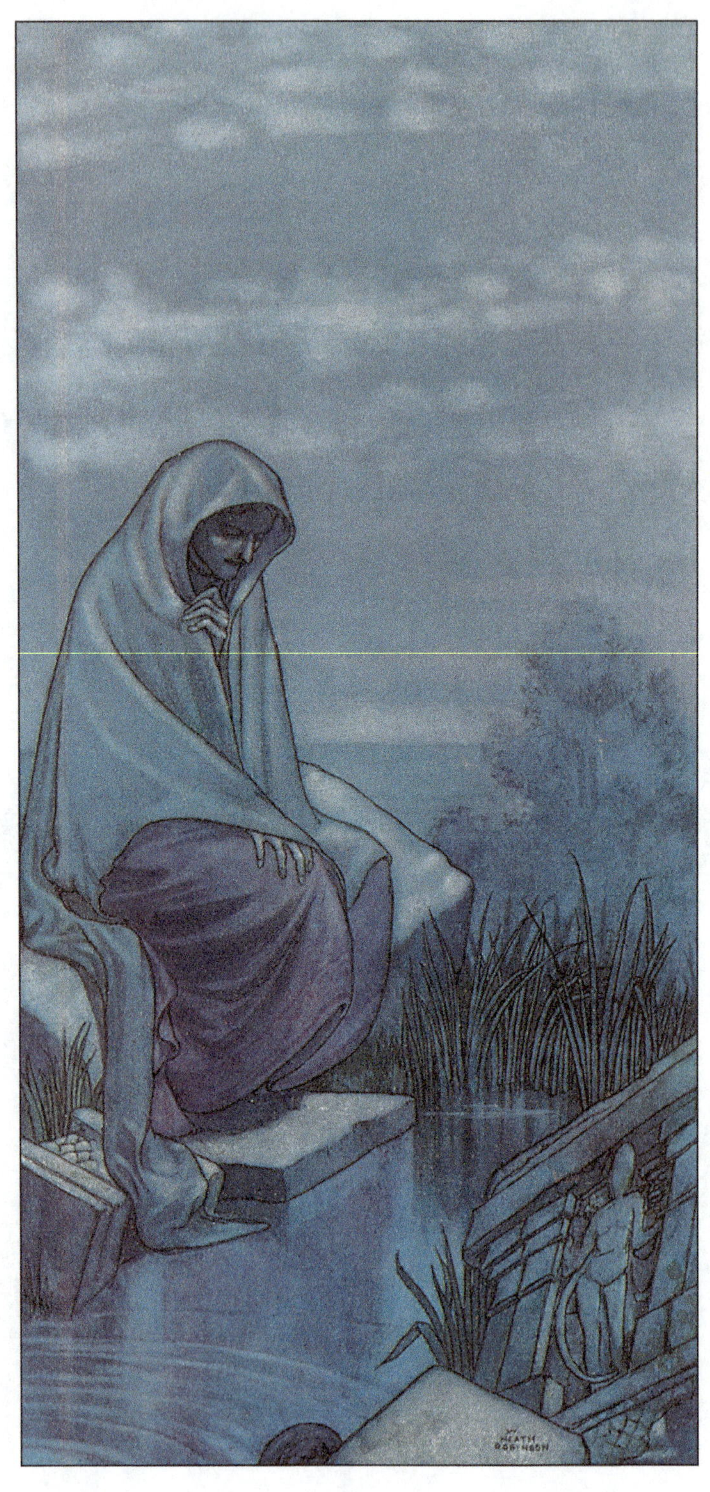

Madras

A Song of the English, 1909

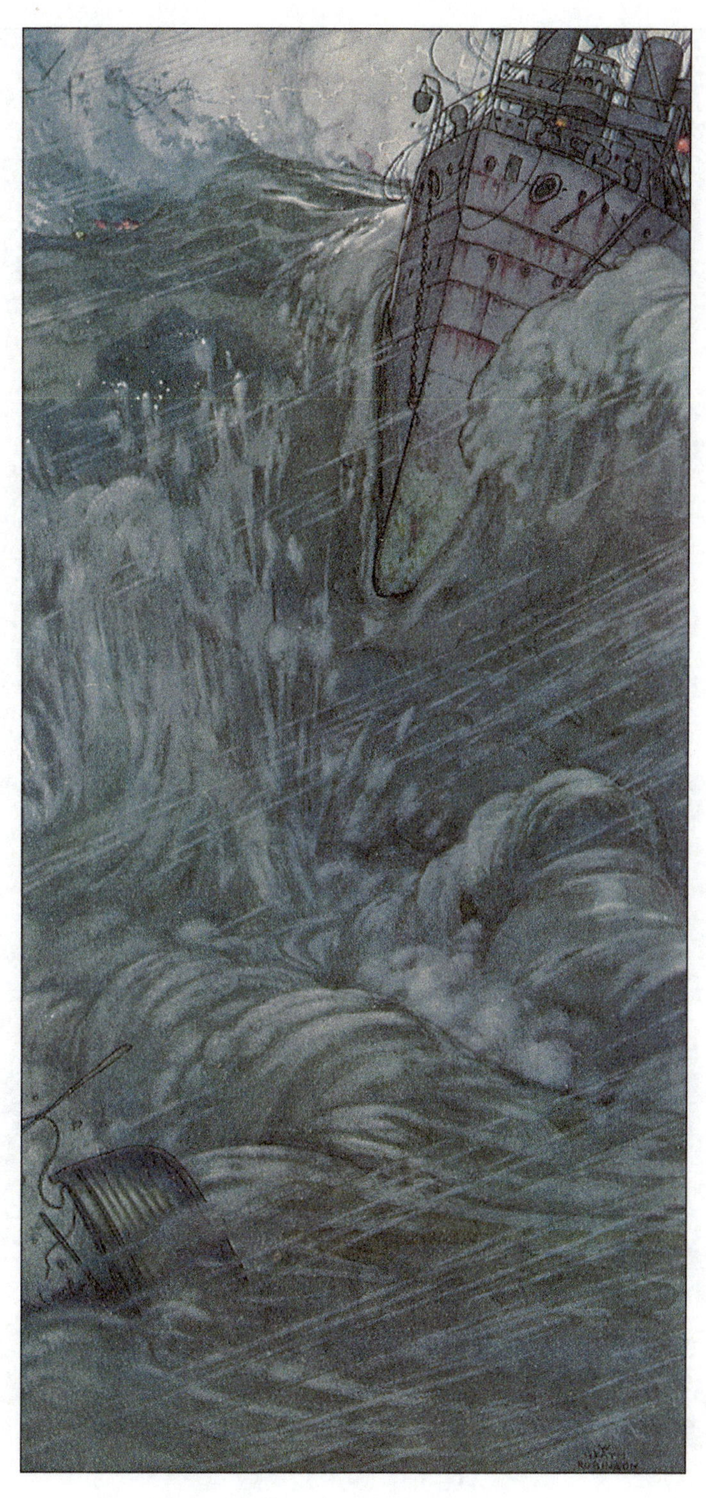

Hong-Kong

A Song of the English, 1909

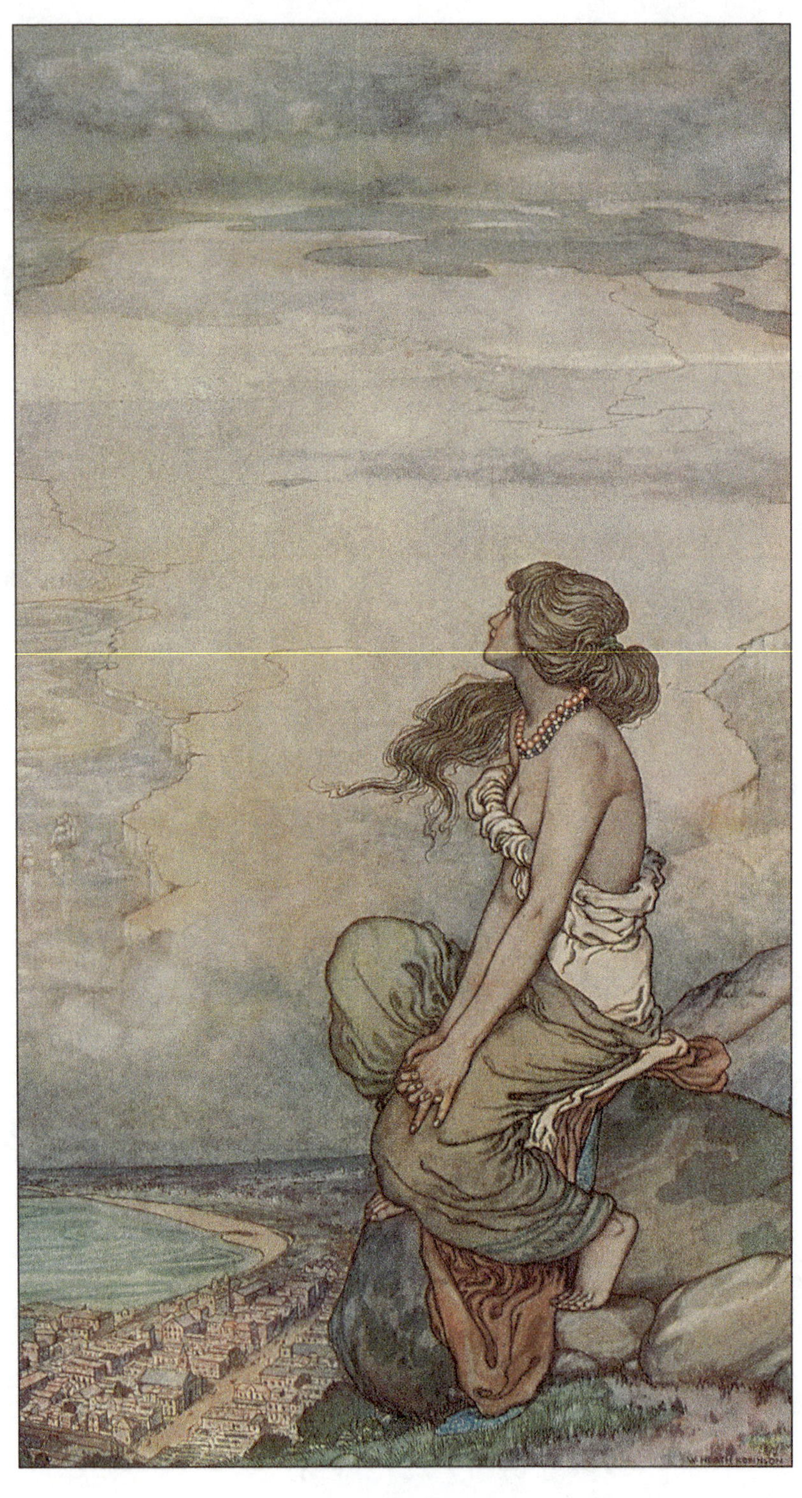

Capetown

A Song of the English, 1909

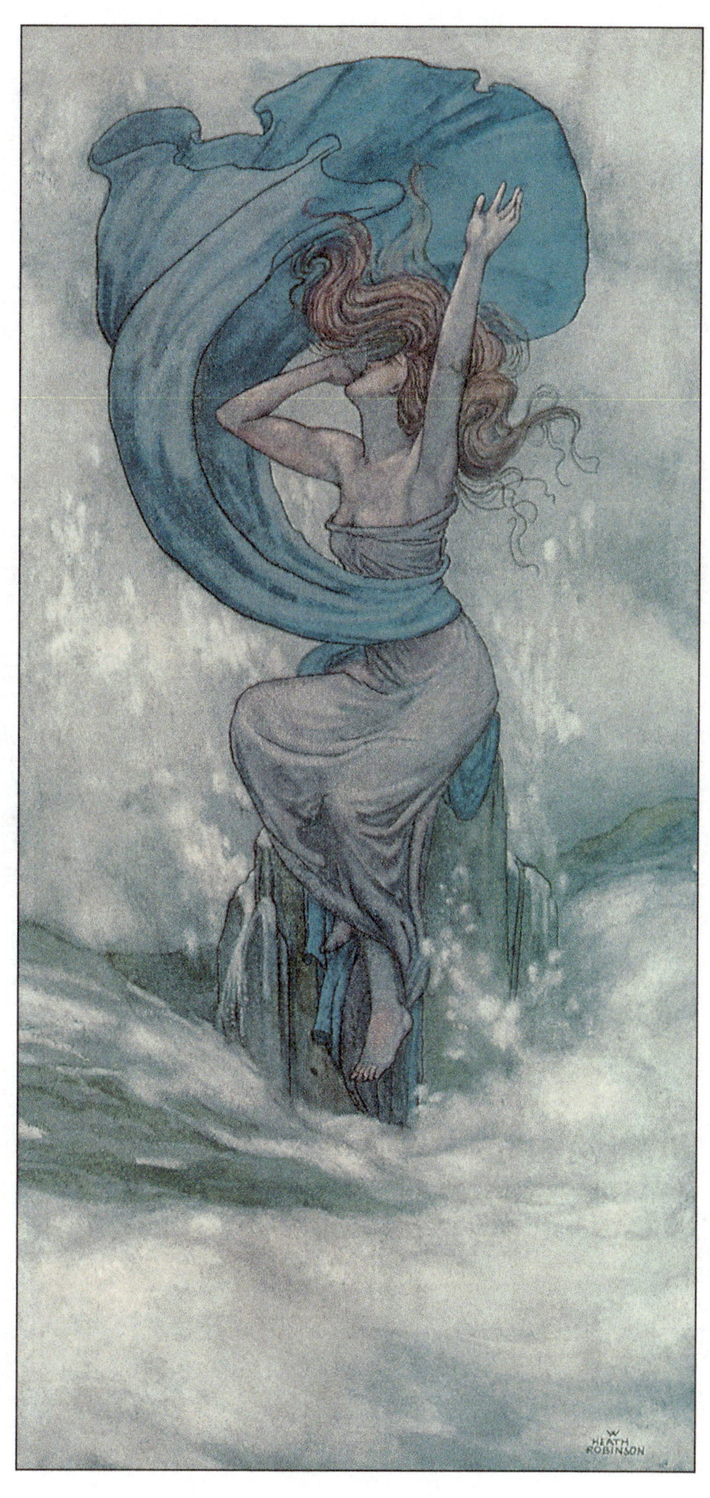

Melbourne

A Song of the English, 1909

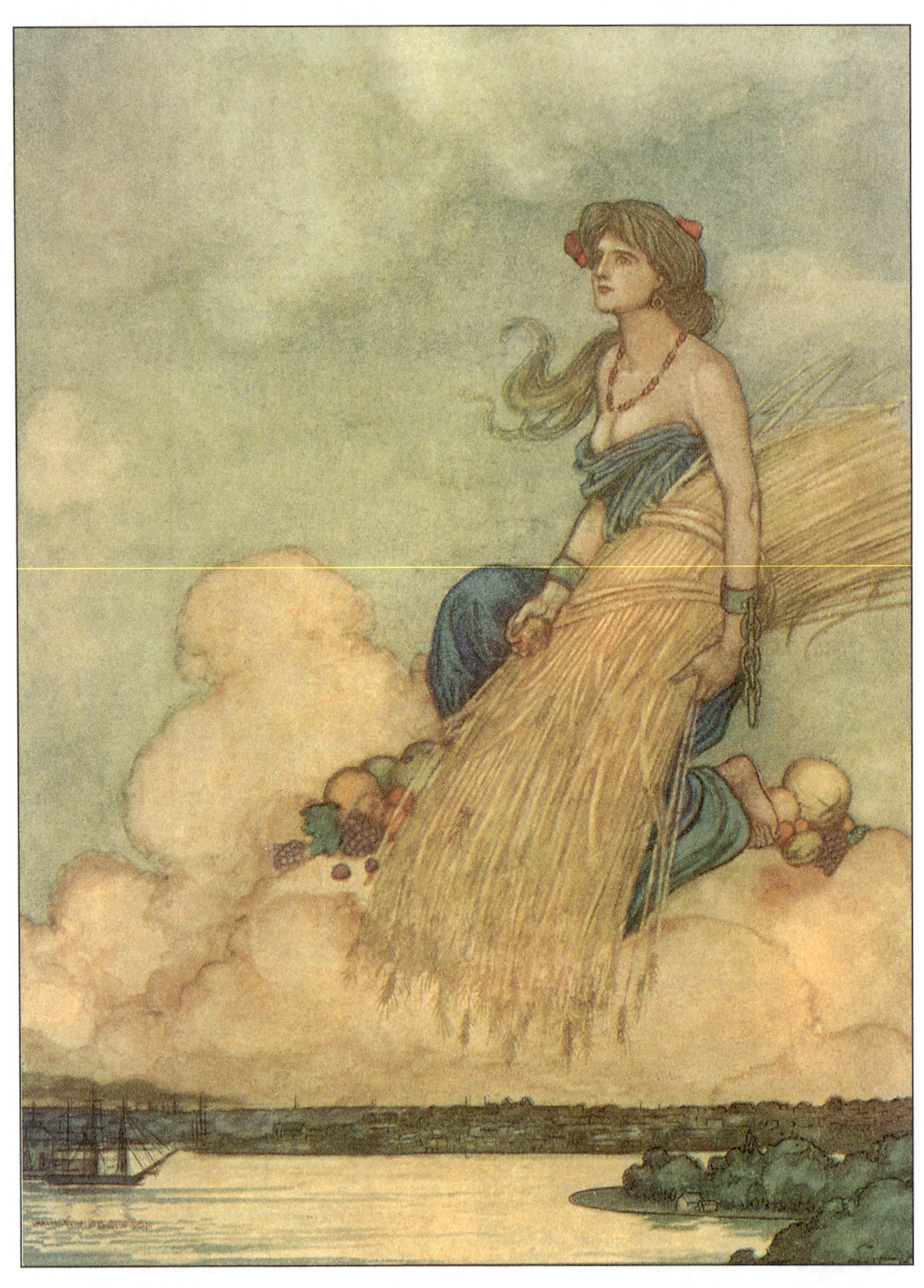

Sydney

A Song of the English, 1909

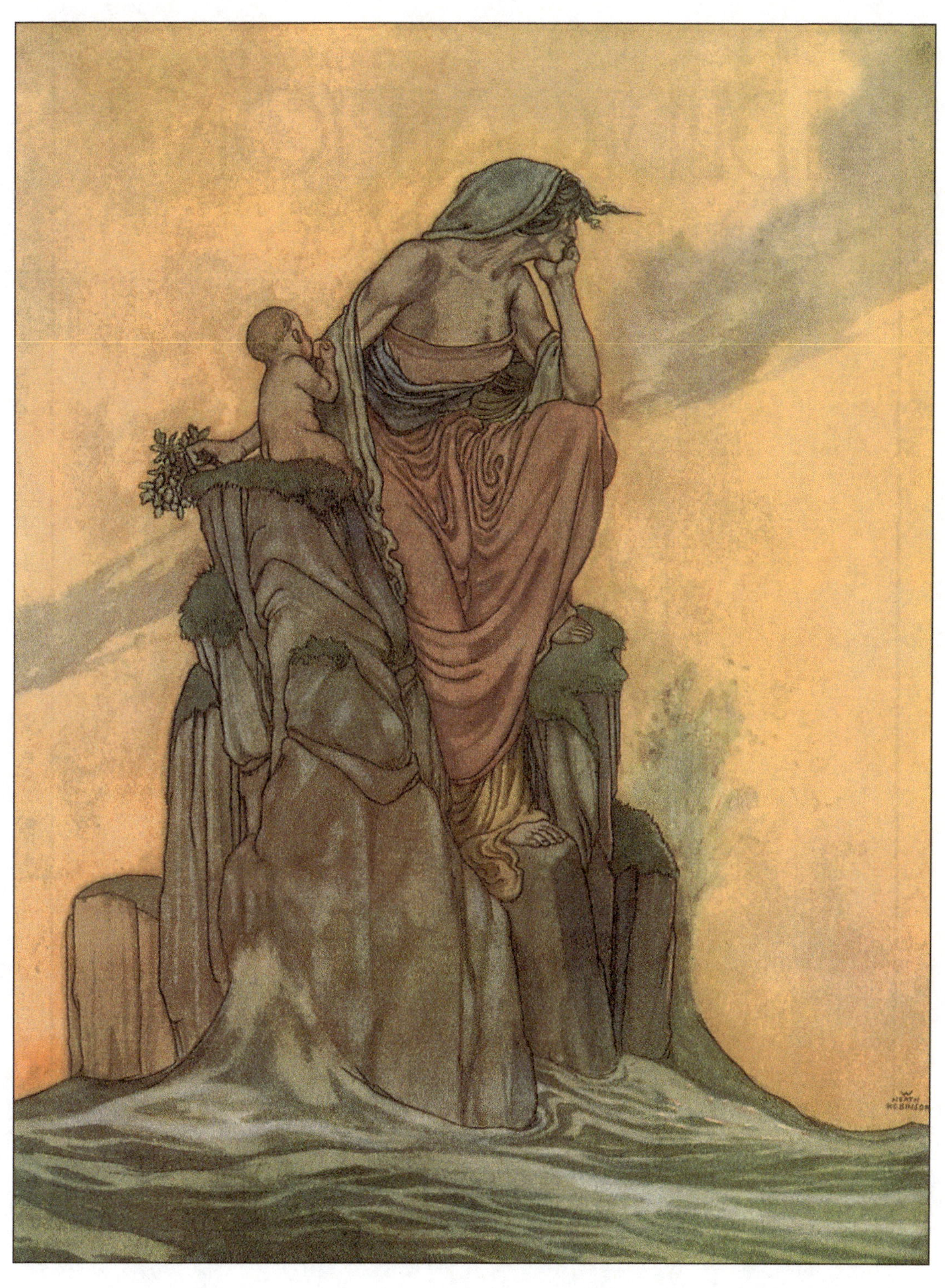

My arm is nothing weak. My strength is not gone by

A Song of the English, 1909

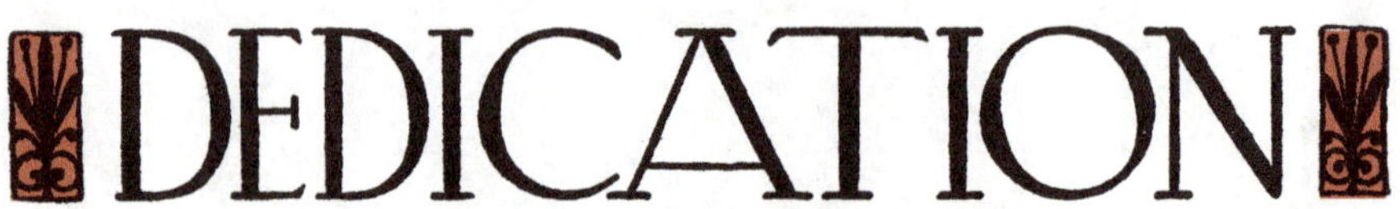

FROM "BARRACK ROOM BALLADS"

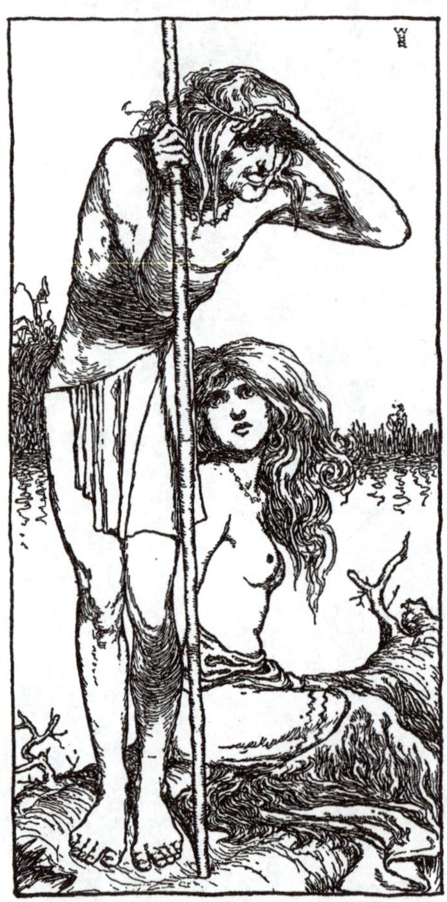

THE·FIRST·CHANTEY·

Section introduction

Collected Verse of Rudyard Kipling, 1910

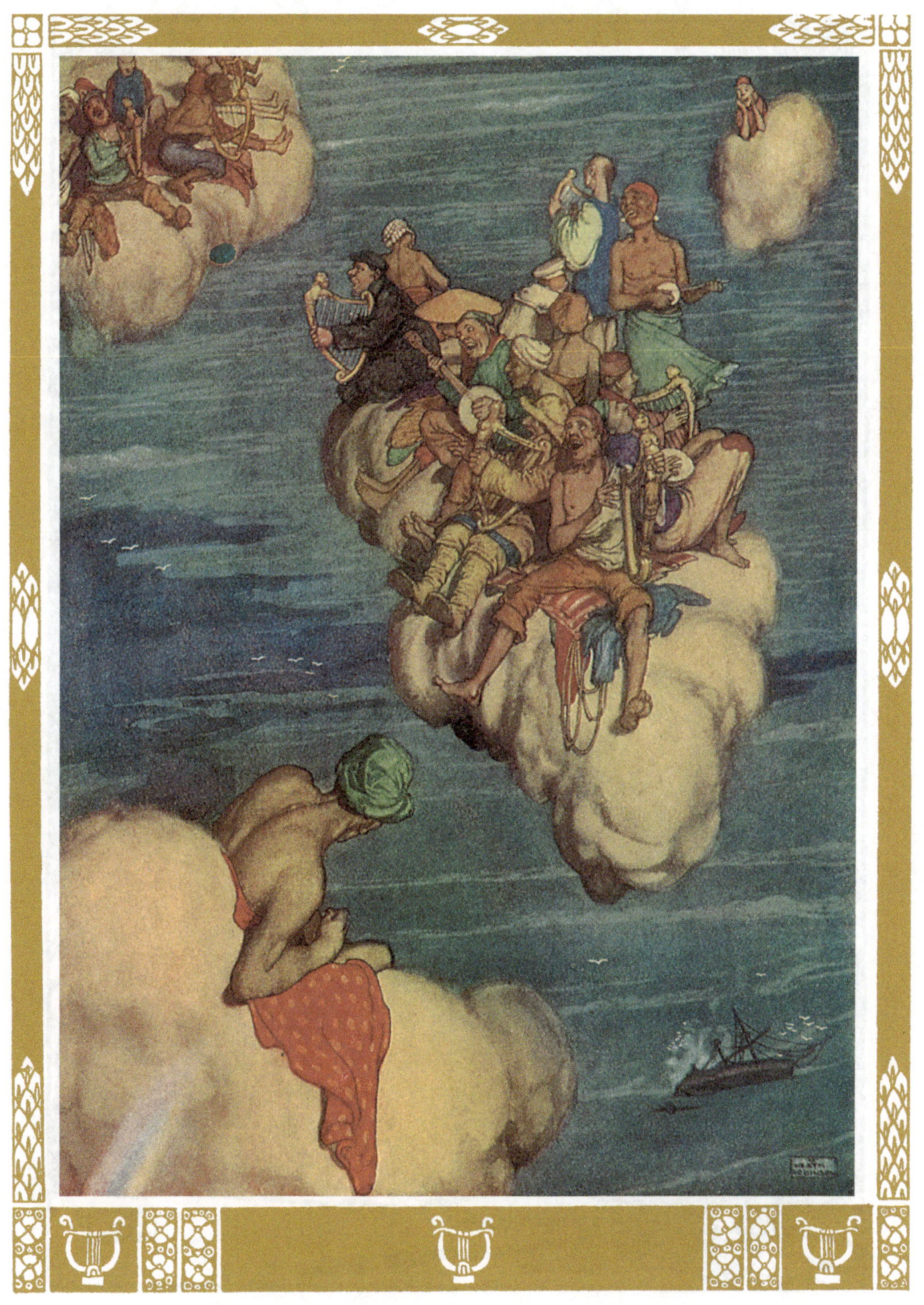

Loud sang the souls of the jolly, jolly mariners

Collected Verse of Rudyard Kipling, 1910

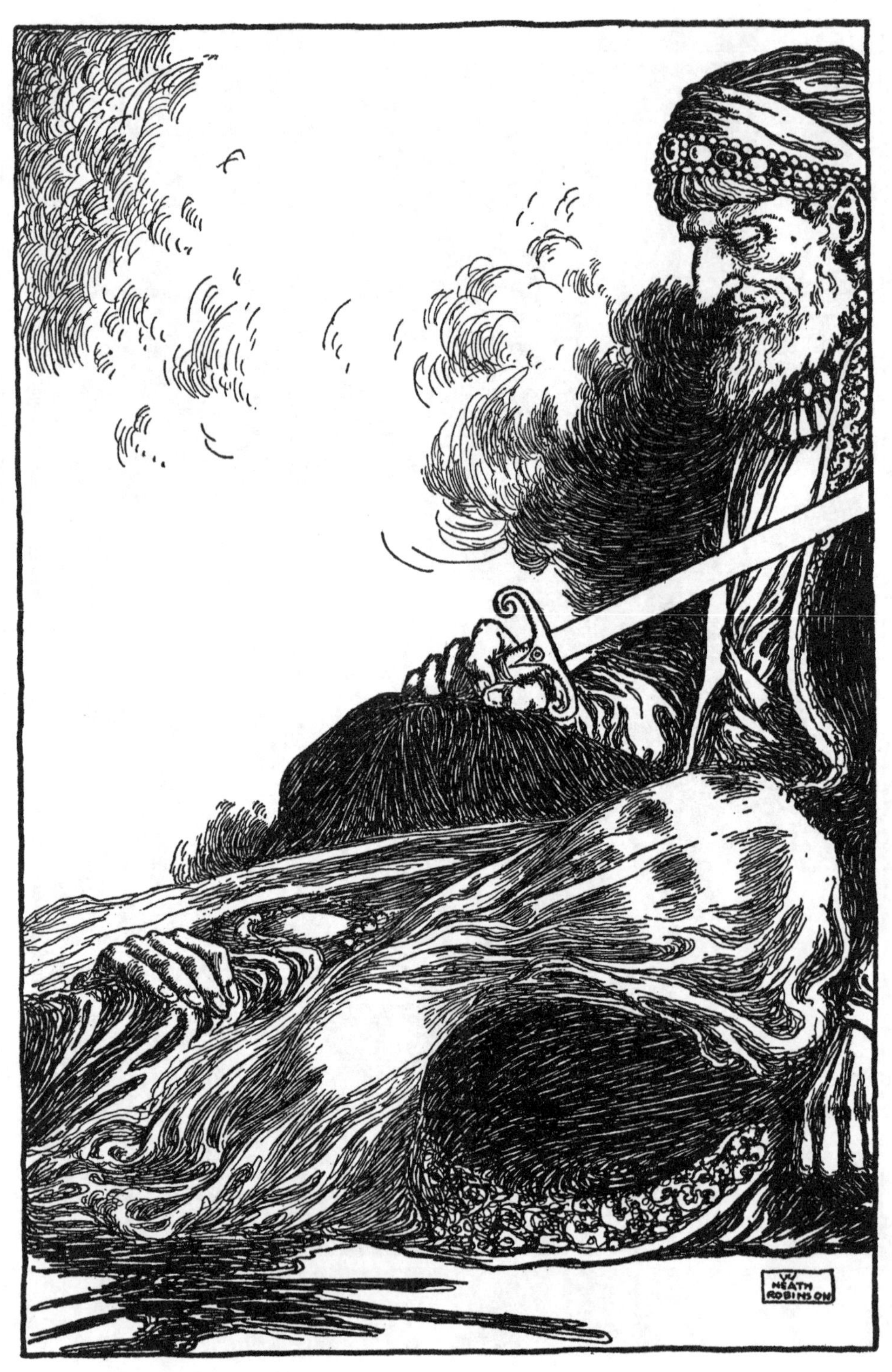

"Sister of mine, pass, free from shame.
"Pass with thy king to rest!"

Collected Verse of Rudyard Kipling, 1910

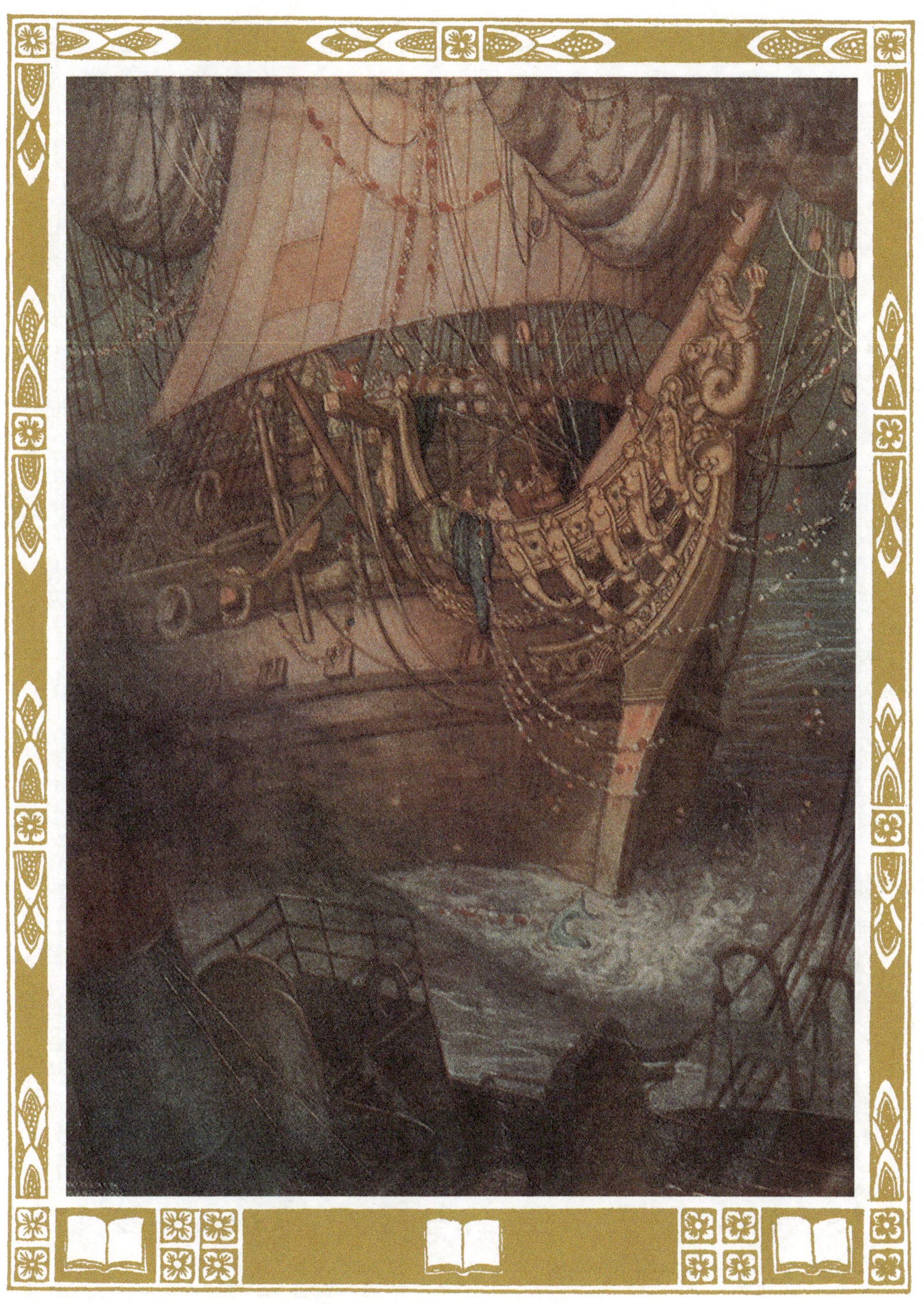

The three-decker

Collected Verse of Rudyard Kipling, 1910

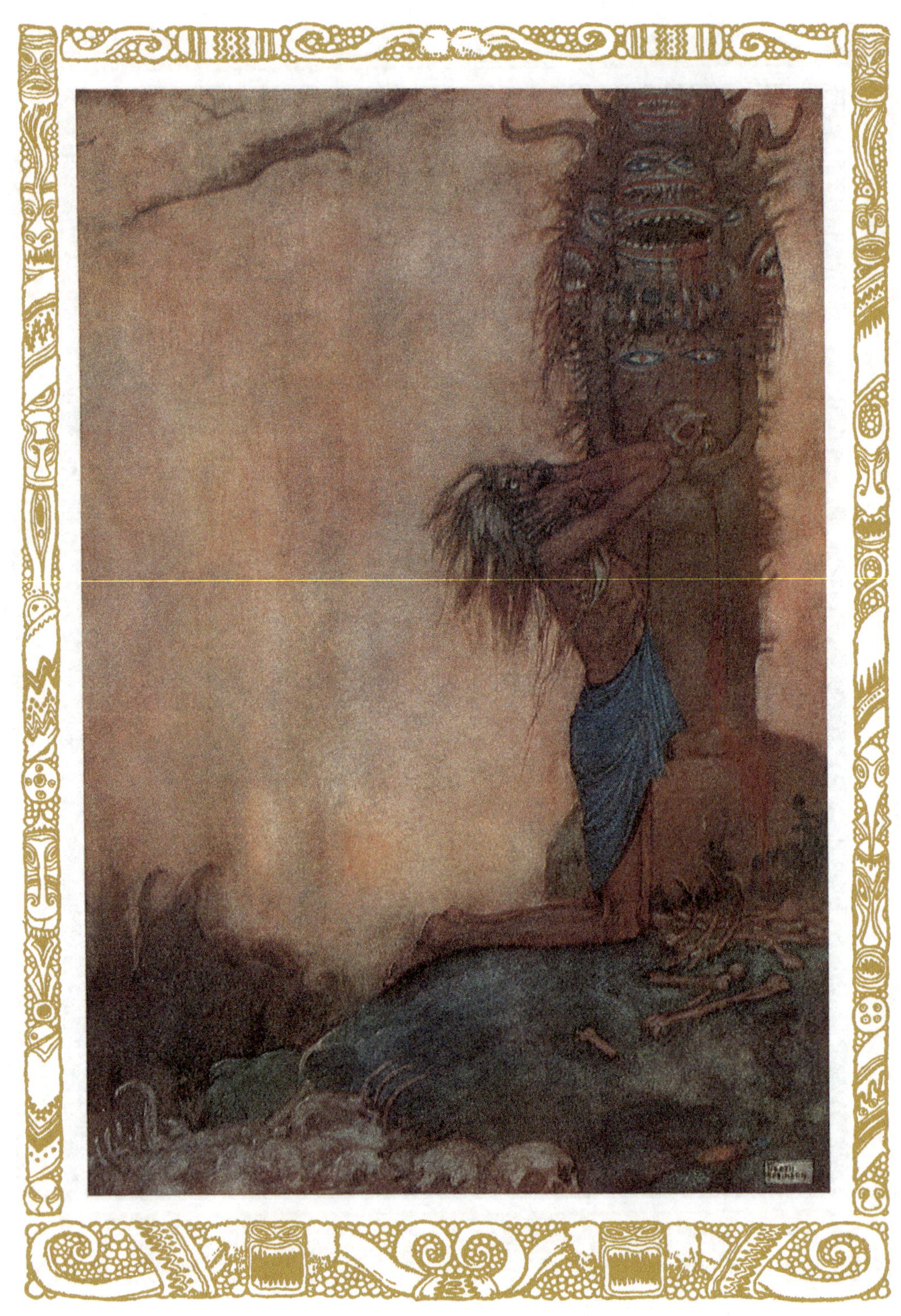

"Thus gods are made,
"And whoso makes them otherwise shall die"

Collected Verse of Rudyard Kipling, 1910

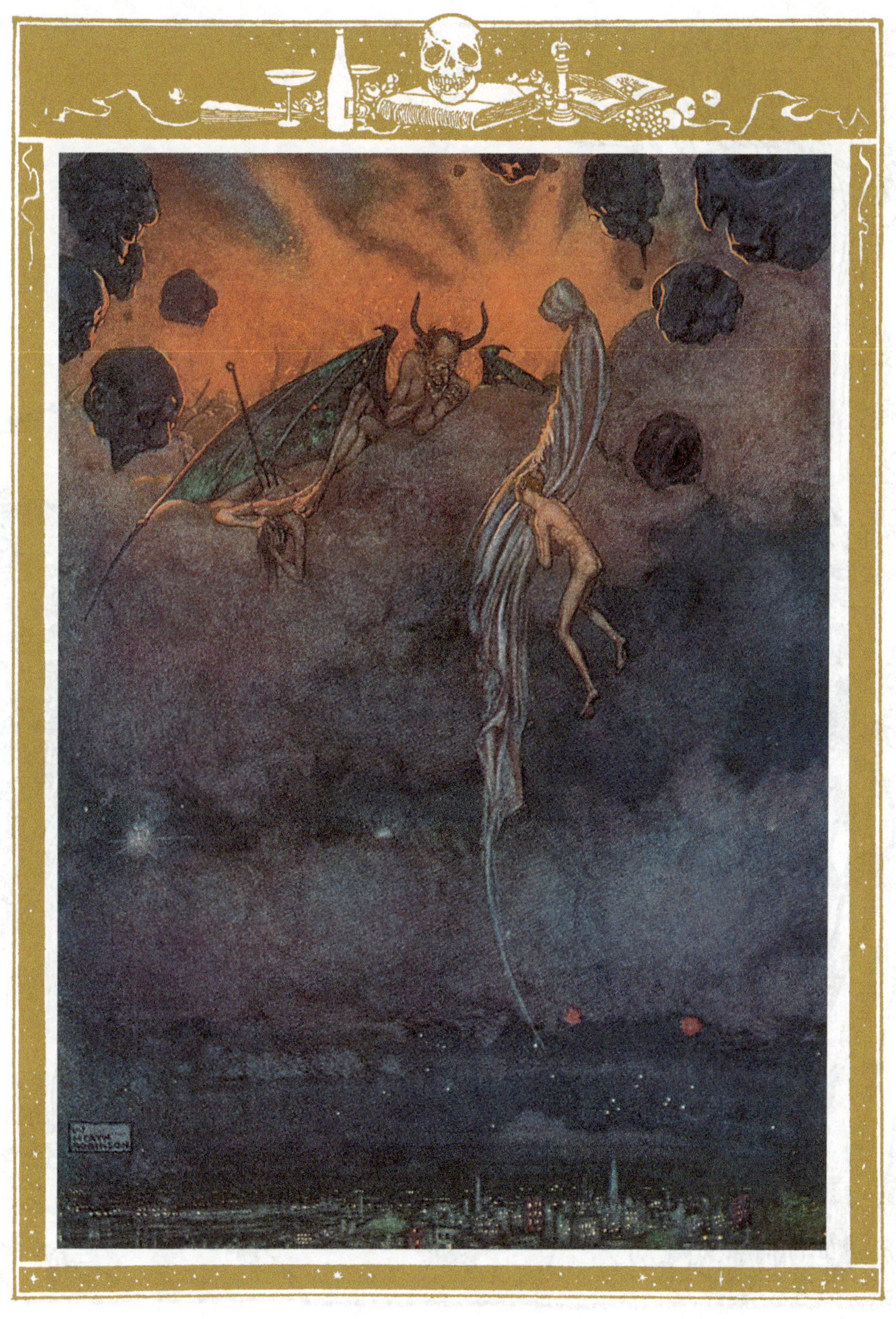

Tomlinson

Collected Verse of Rudyard Kipling, 1910

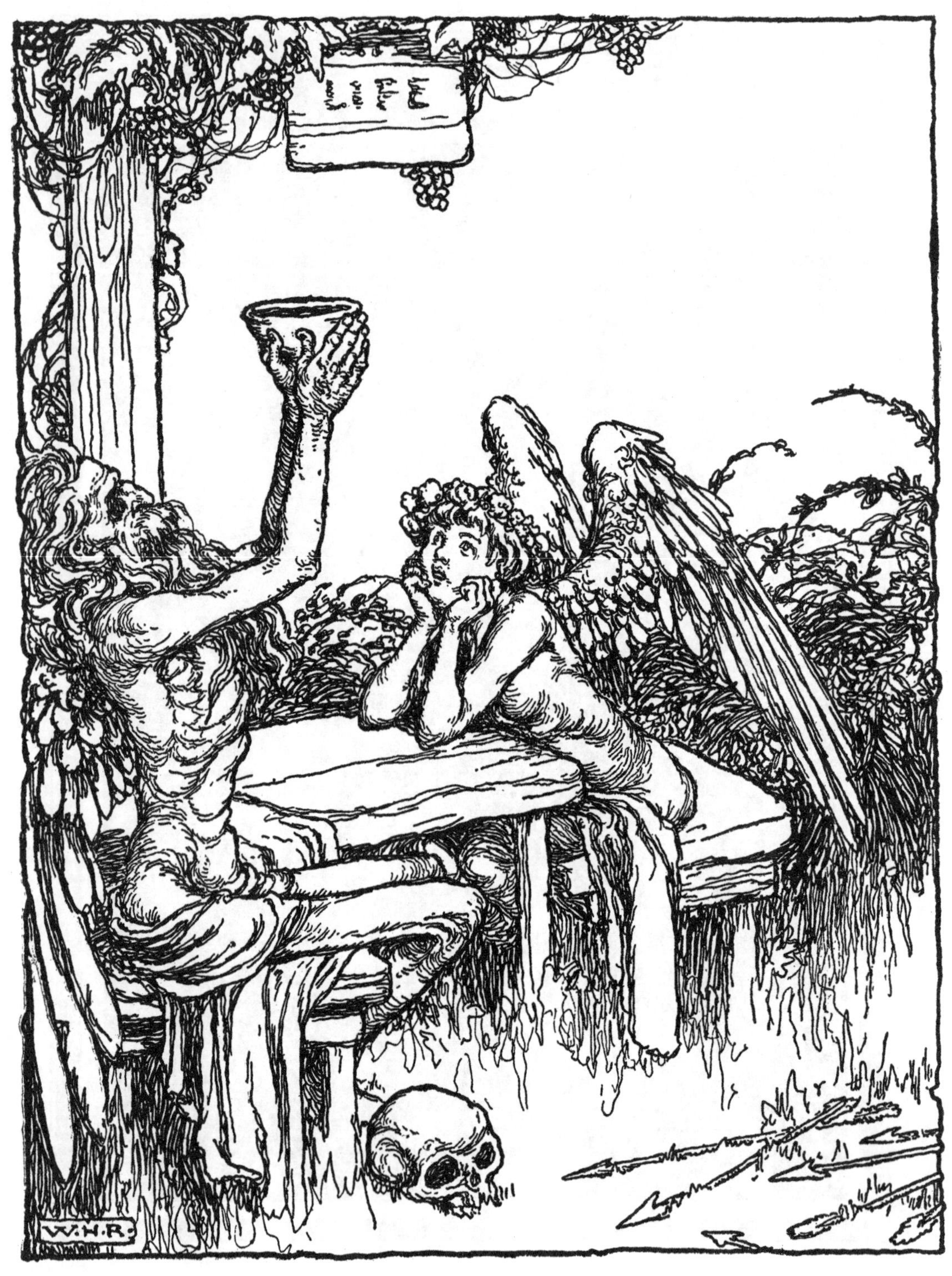

The explanation

Collected Verse of Rudyard Kipling, 1910

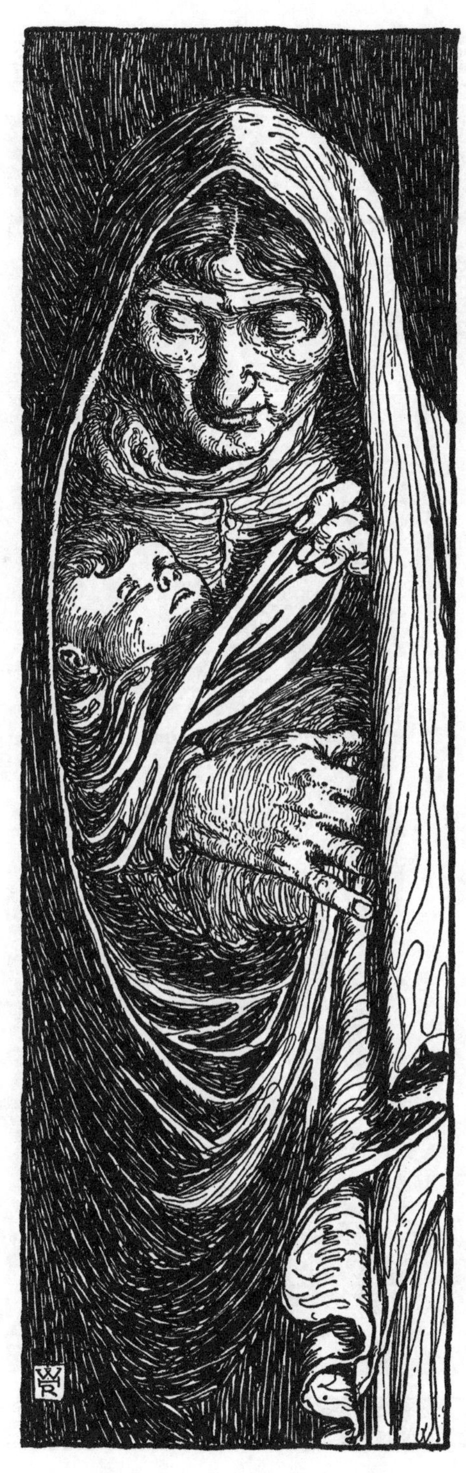

She laid it into her breast

Collected Verse of Rudyard Kipling, 1910

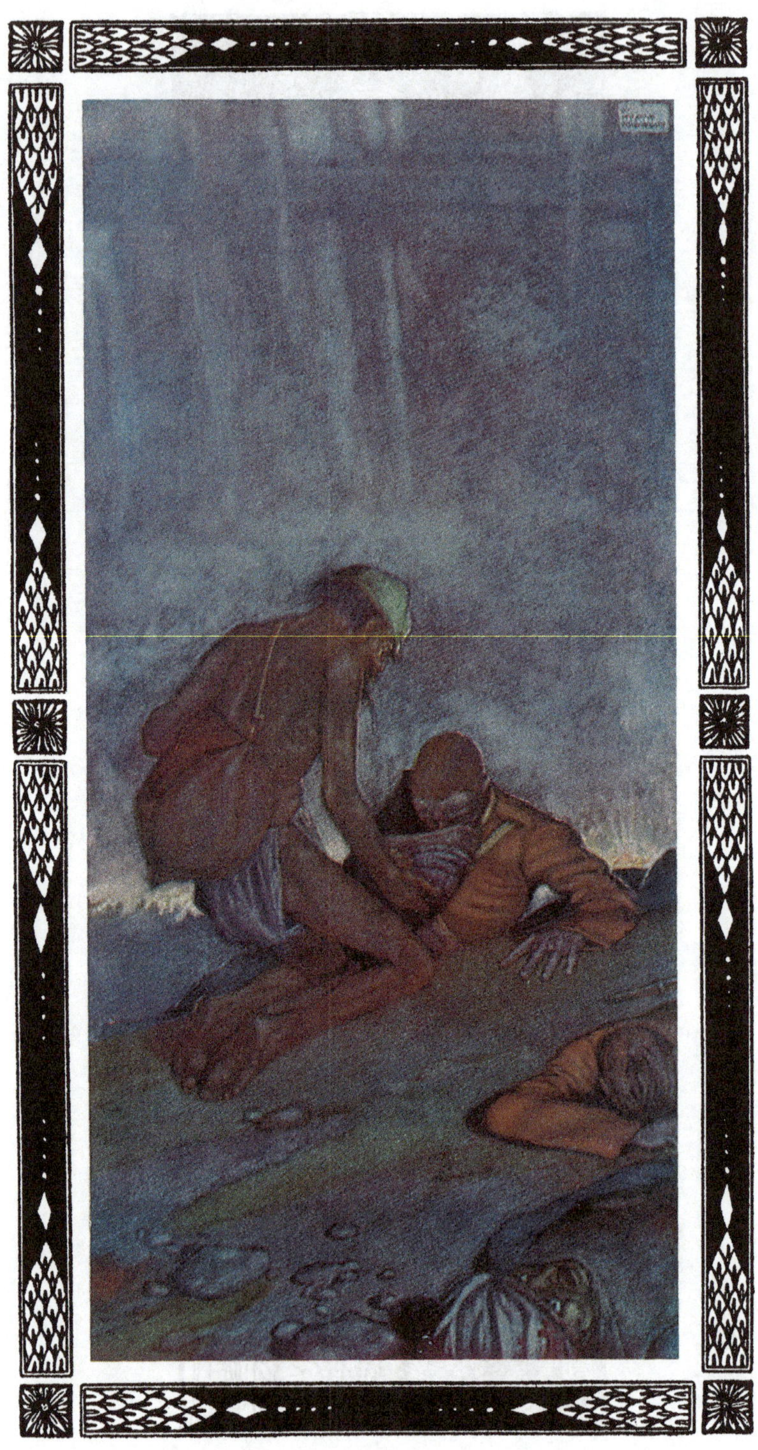

An' the man that spied me first was our good old grinnin', gruntin' gunga din

Collected Verse of Rudyard Kipling, 1910

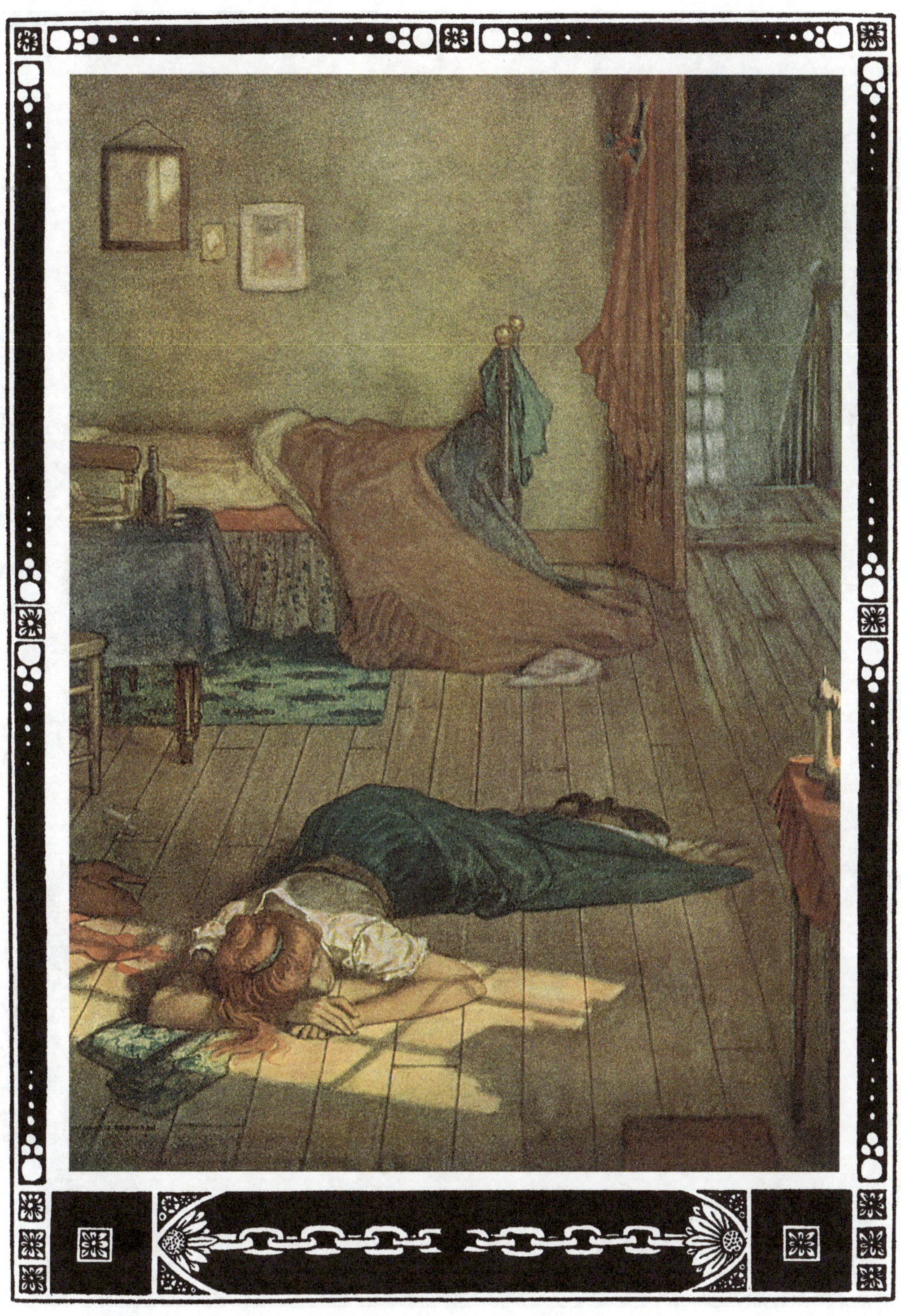

"Mary, pity women!"

Collected Verse of Rudyard Kipling, 1910

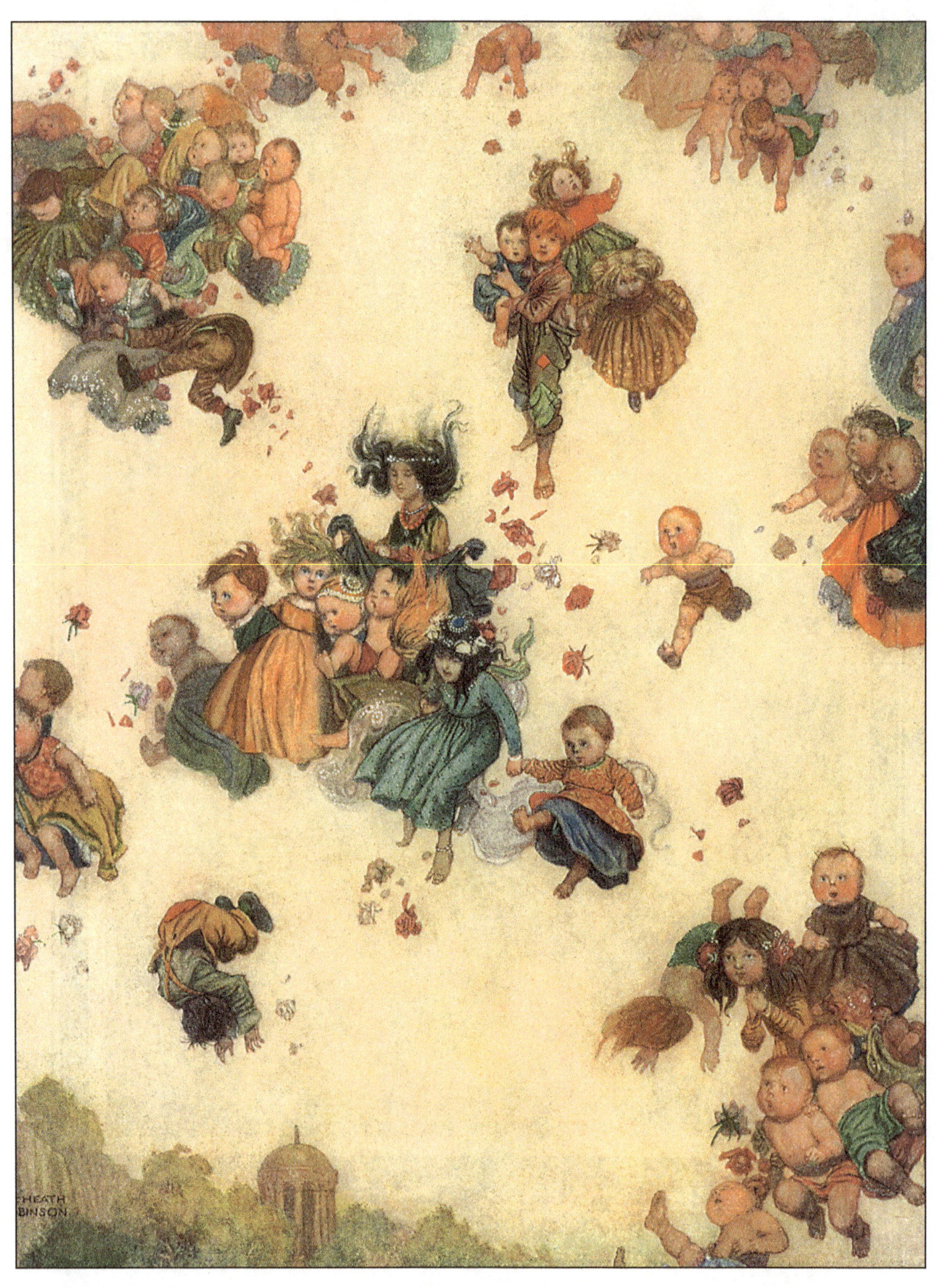

Frontispiece

Bill the Minder, 1912

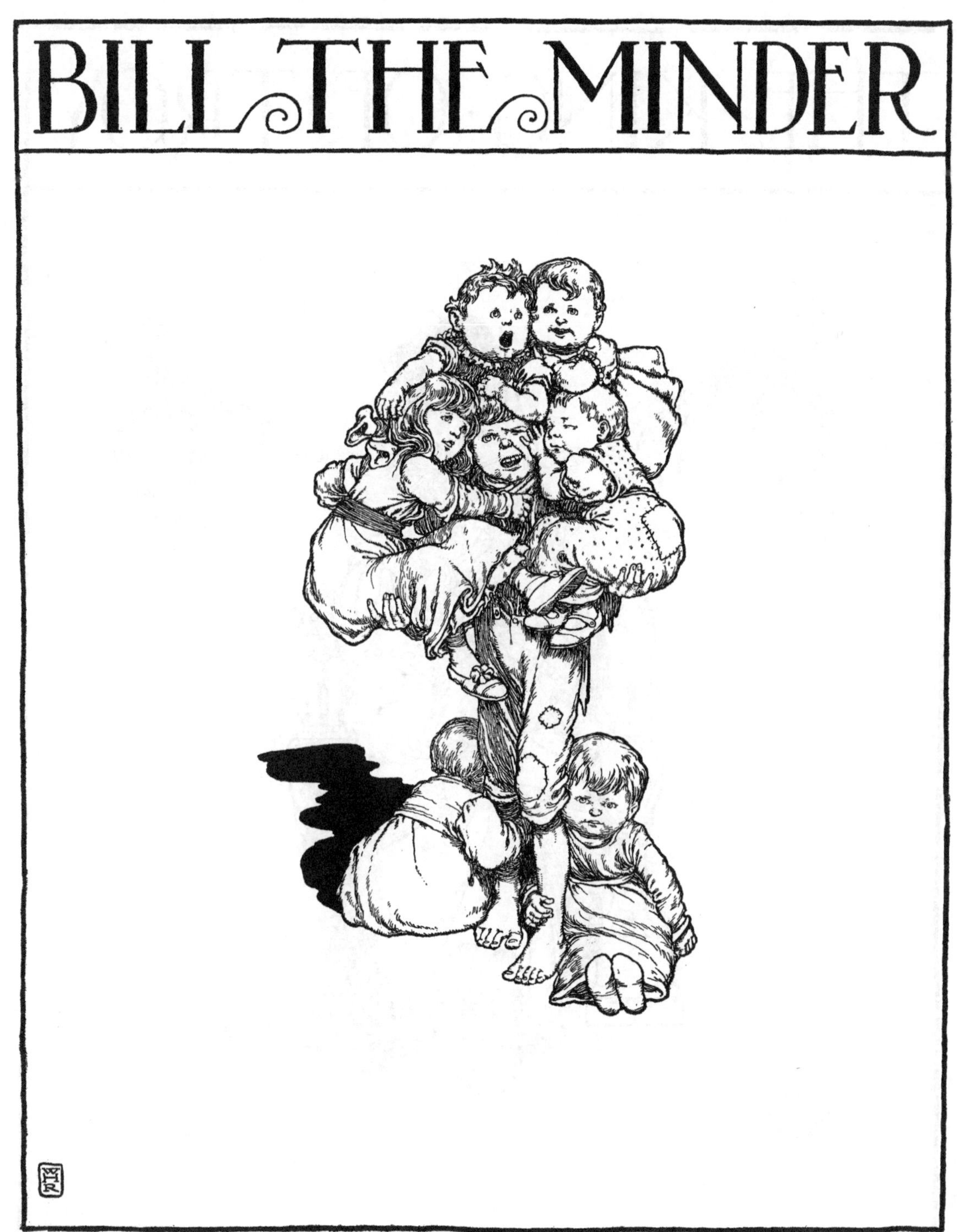

Bill the Minder

Bill the Minder, 1912

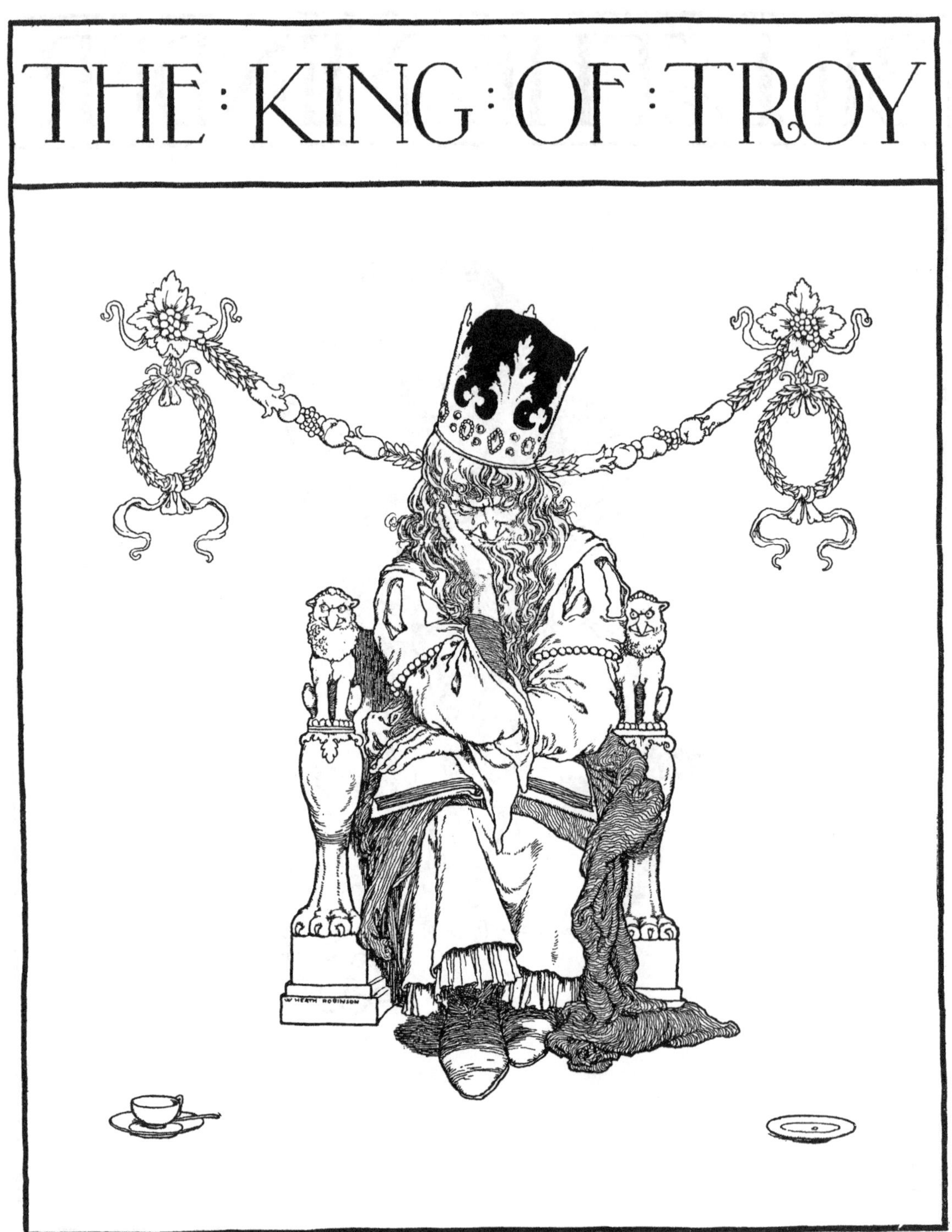

The King of Troy

Bill the Minder, 1912

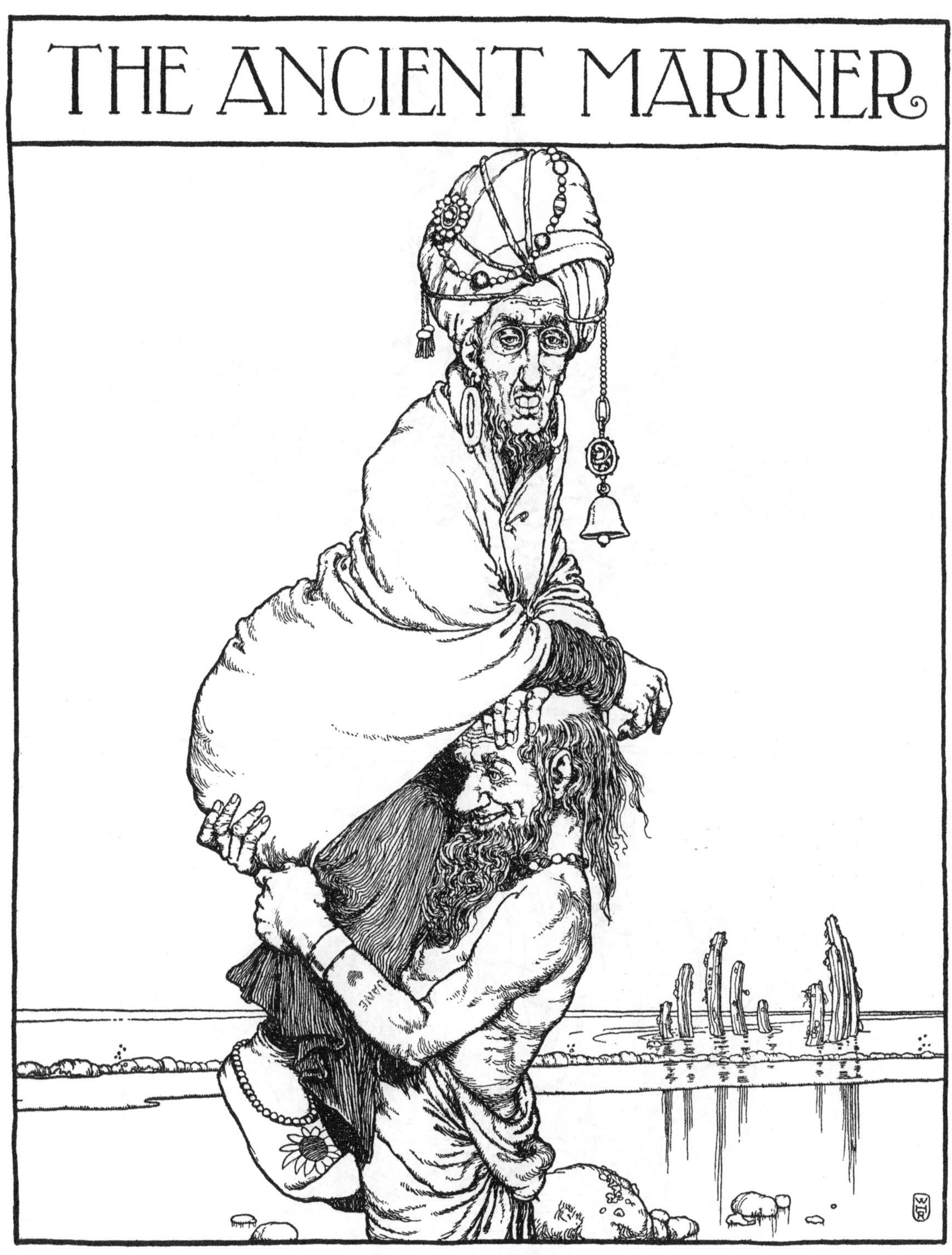

The Ancient Mariner

Bill the Minder, 1912

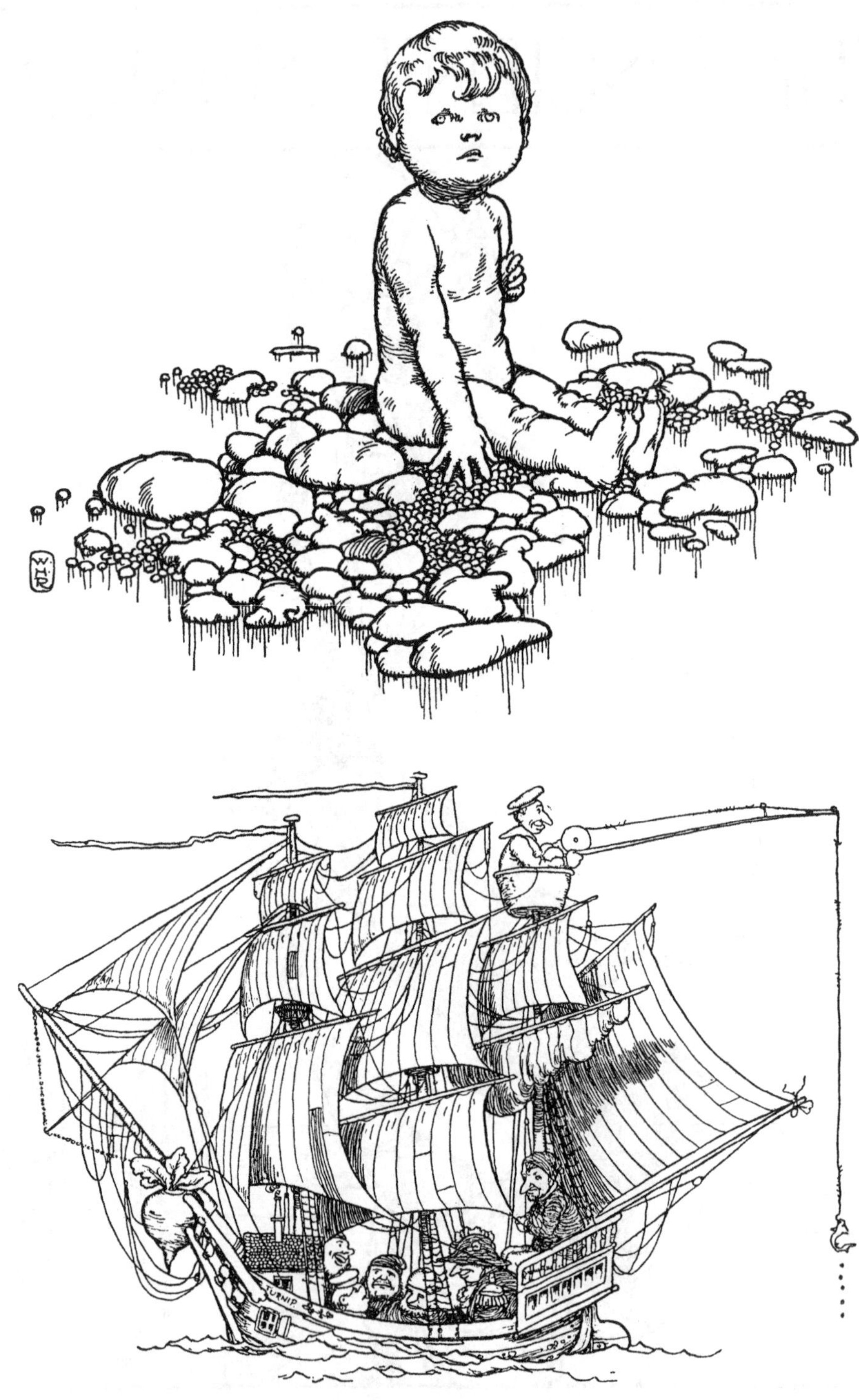

Top. Headpiece, Bill the Minder
Bottom. For years we sailed

Bill the Minder, 1912

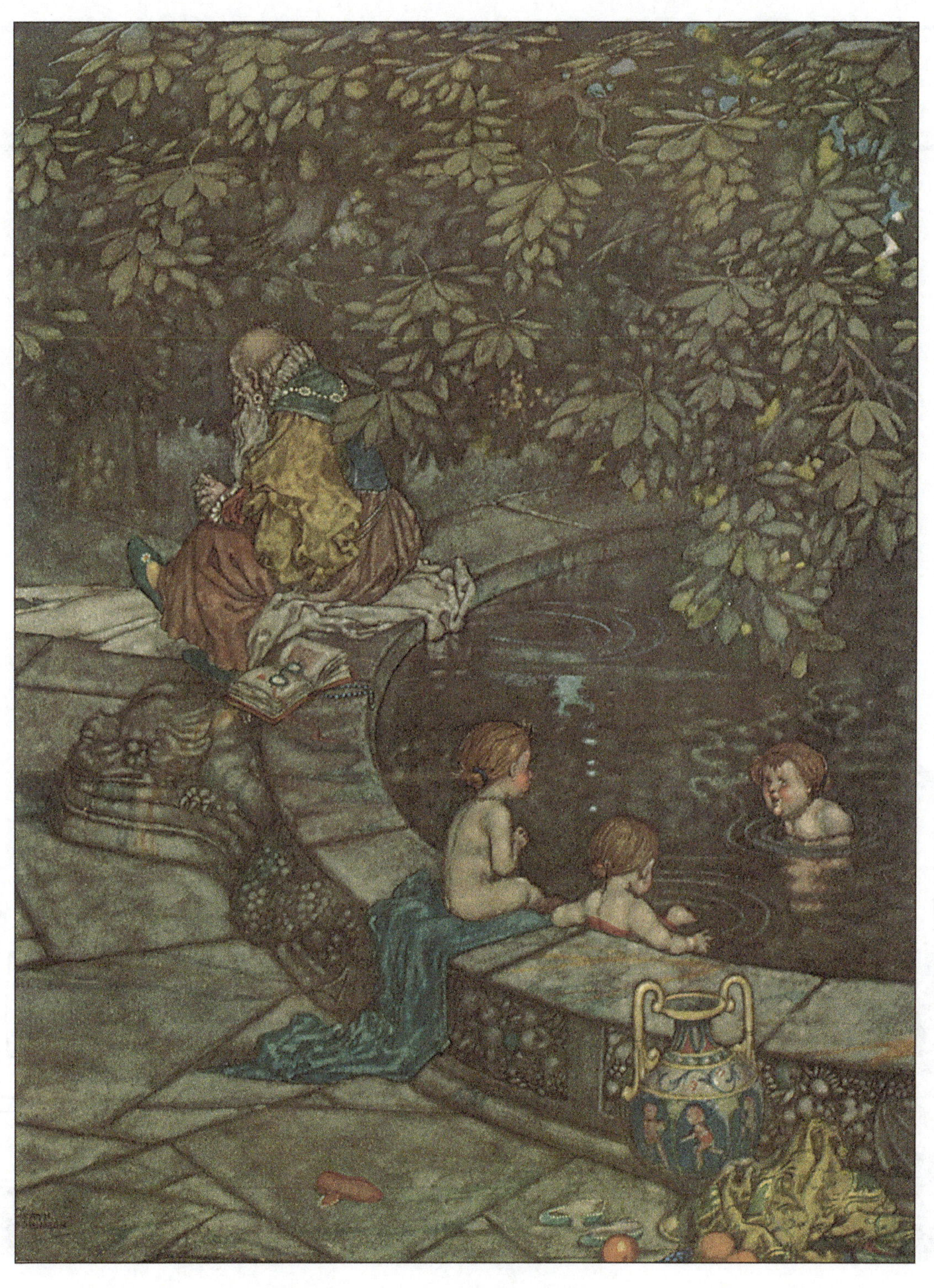

He was always at hand

Bill the Minder, 1912

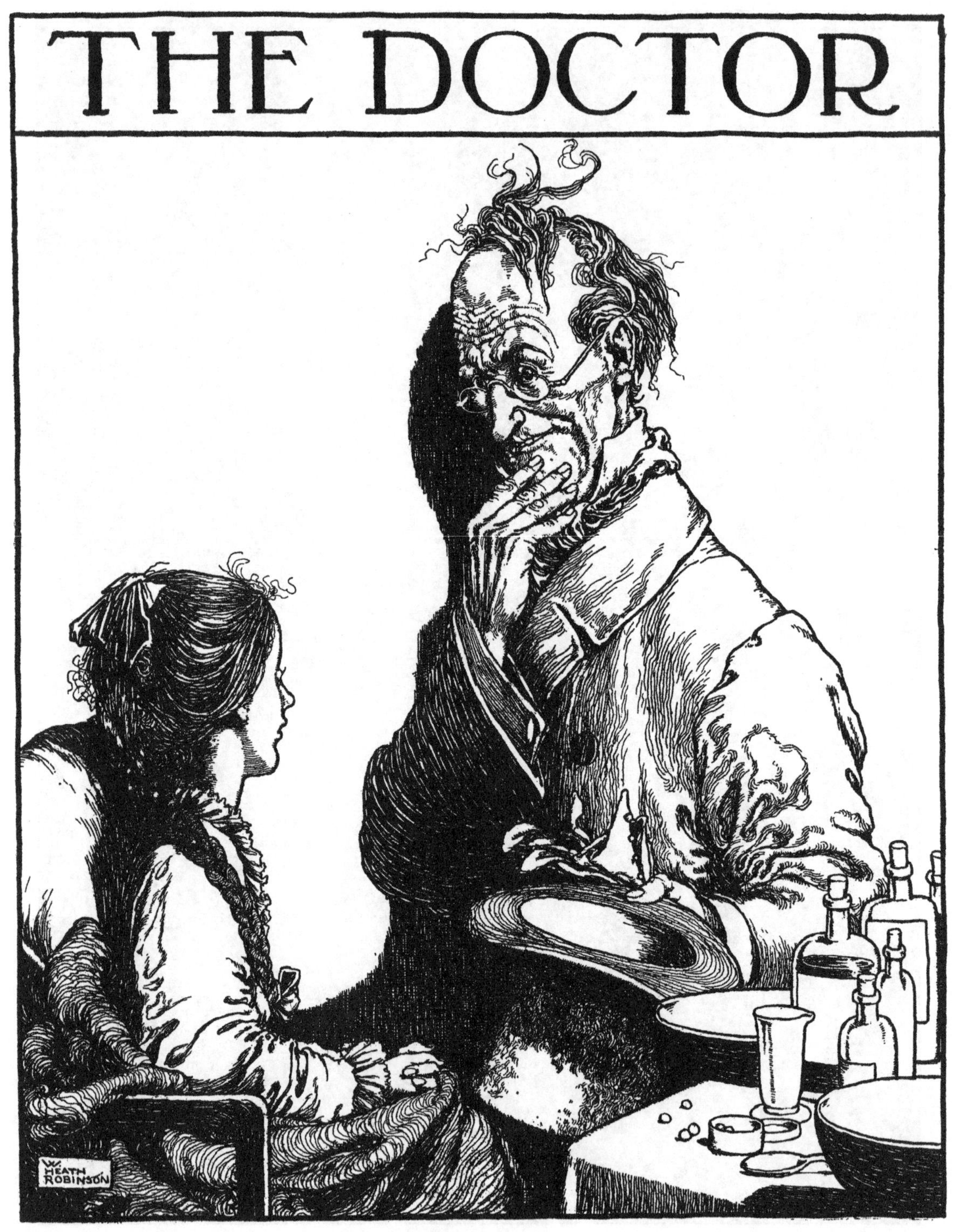

The Doctor

Bill the Minder, 1912

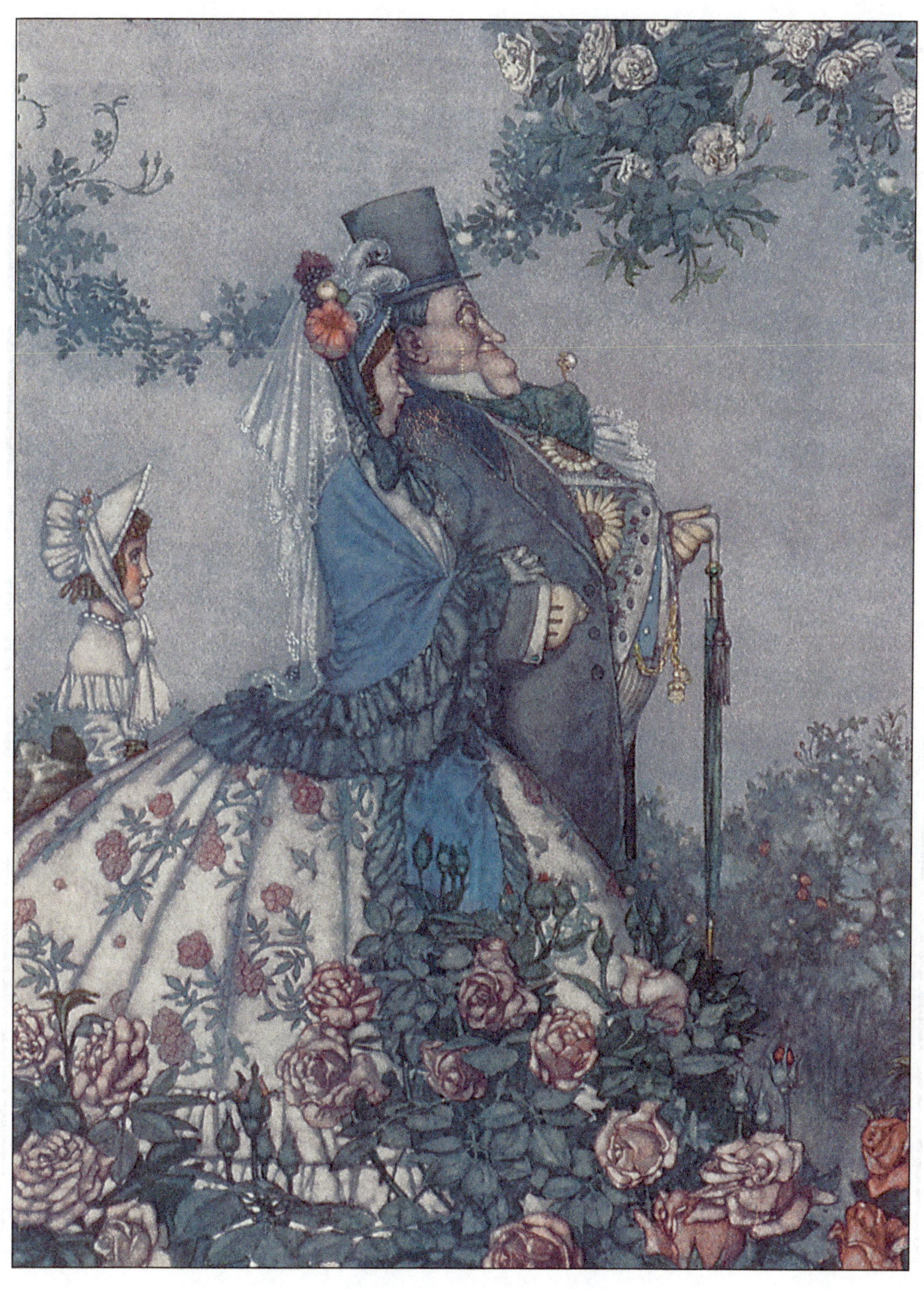

The Respectable Gentleman

Bill the Minder, 1912

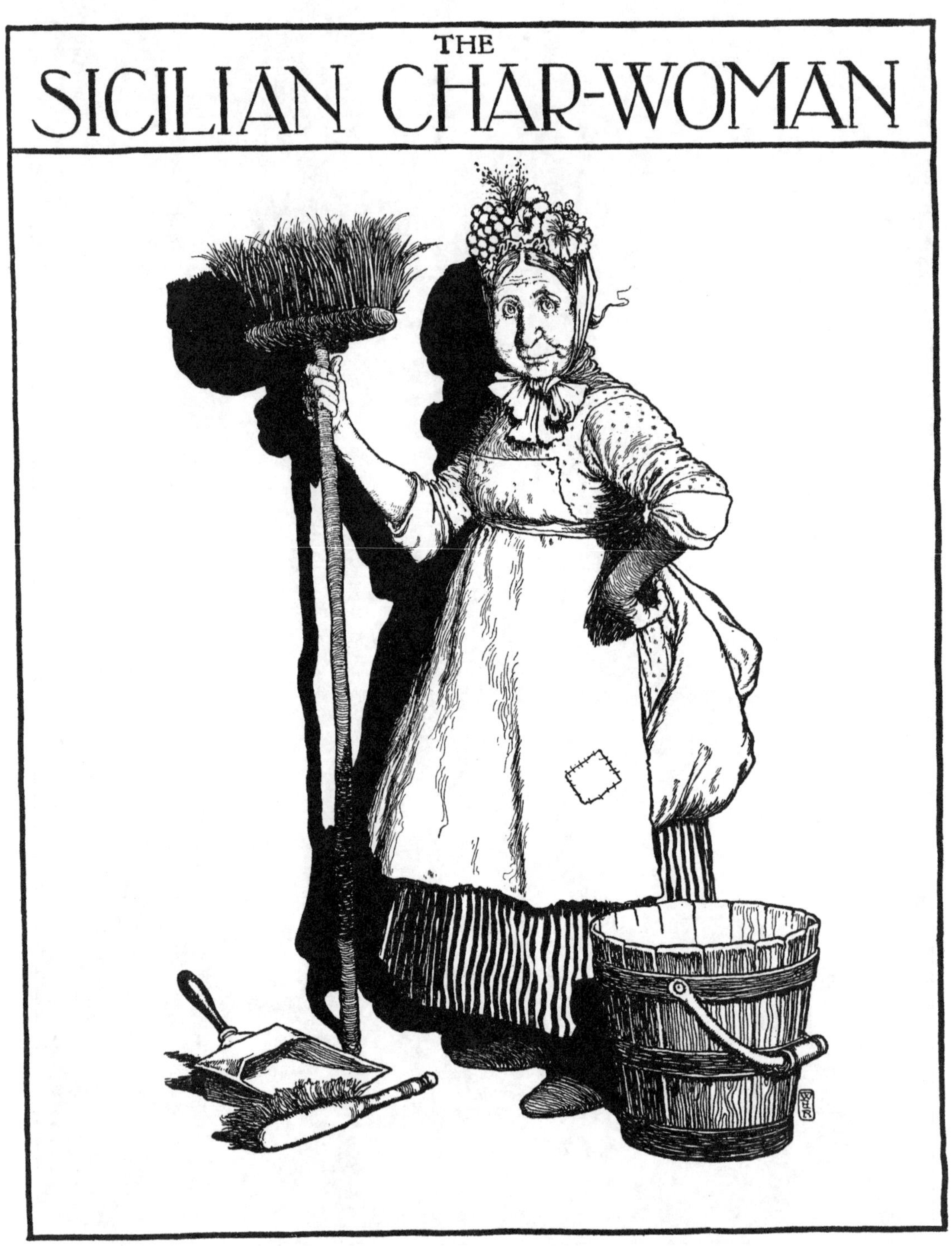

The Sicilian Char-woman

Bill the Minder, 1912

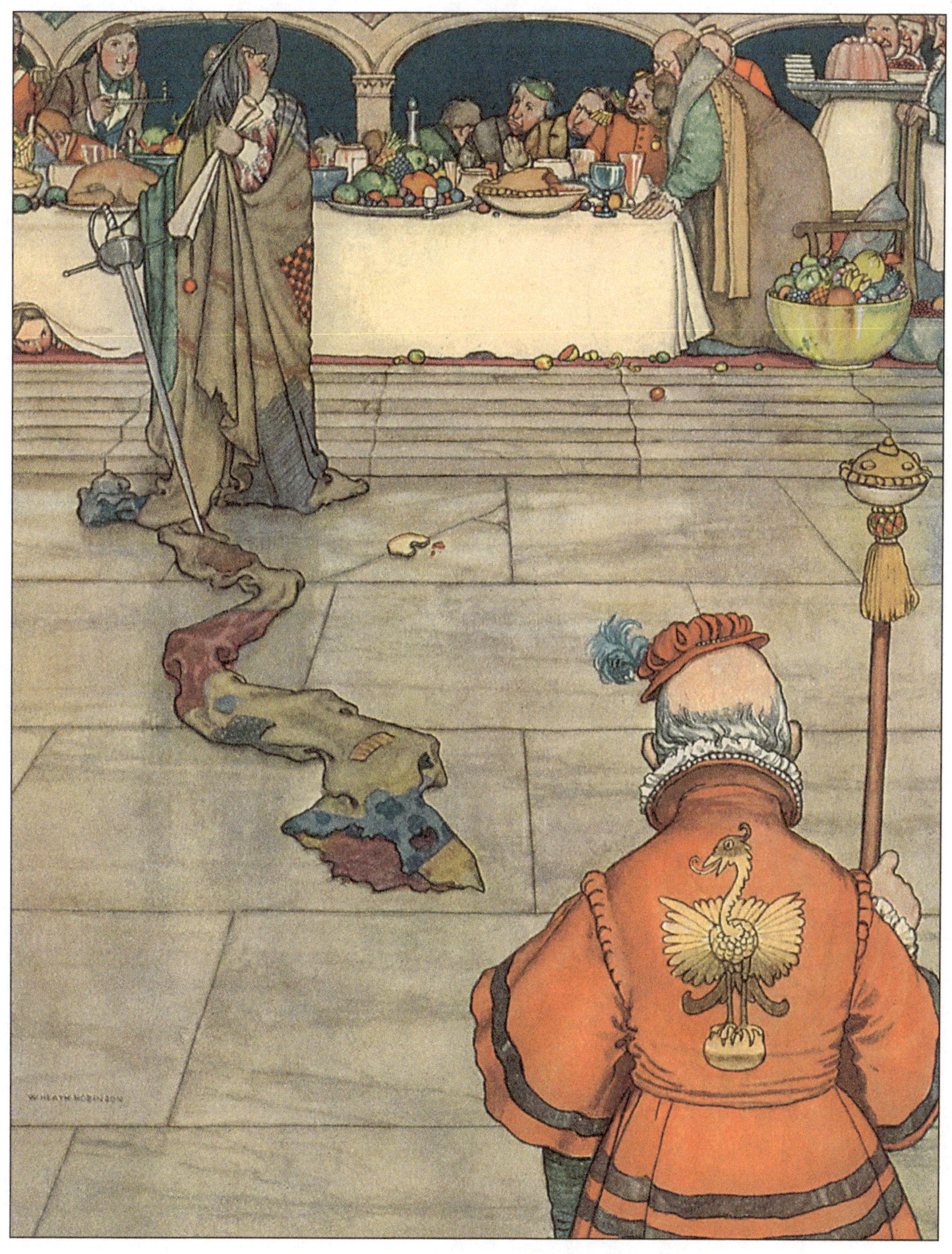

Reginald completely lost his temper

Bill the Minder, 1912

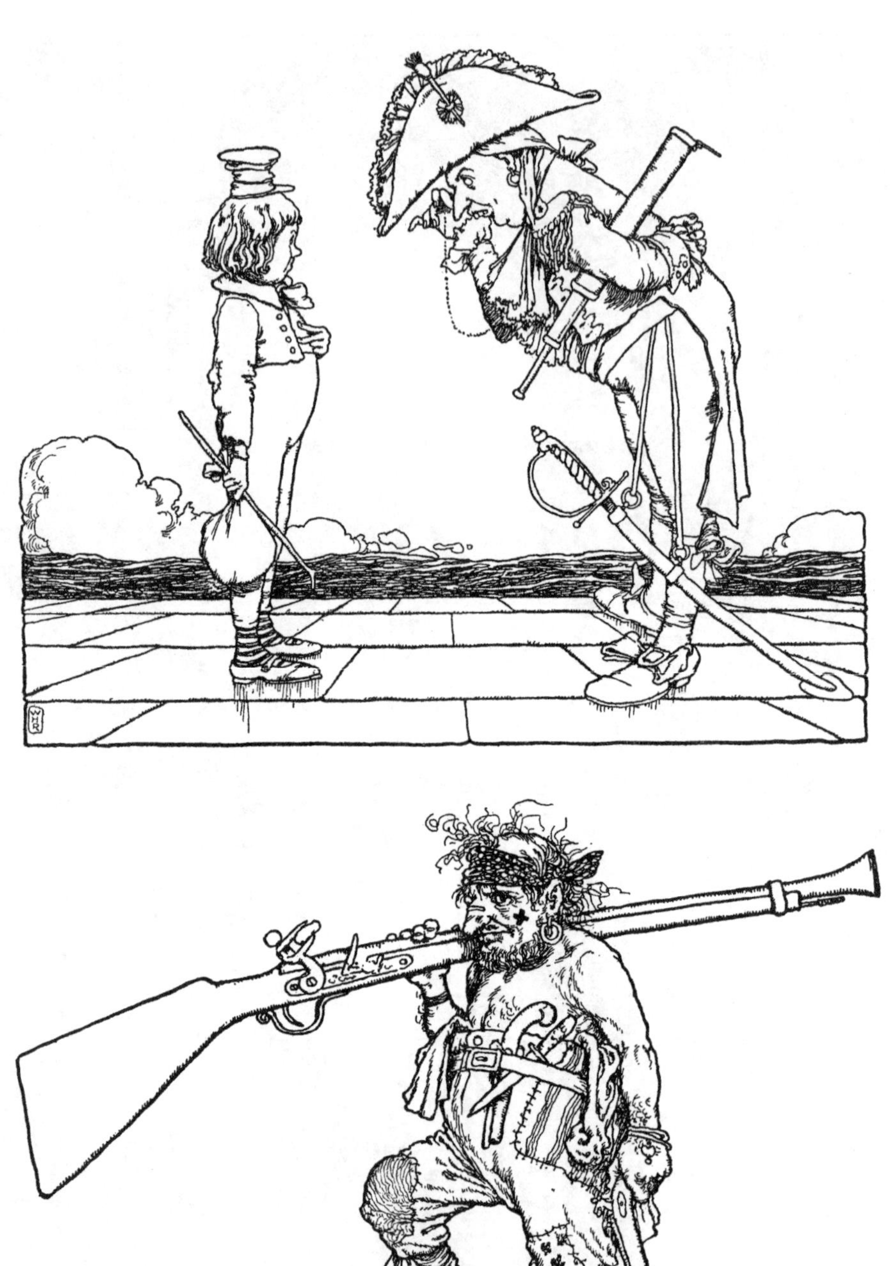

Top. I sign on as cabin boy
Bottom. In expectation of their leader

BILL THE MINDER, 1912

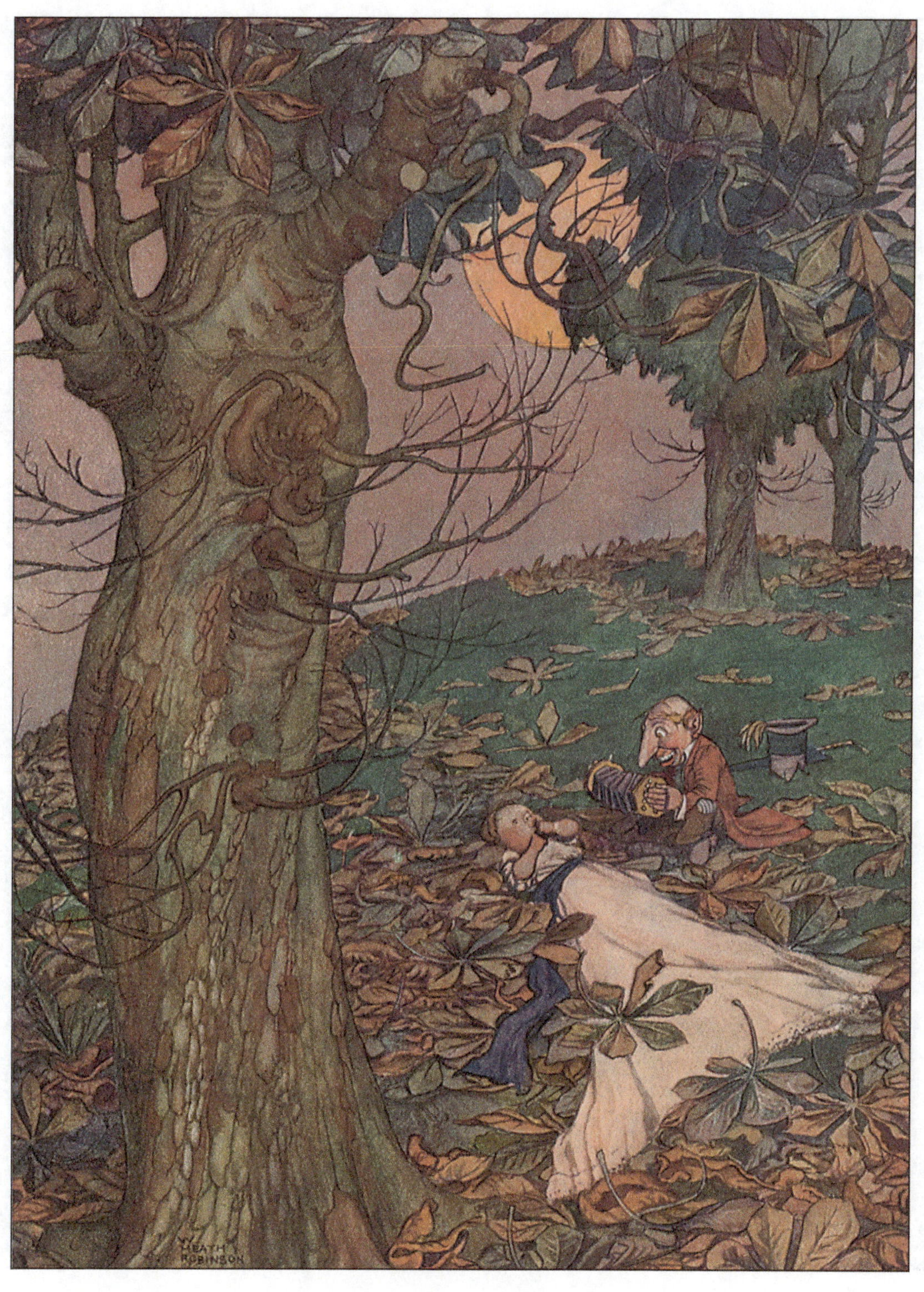

And played it for my delight

Bill the Minder, 1912

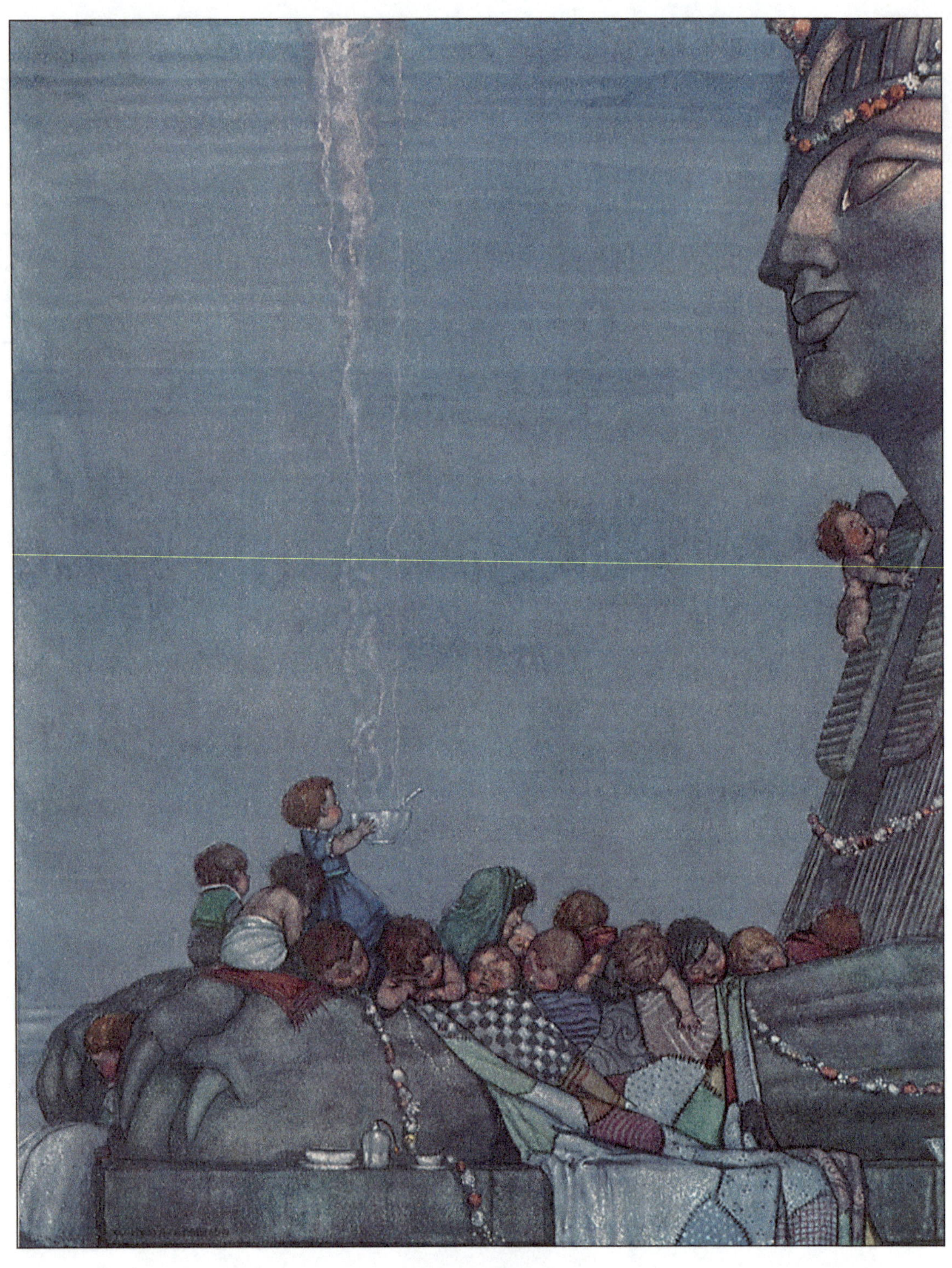

They came upon a great stone sphinx

Bill the Minder, 1912

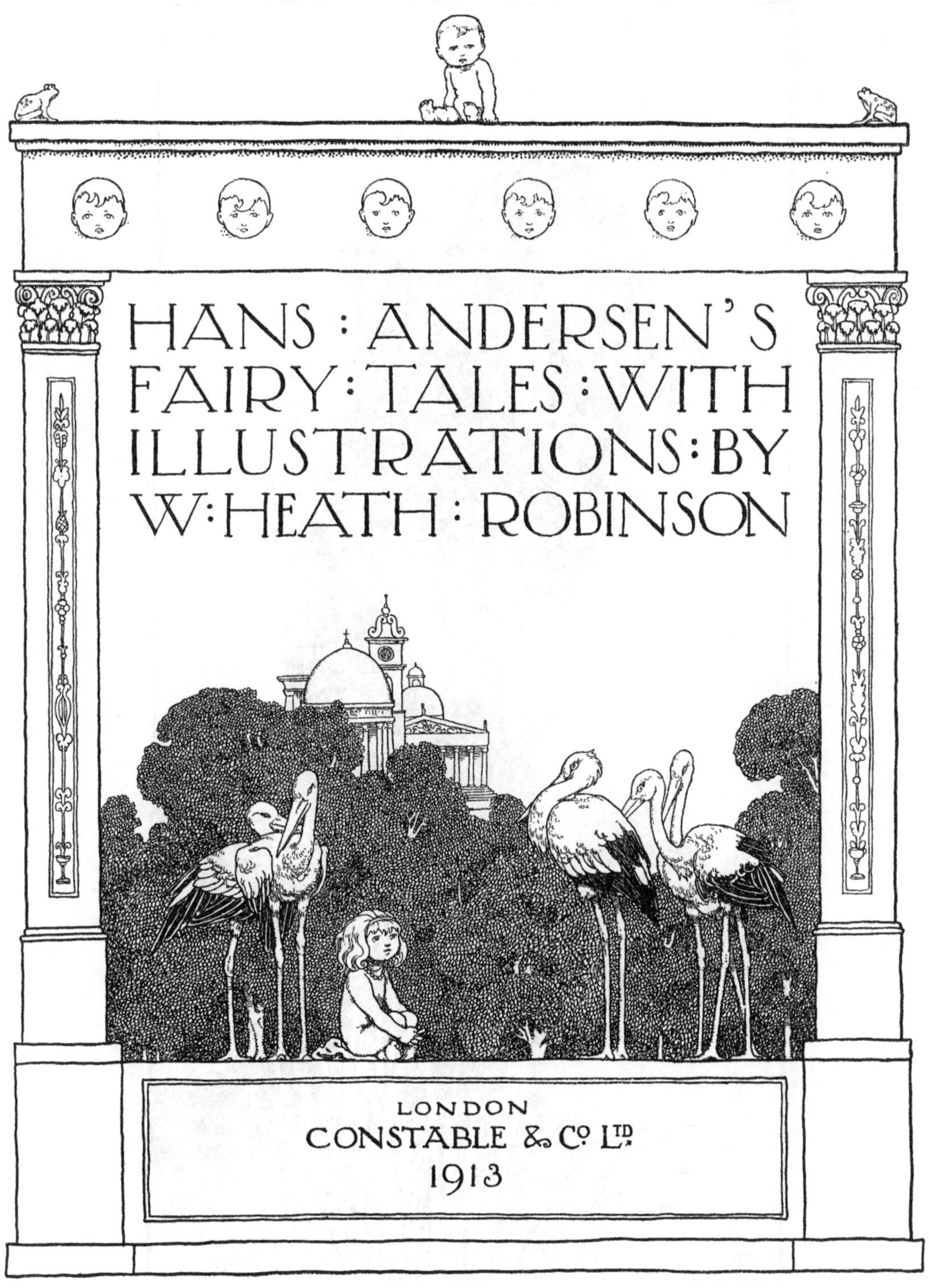

Title page

Hans Andersen's Fairy Tales, 1913

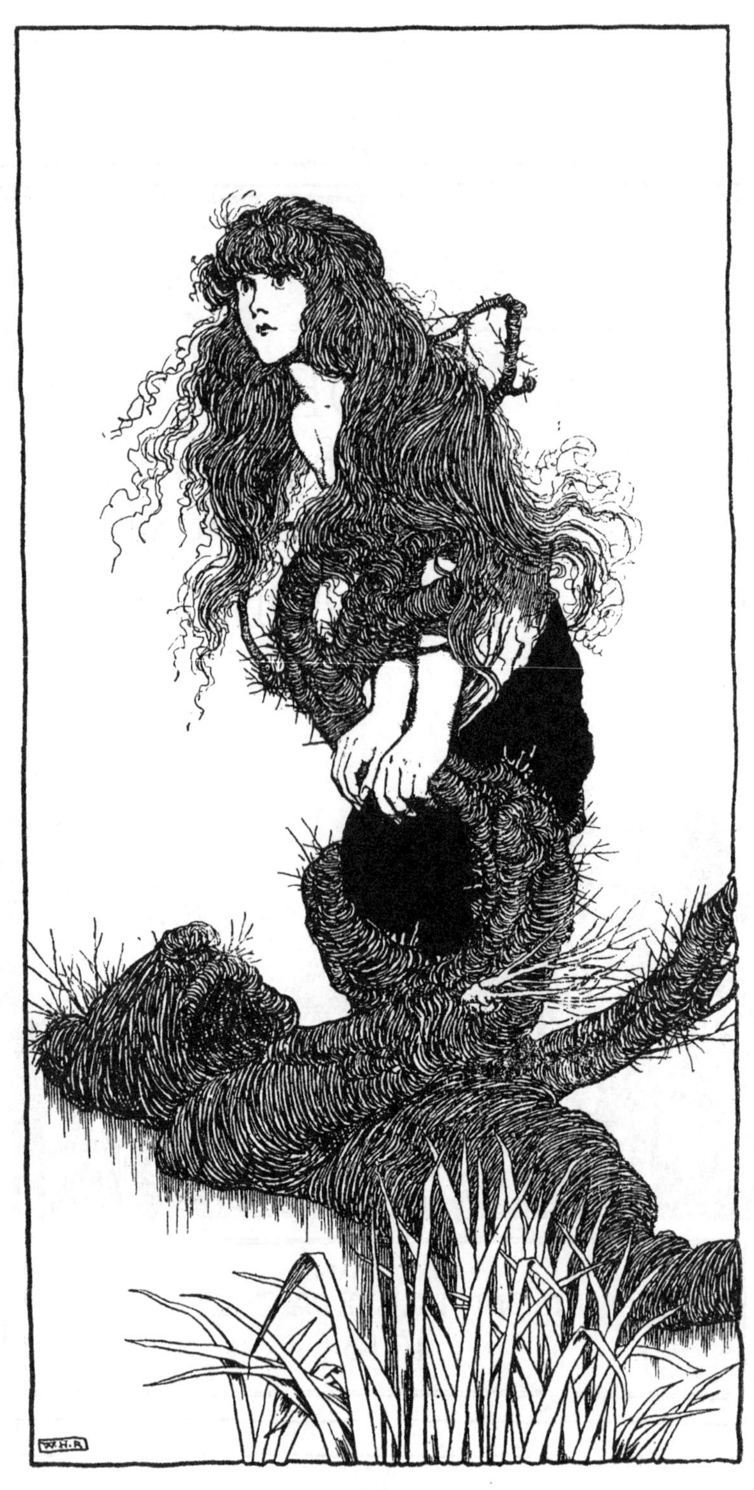

It was he who pulled her down

Hans Andersen's Fairy Tales, 1913

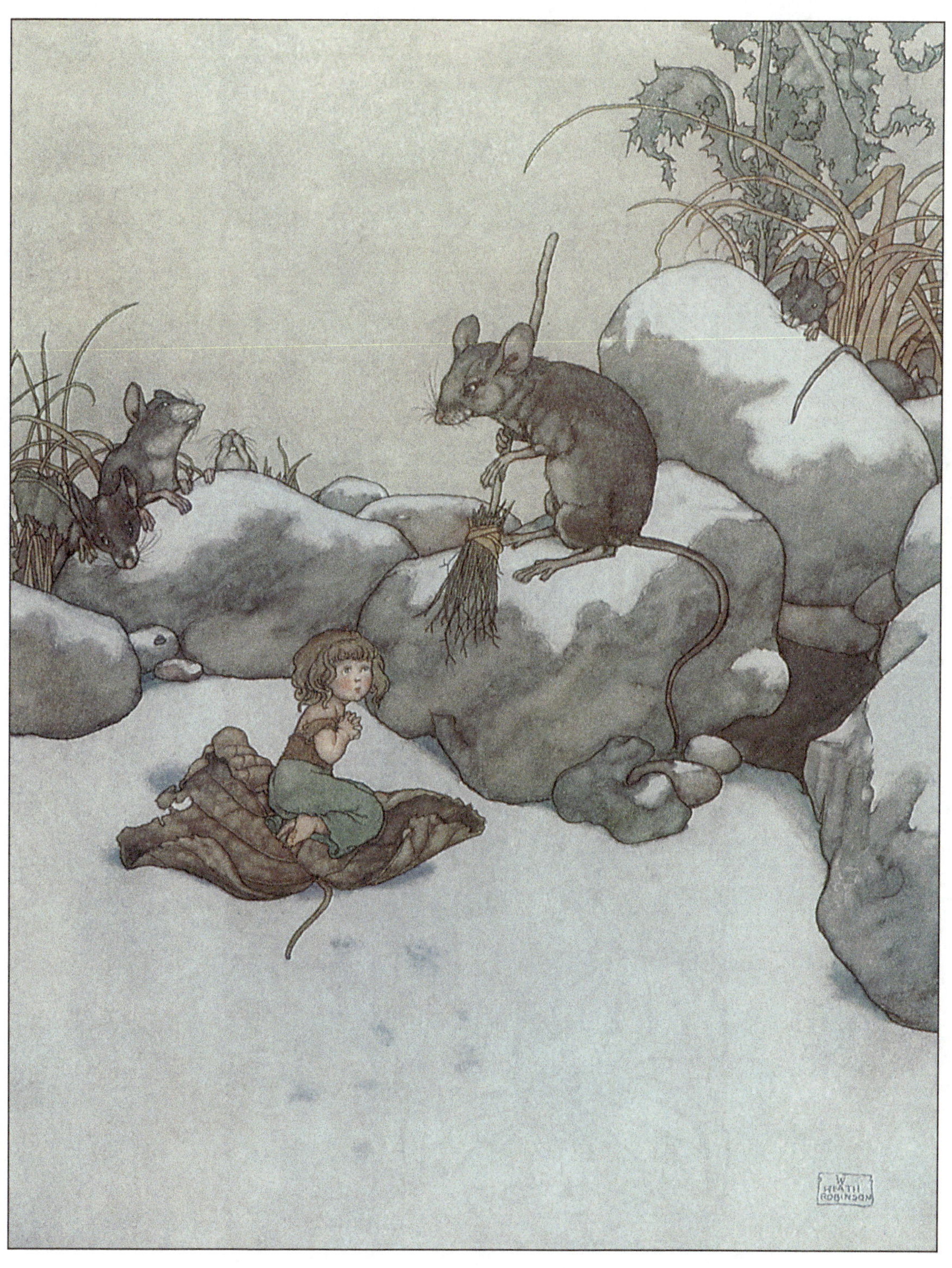

She stood at the door and begged for a piece of barley-corn

Hans Andersen's Fairy Tales, 1913

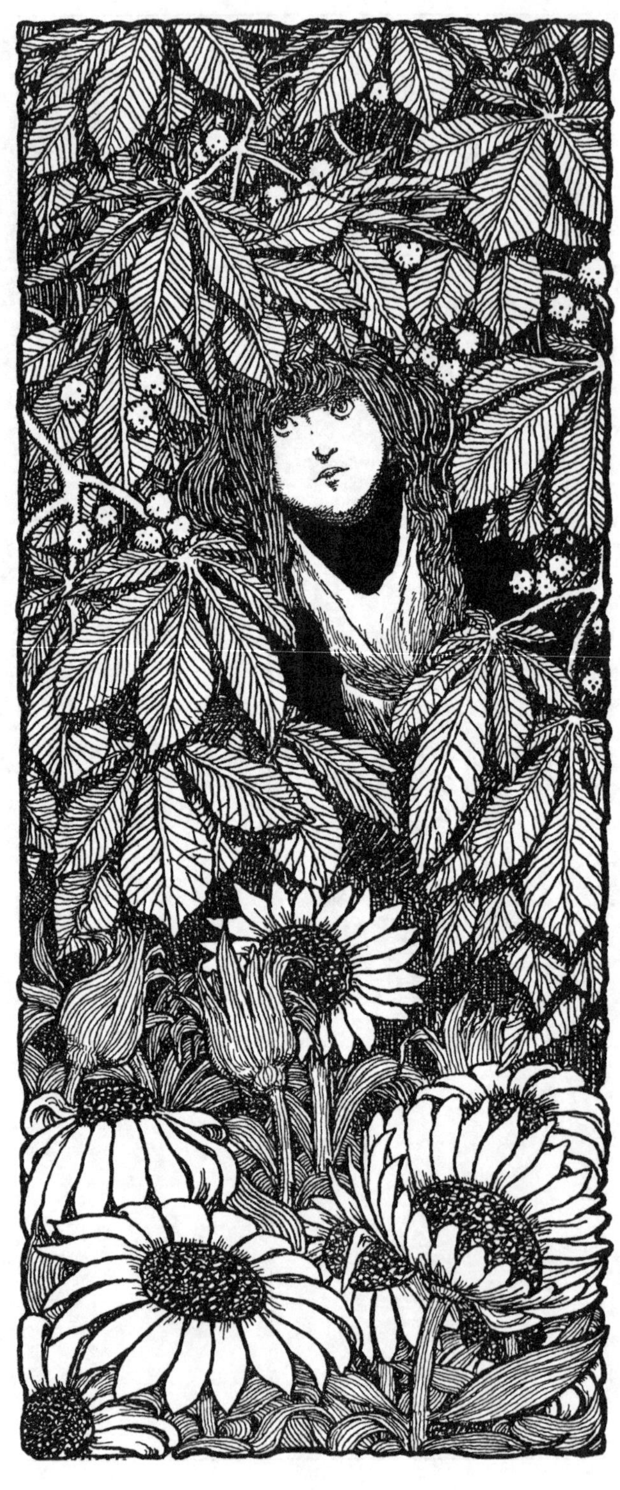

The little robber-maiden

Hans Andersen's Fairy Tales, 1913

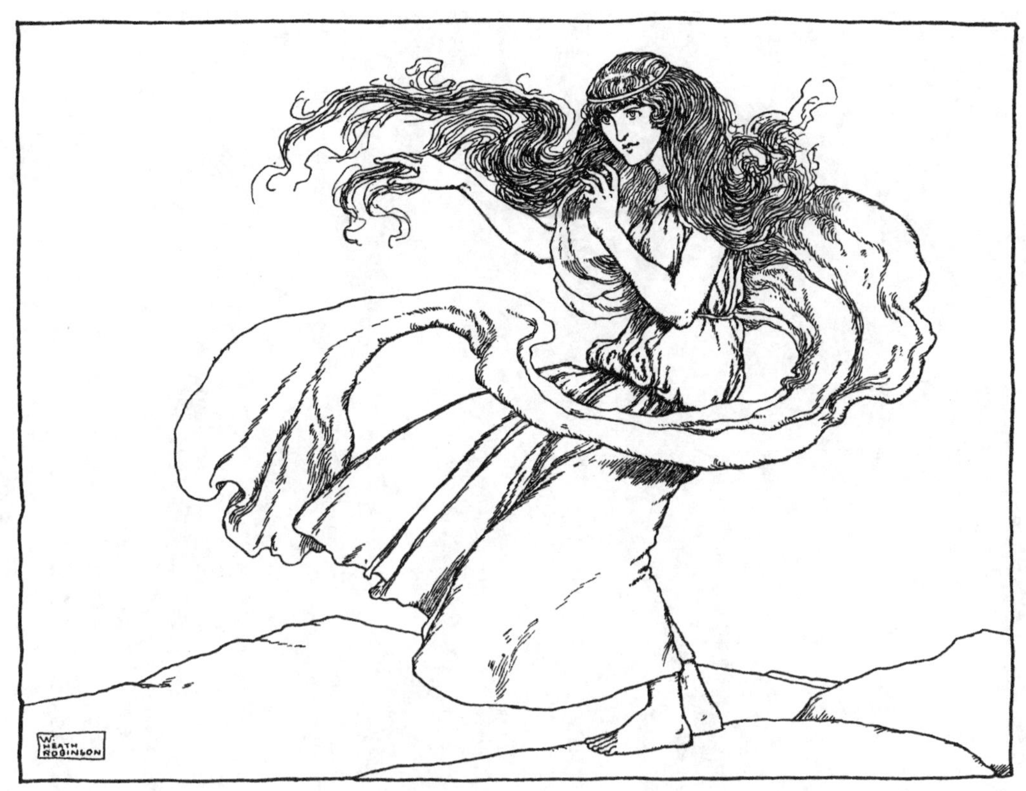

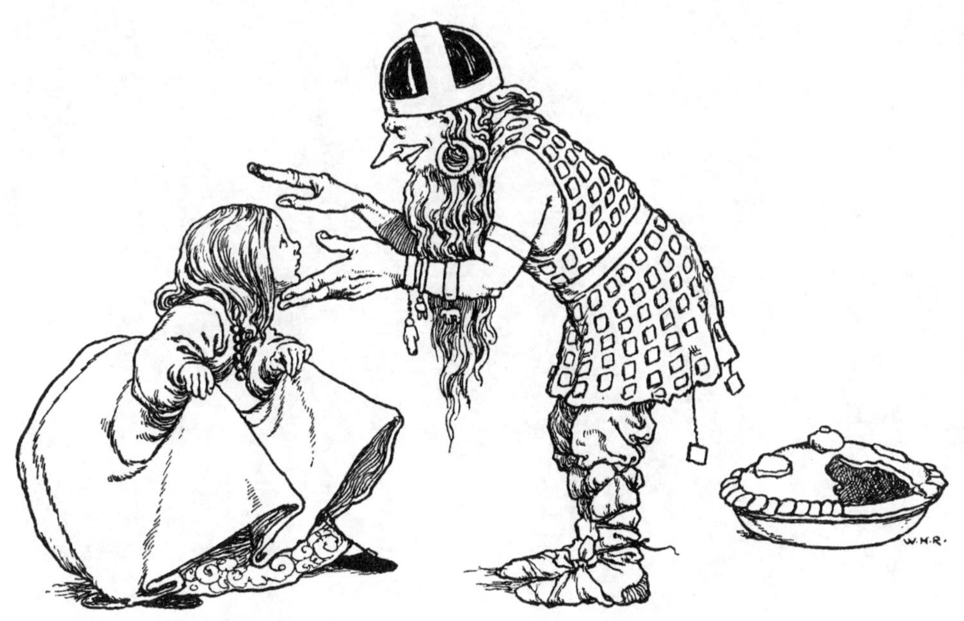

Top. Headpiece, The Snow Queen
Bottom. I will have thee myself to wife

Hans Andersen's Fairy Tales, 1913

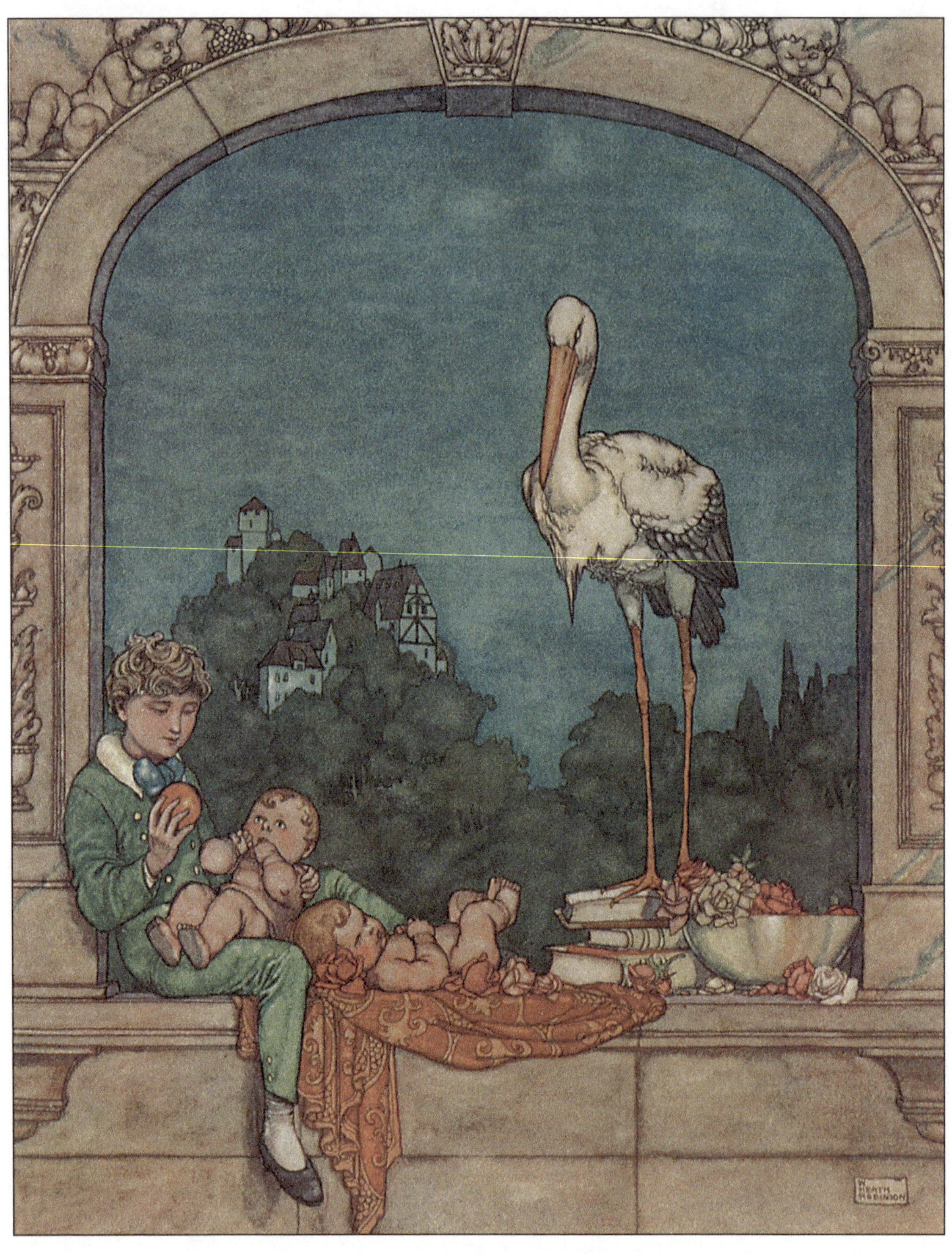

We will bring him two little ones, a brother and a sister

Hans Andersen's Fairy Tales, 1913

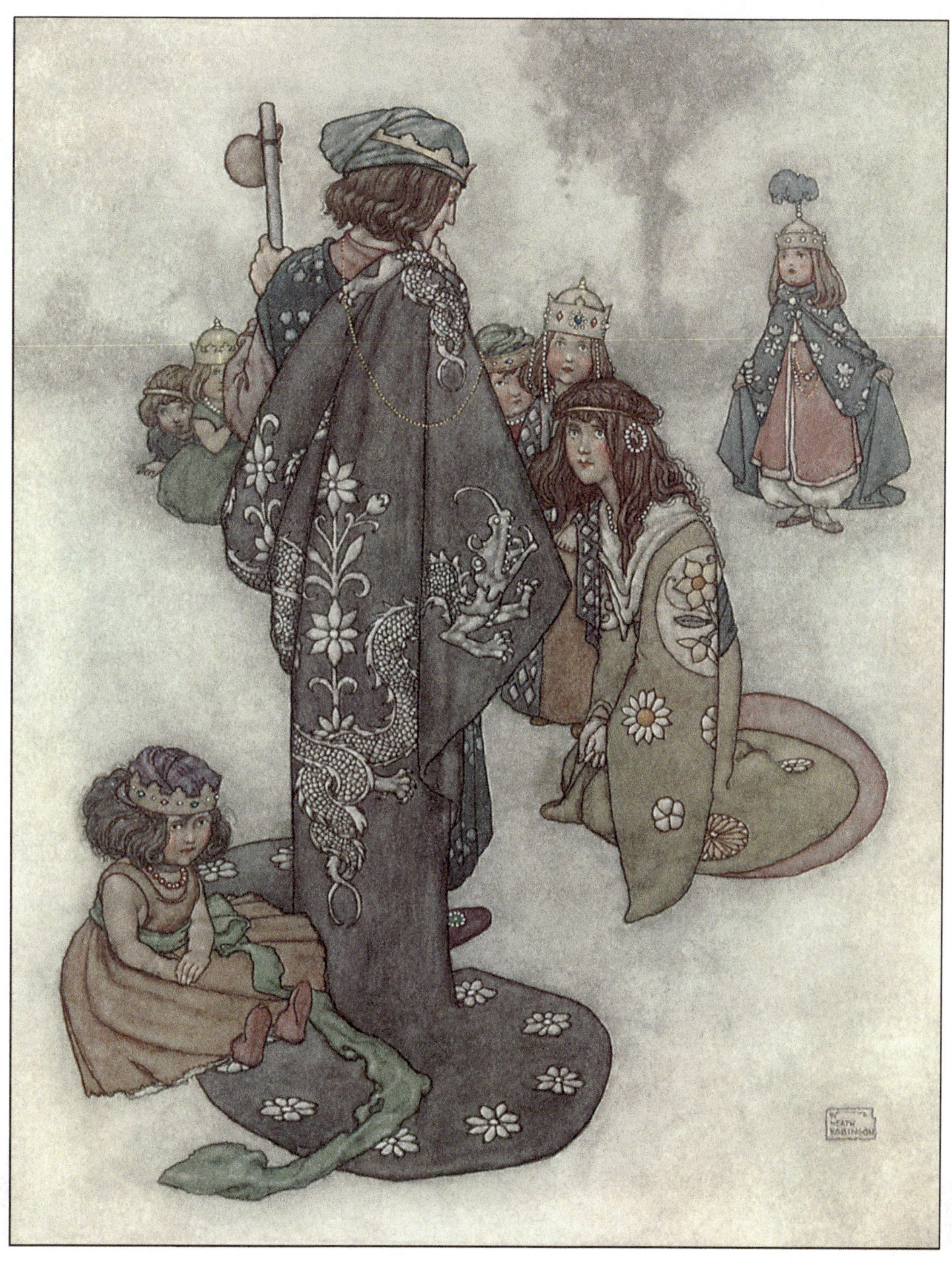

Princesses he found in plenty, but whether they were real Princesses
it was impossible for him to decide

HANS ANDERSEN'S FAIRY TALES, 1913

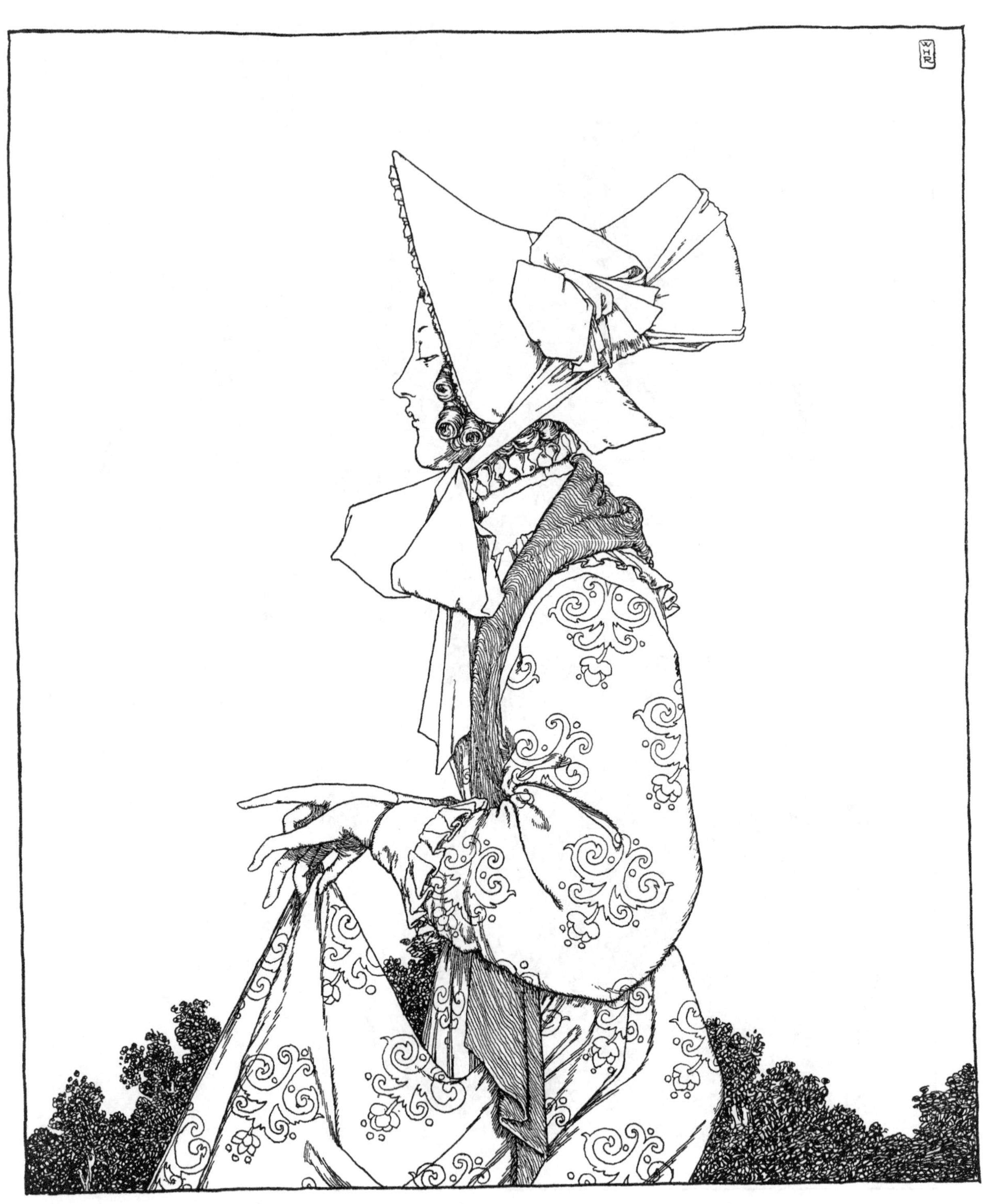

Karen

Hans Andersen's Fairy Tales, 1913

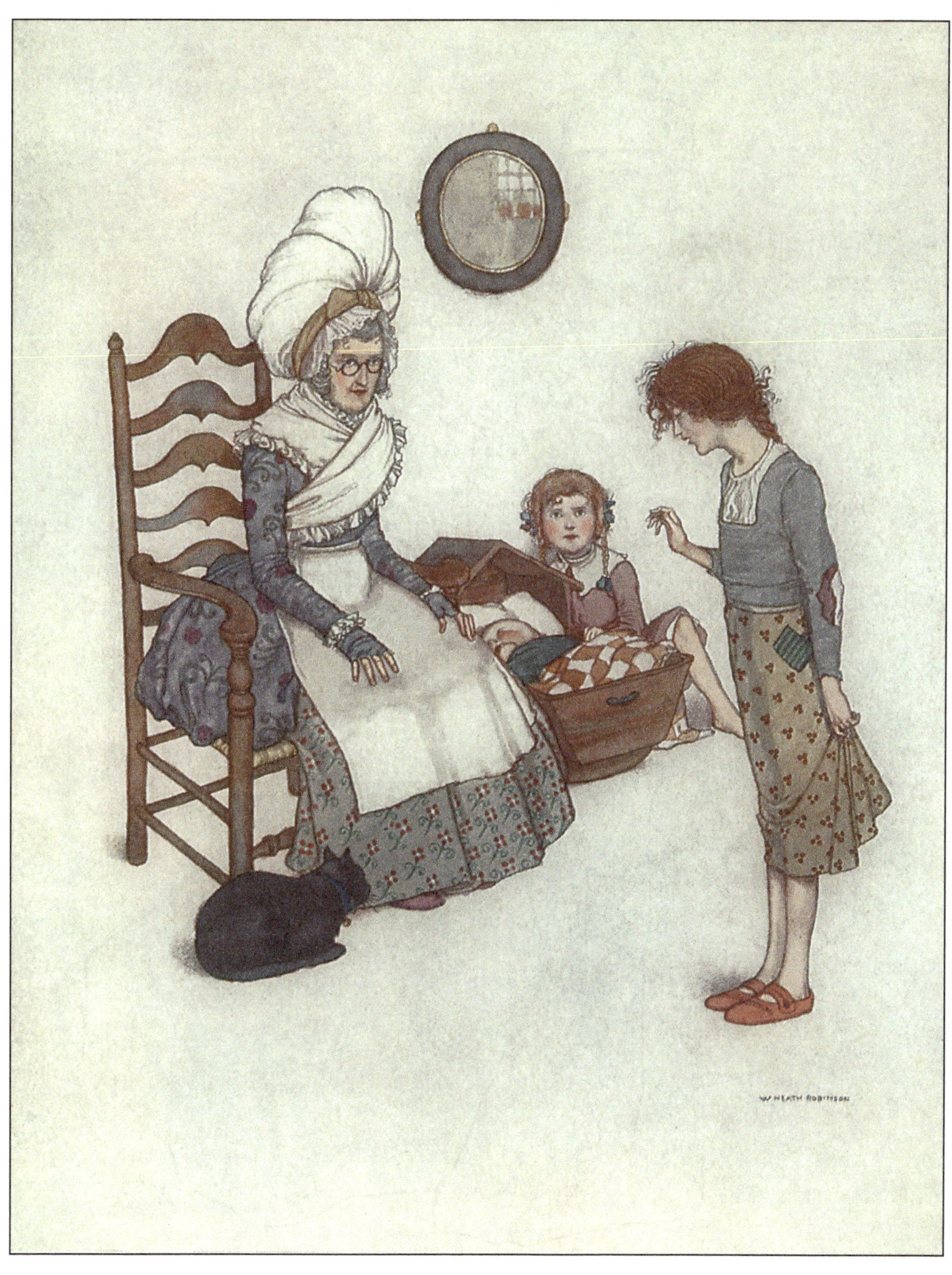

She sat down one day and made out of some old pieces of red cloth,
a pair of little shoes

Hans Andersen's Fairy Tales, 1913

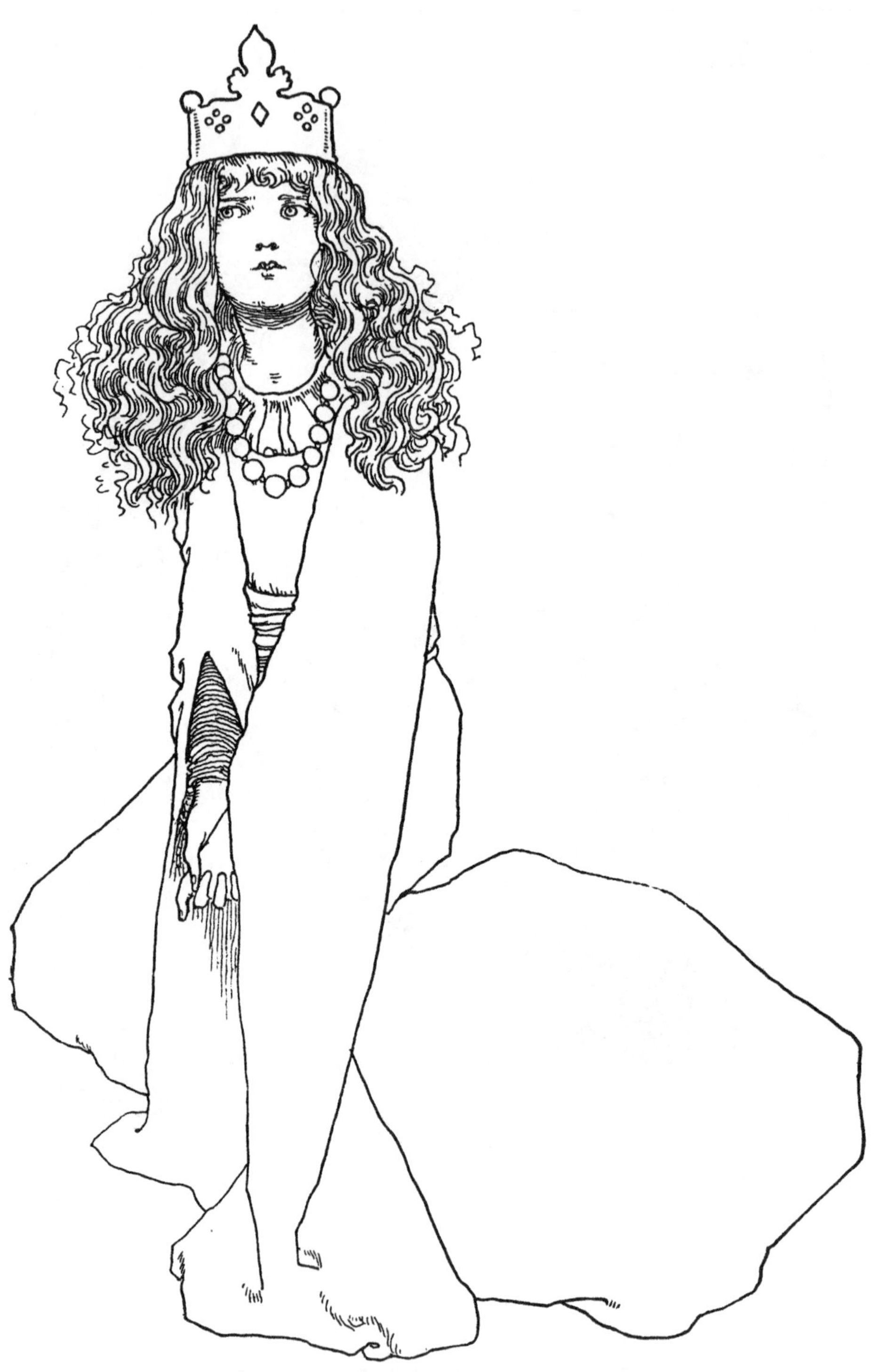

Tailpiece, The Emperor's New Clothes

Hans Andersen's Fairy Tales, 1913

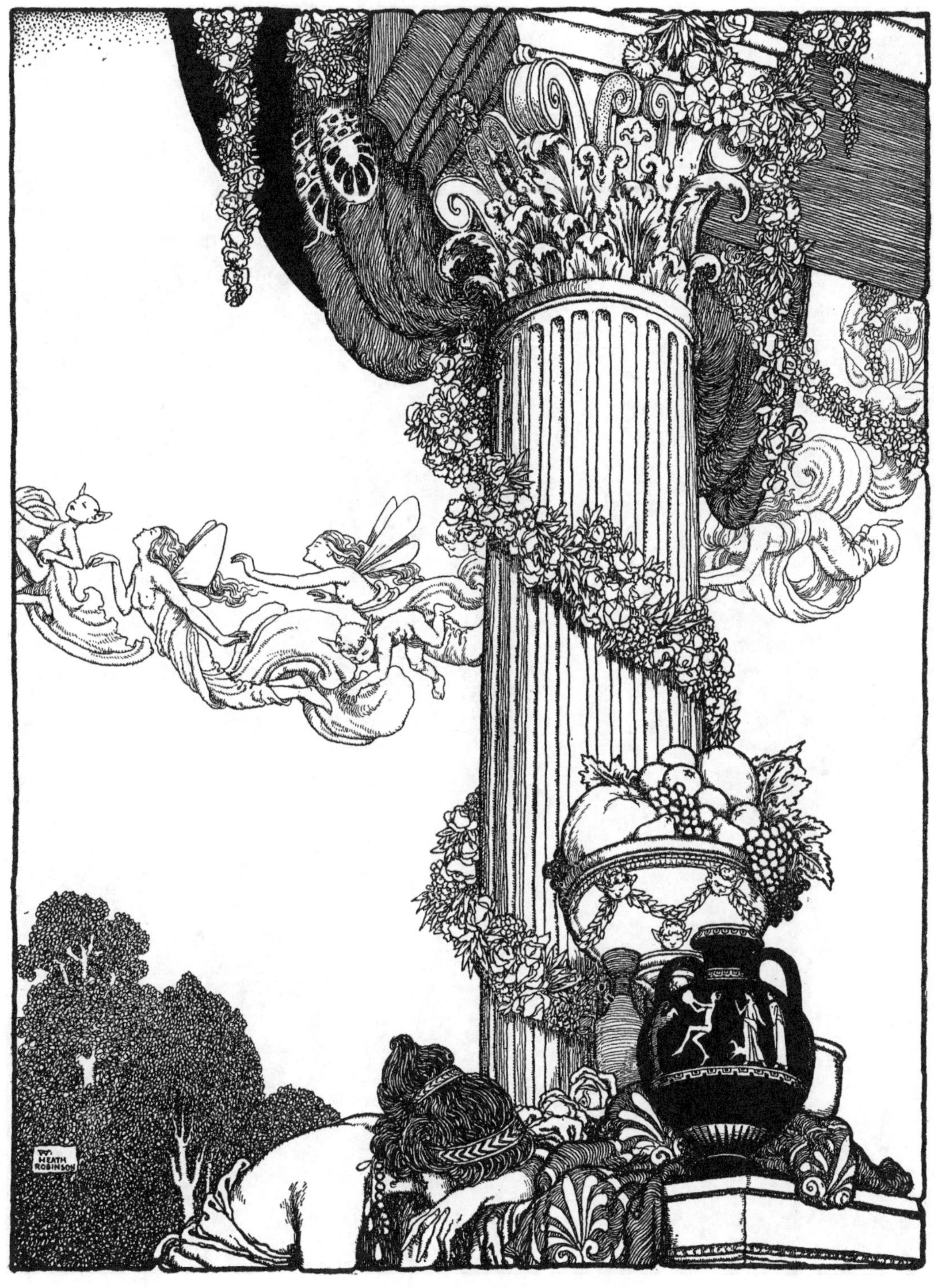

Lysander. . . . . and she, sweet lady, dotes,/Devoutly dotes, dotes in idolatry,
Upon this spotted and inconstant man.

A Midsummer Night's Dream, 1914

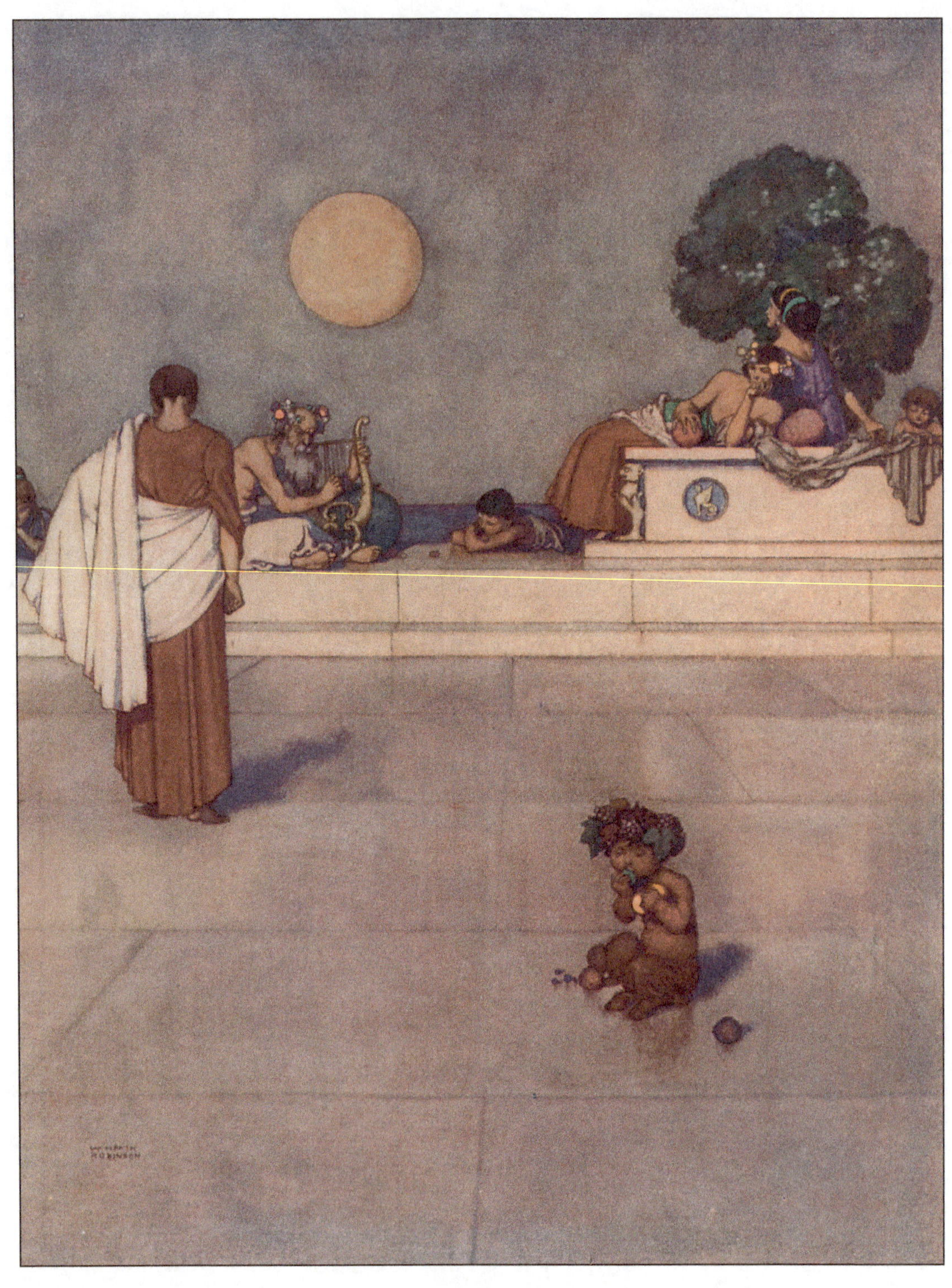

Hippolyta: "Four days will quickly steep themselves in night."

A Midsummer Night's Dream, 1914

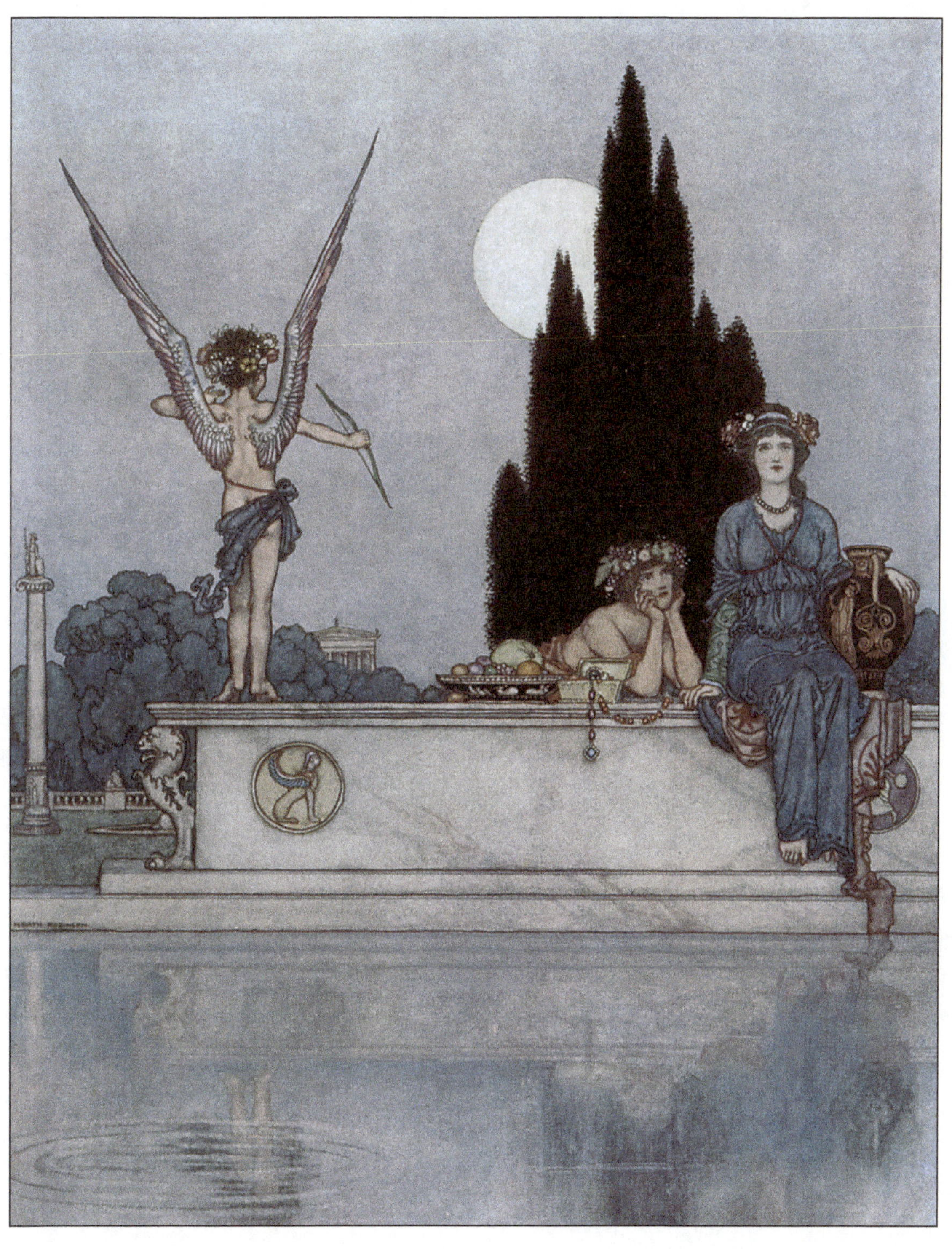

Egeus. "This man hath bewitch'd the bosom of my child."

A Midsummer Night's Dream, 1914

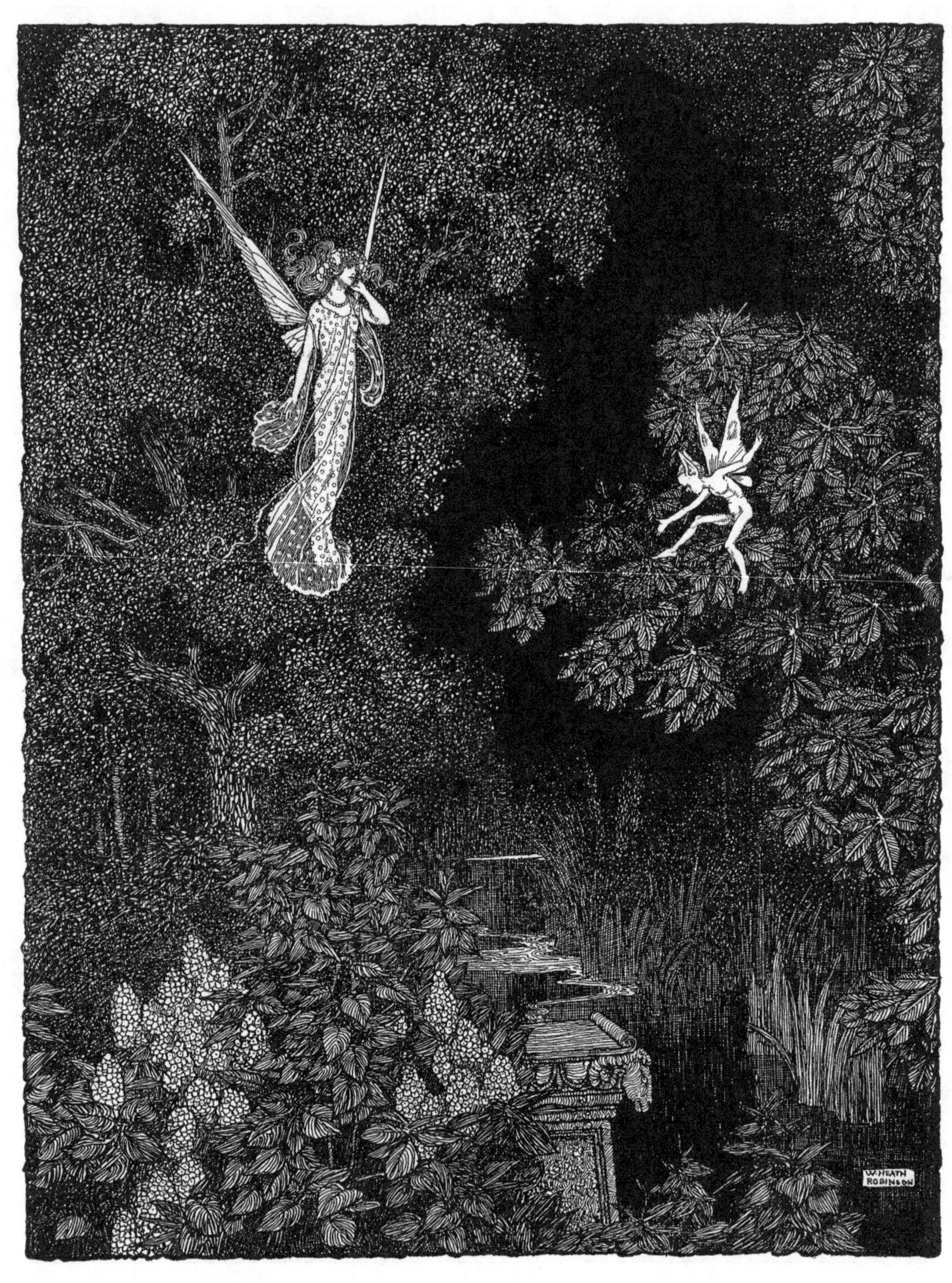

Puck. How now, spirit! whither wander you?

A Midsummer Night's Dream, 1914

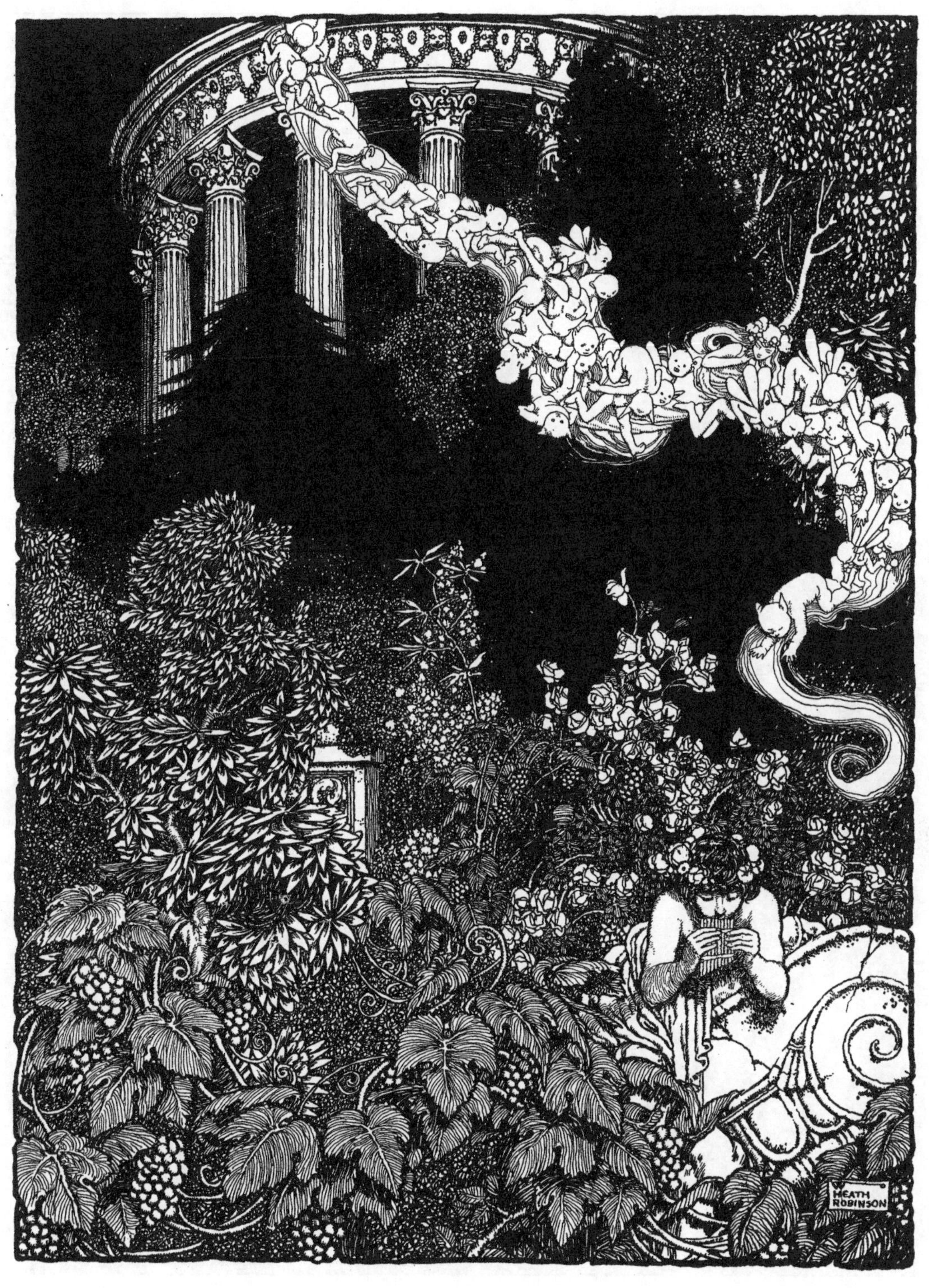

Titania. Playing on pipes of corn, and versing love/To amorous Phillida

A Midsummer Night's Dream, 1914

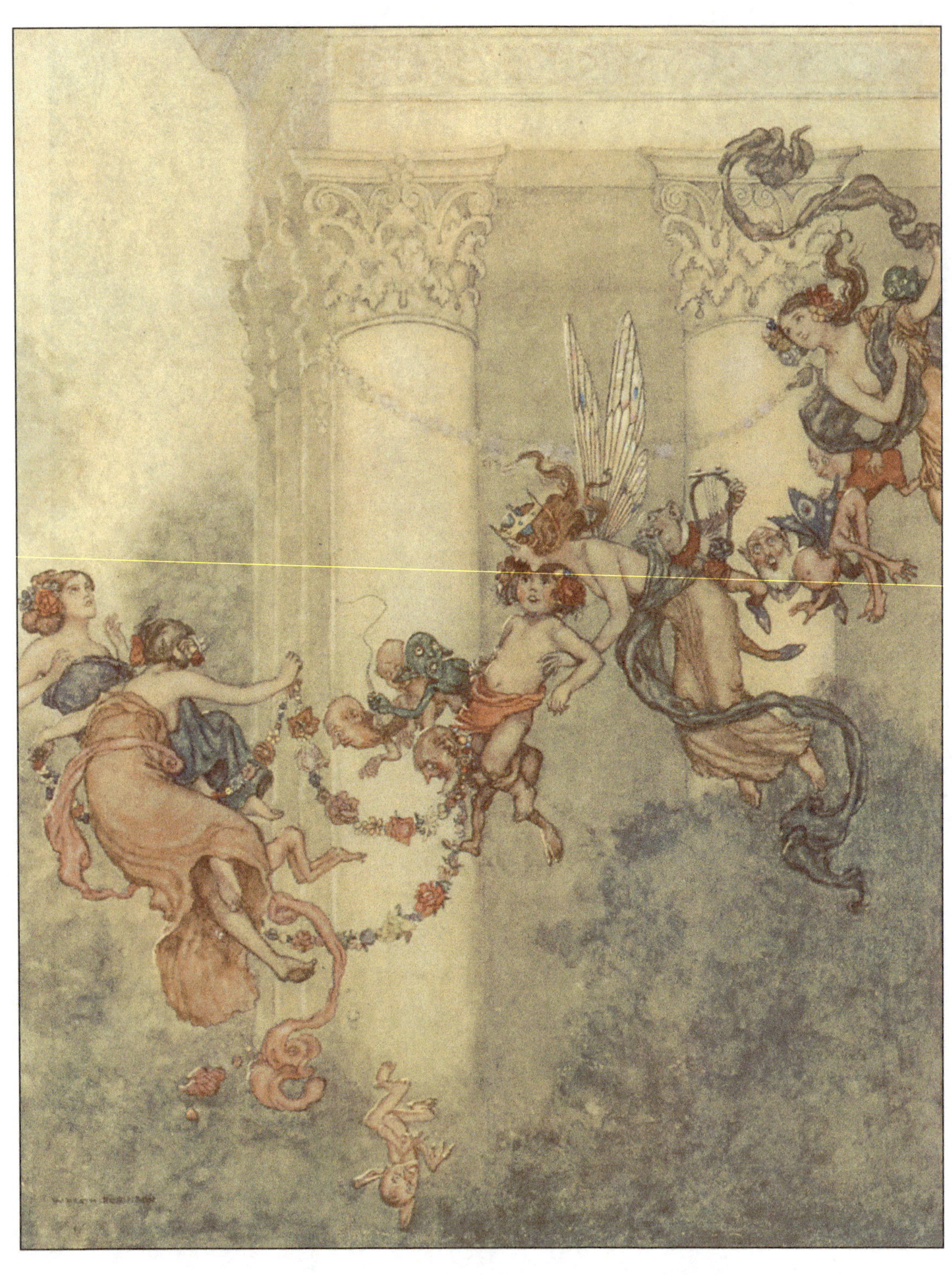

Puck. "She never had so sweet a changeling"

A Midsummer Night's Dream, 1914

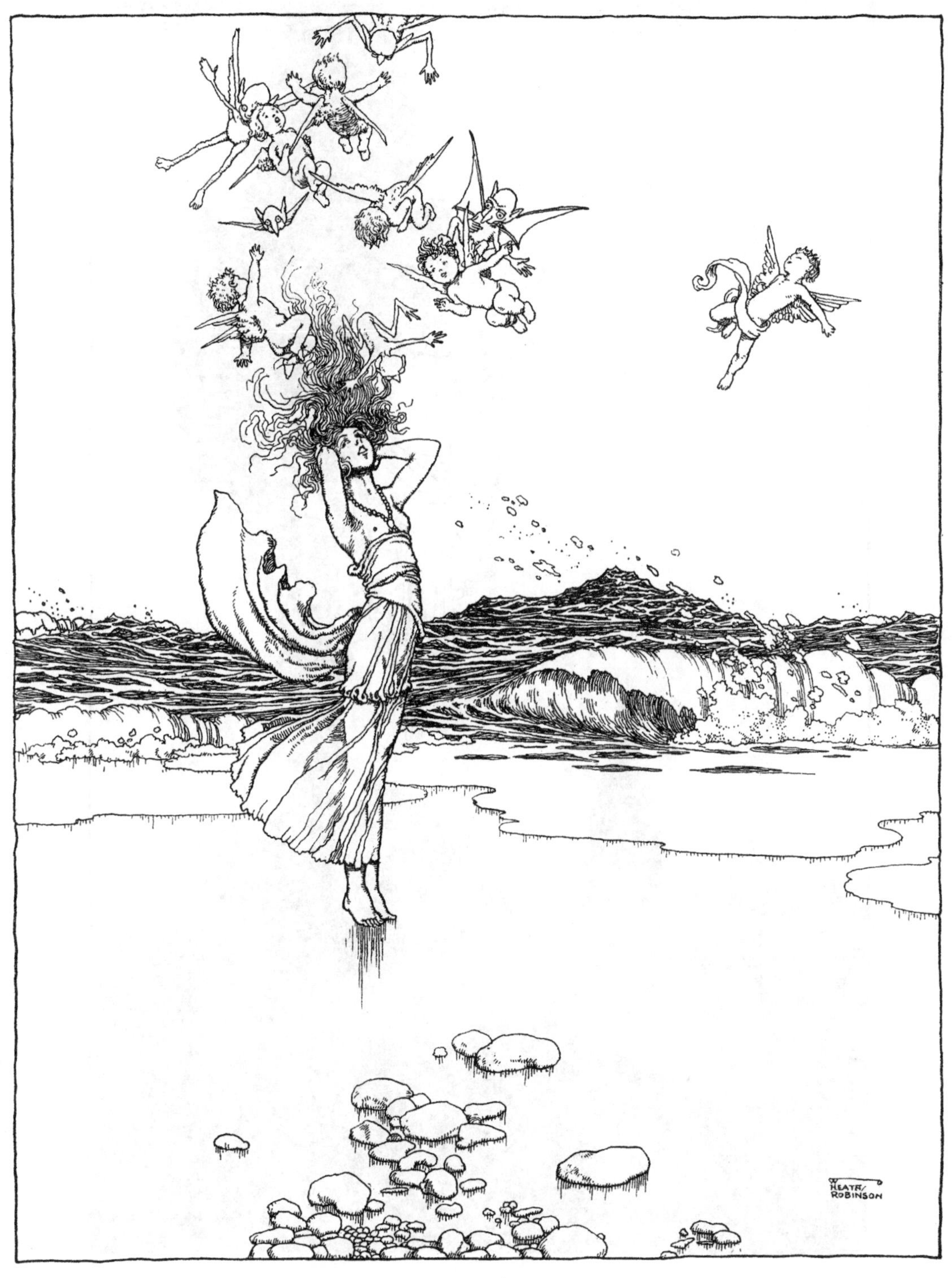

Titania. To dance our ringlets to the whistling wind.

A Midsummer Night's Dream, 1914

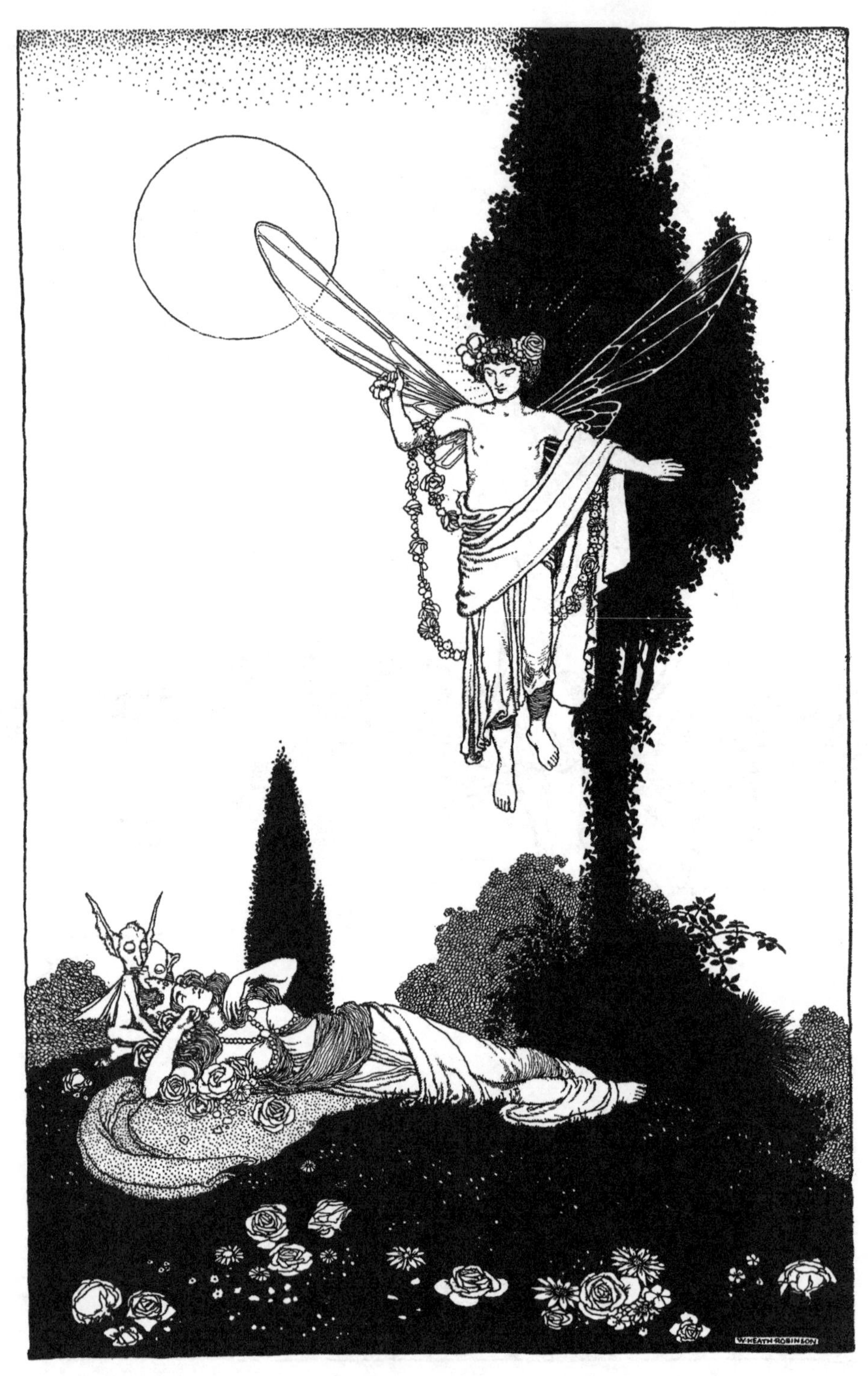

OBERON. What thou seest, when thou dost wake,
Do it for thy true love take.

A MIDSUMMER NIGHT'S DREAM, 1914

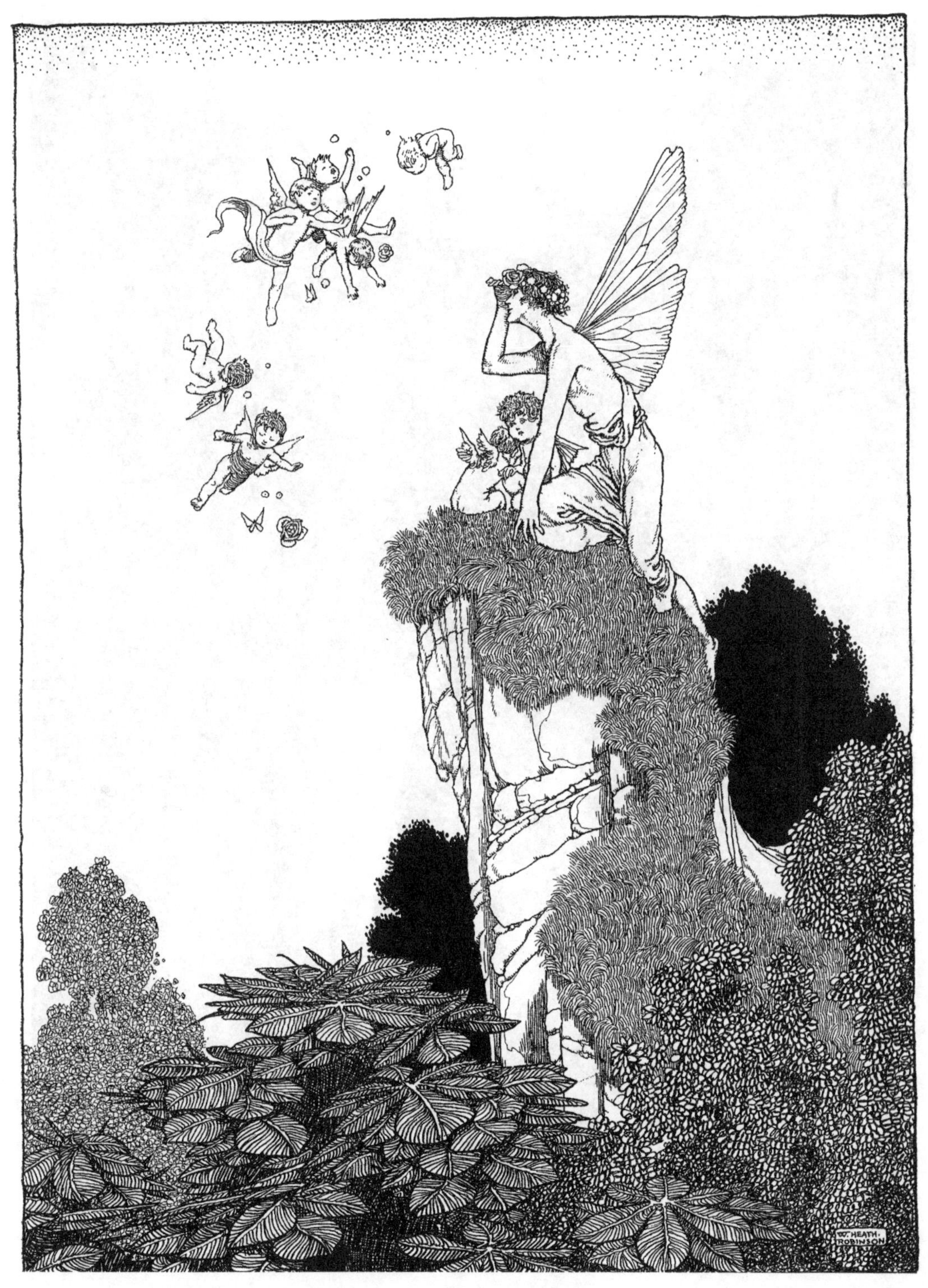

OBERON. I with the morning's love have oft made sport

A MIDSUMMER NIGHT'S DREAM, 1914

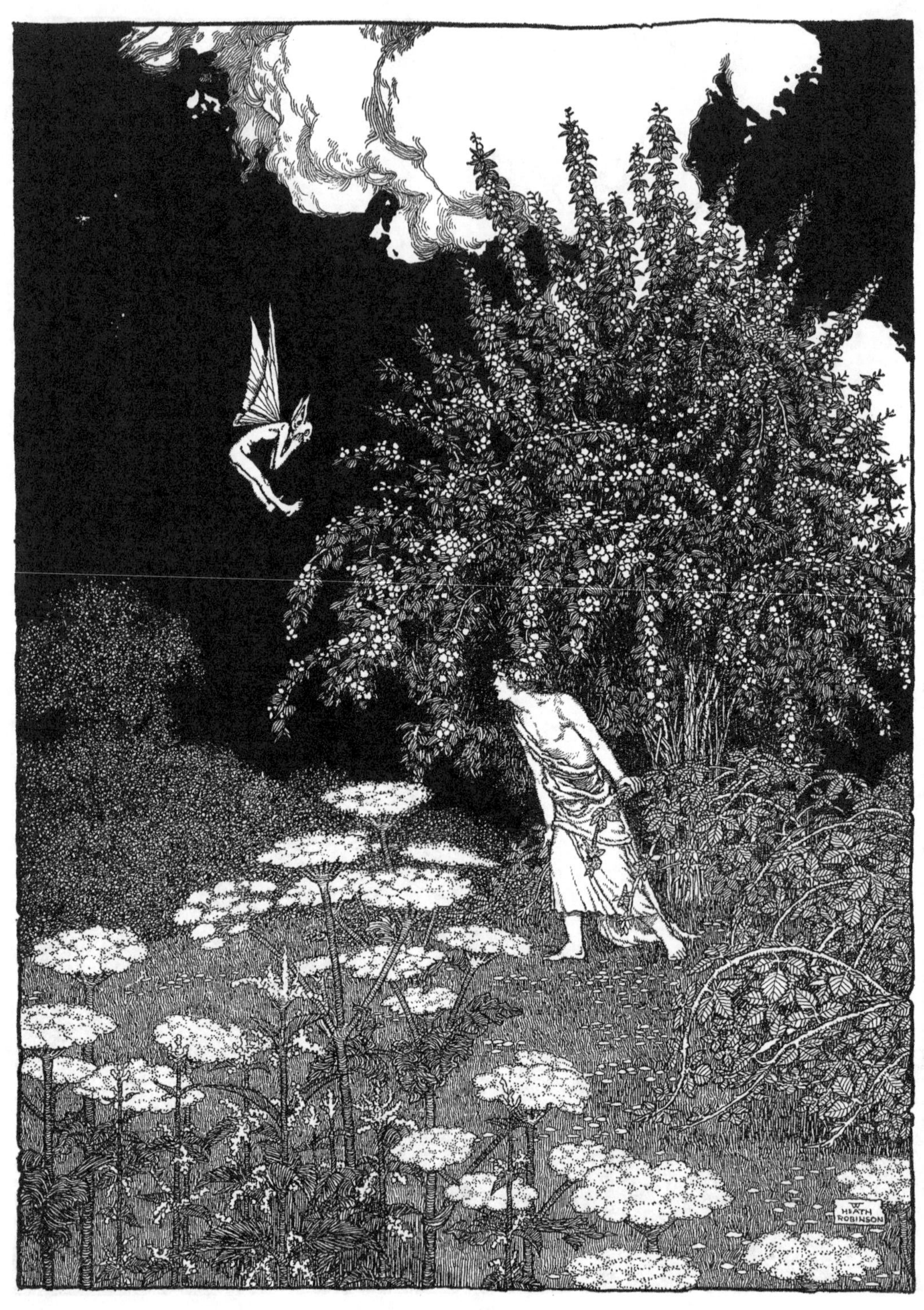

Demetrius. Thou runaway, thou coward, art thou fled?

A Midsummer Night's Dream, 1914

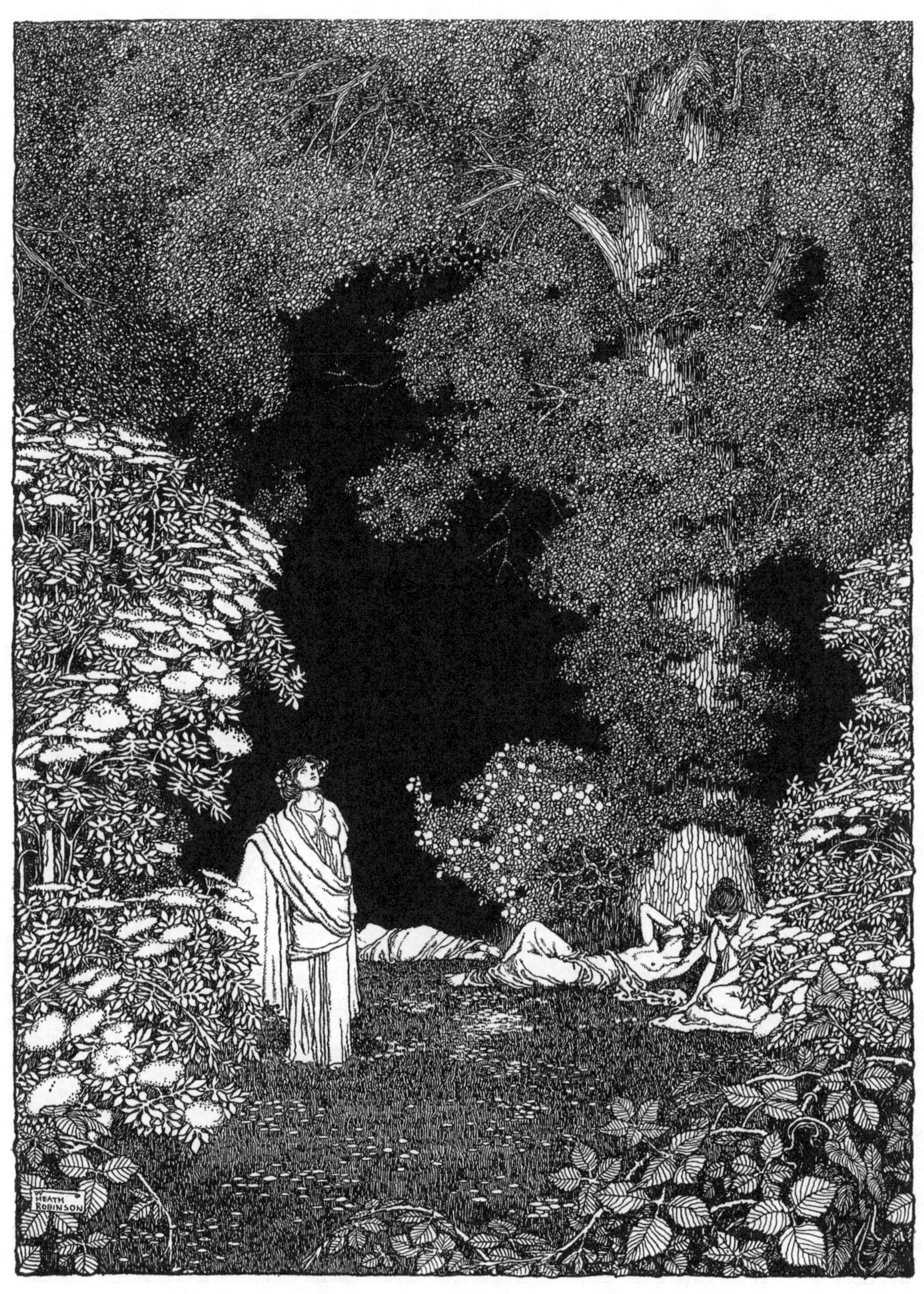

Helena. O weary night, O long and tedious night

A Midsummer Night's Dream, 1914

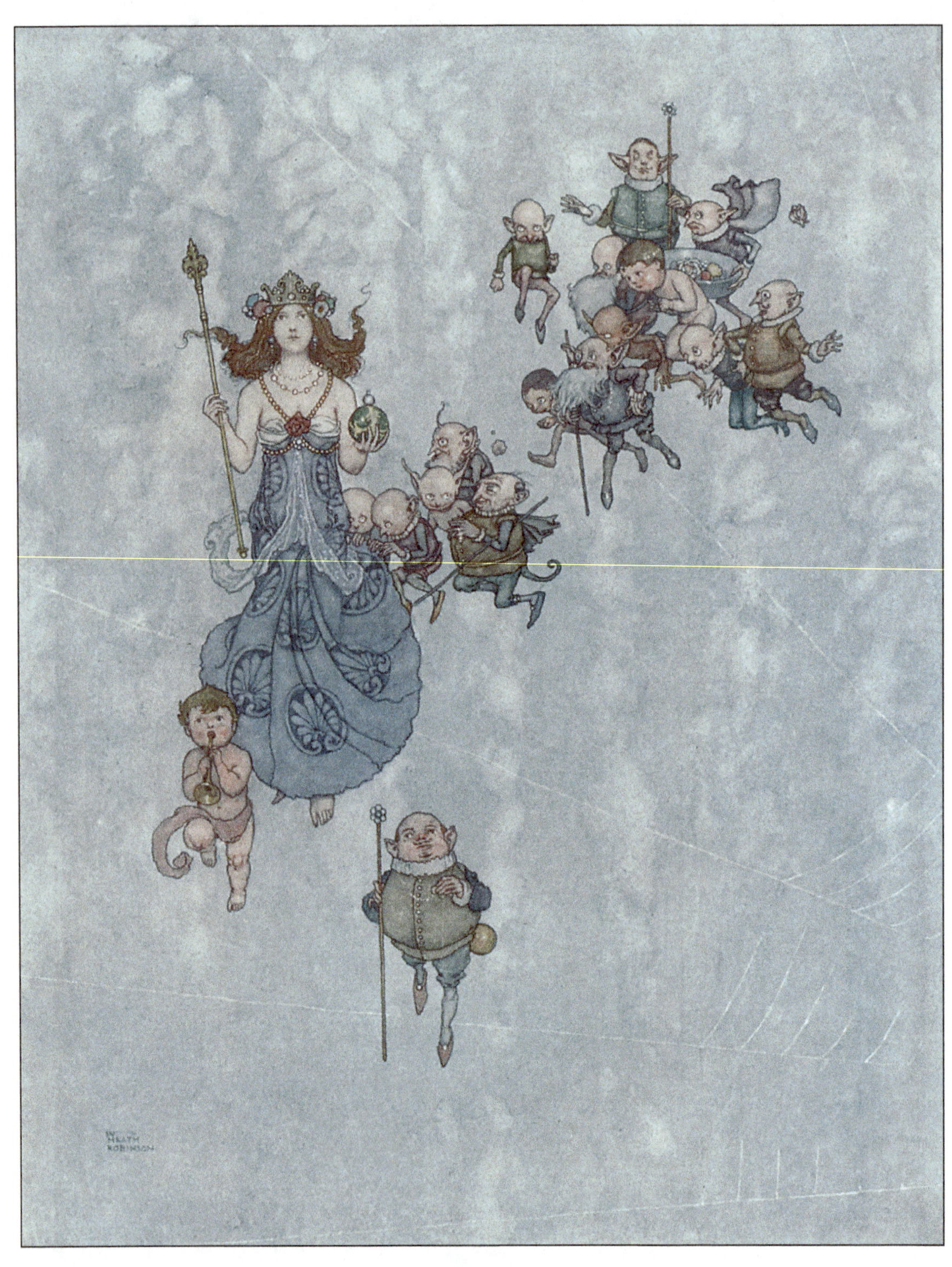

Titania [Act IV.]

A Midsummer Night's Dream, 1914

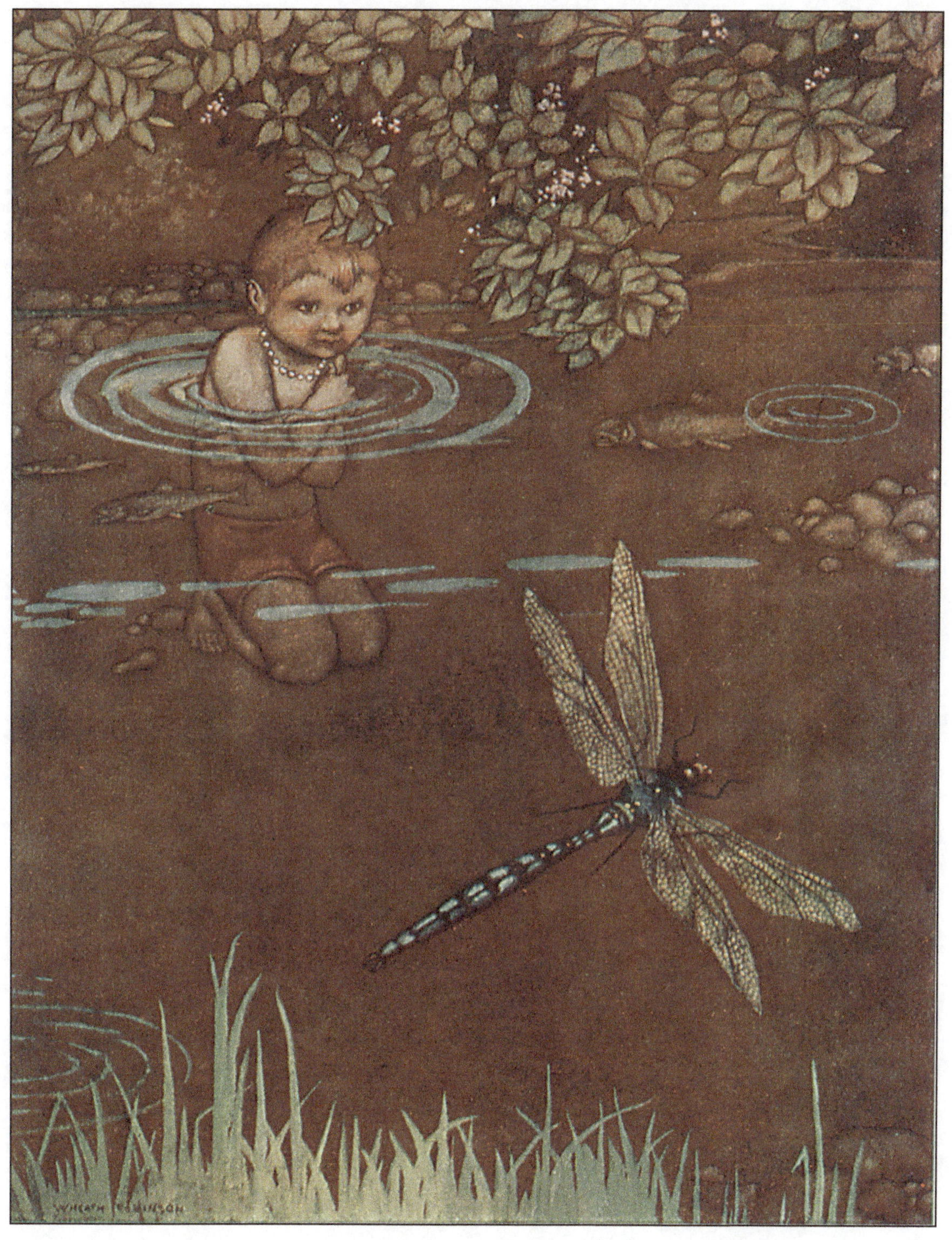

He was a little conceited about his fine colours and his large wings

The Water-Babies, 1915

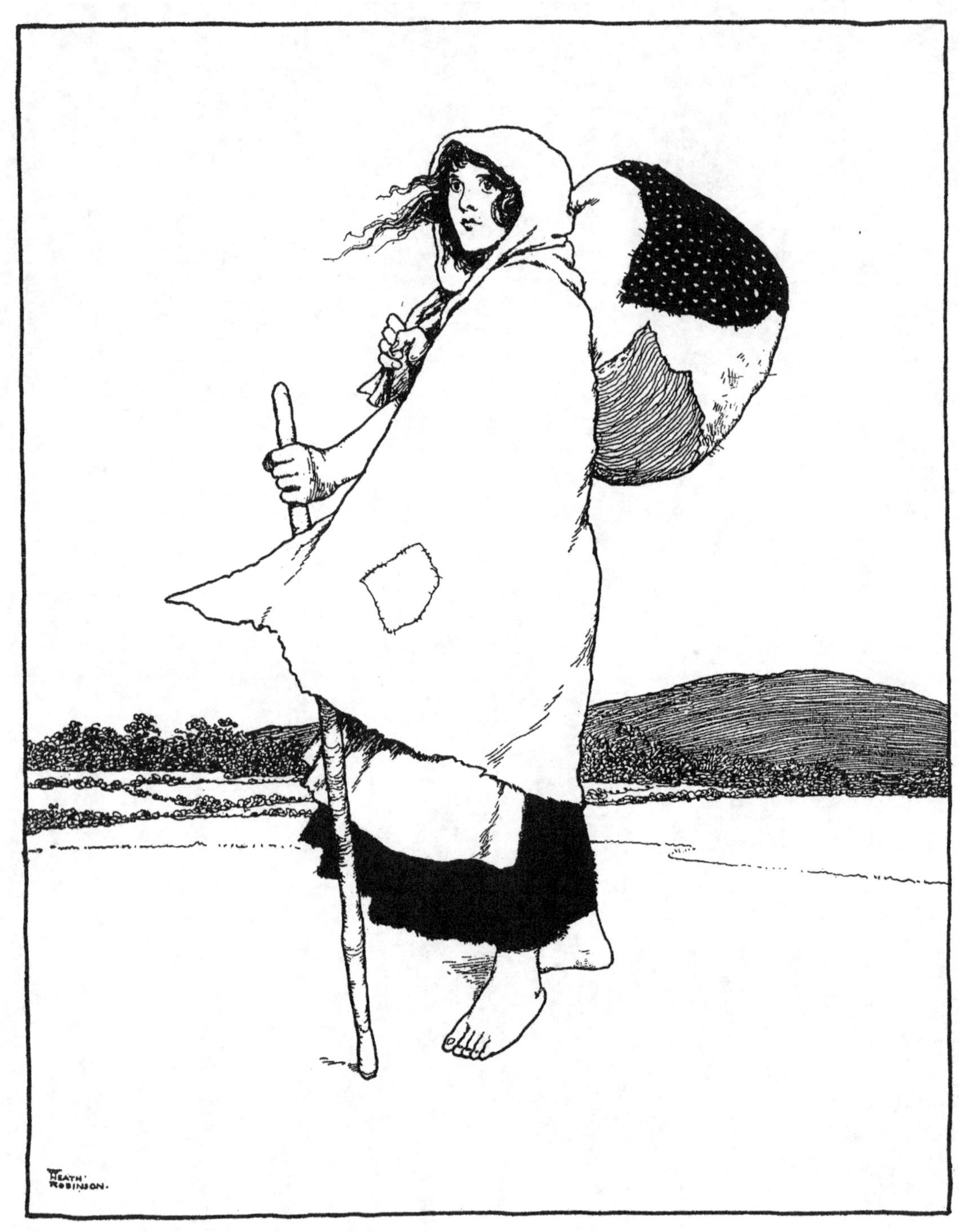

Trudging along with a bundle at her back

The Water-Babies, 1915

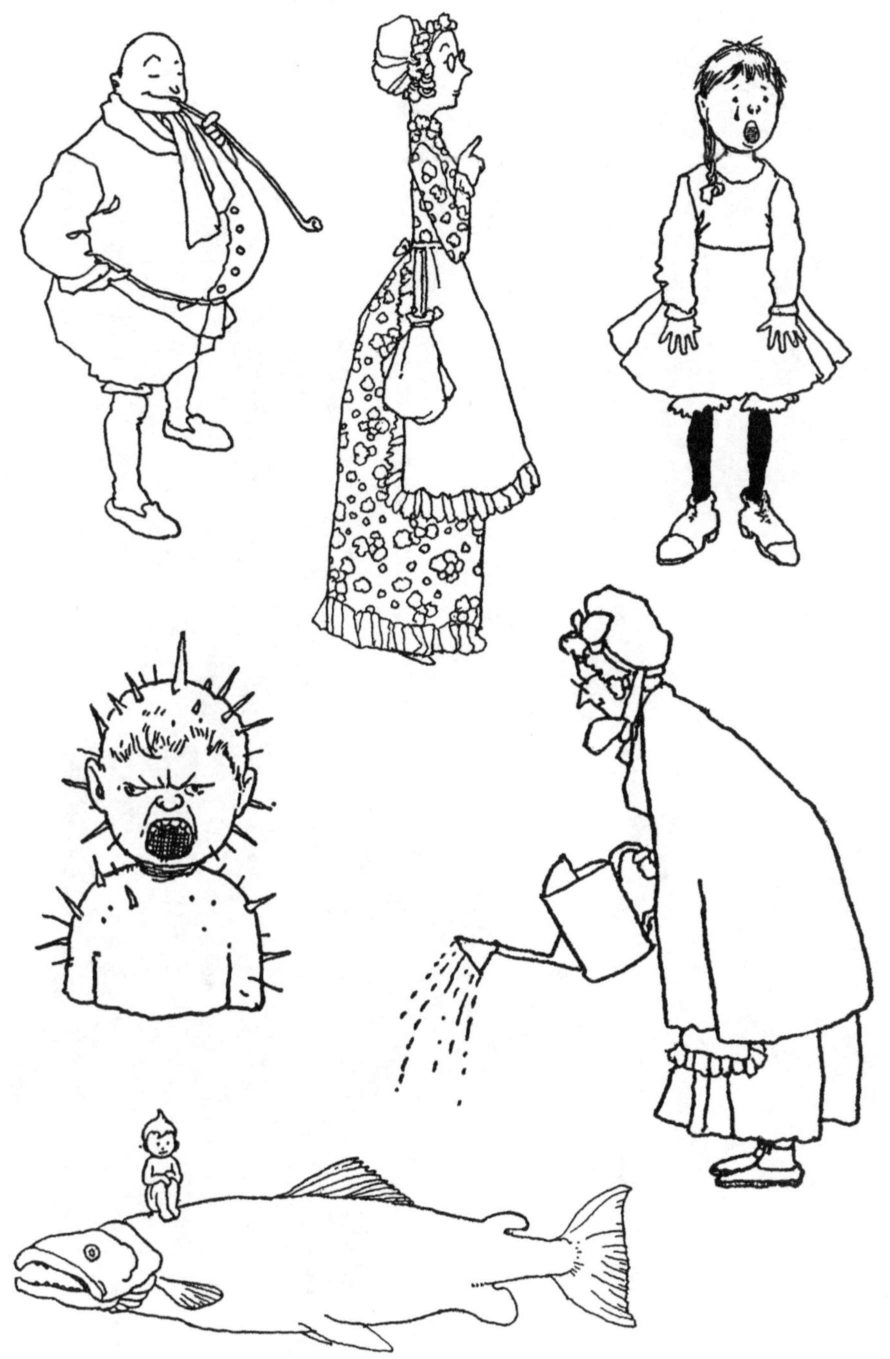

Six small spot illustrations

THE WATER-BABIES, 1915

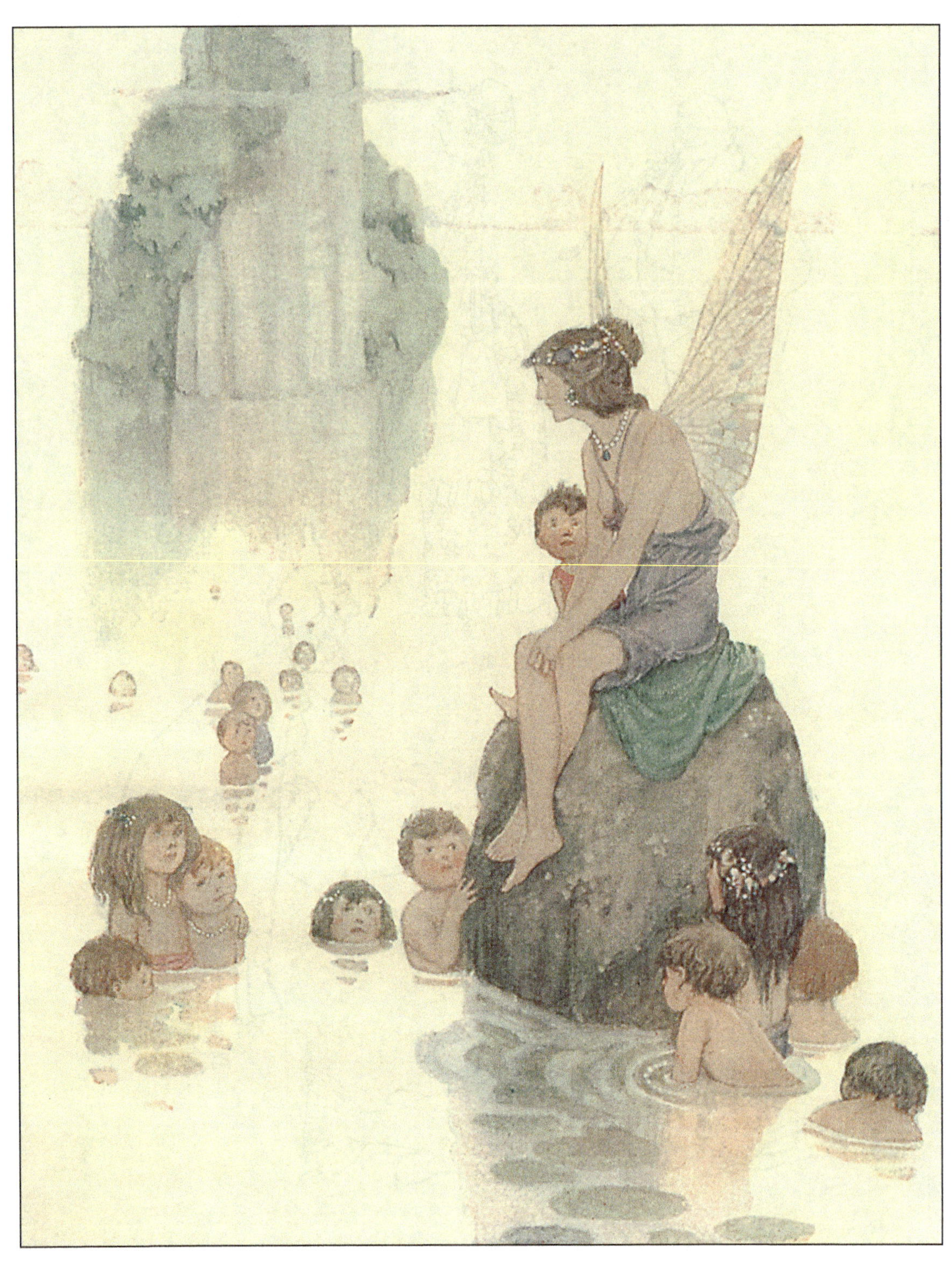

But the fairies took to the water-babies

The Water-Babies, 1915

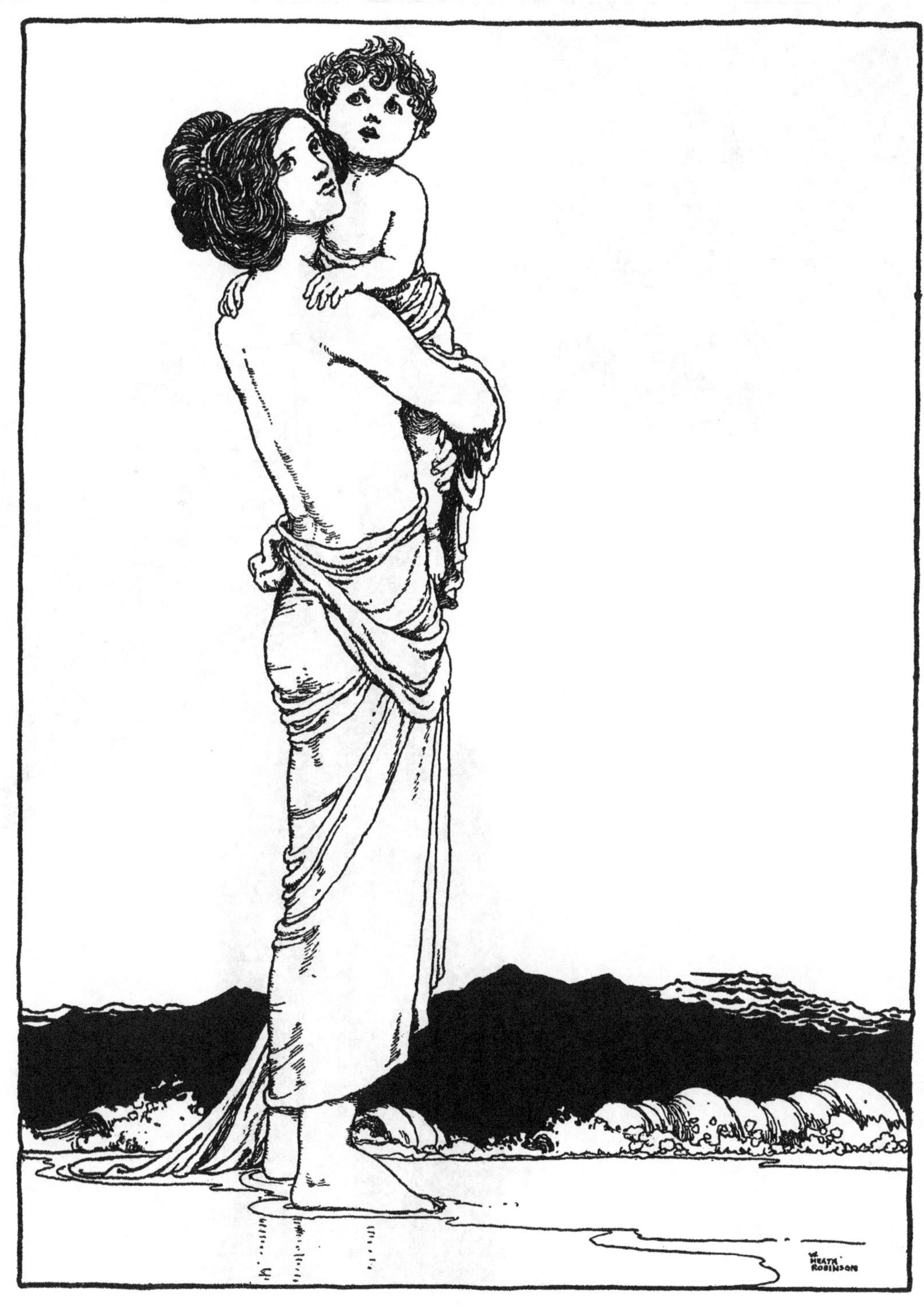

Play by me, bathe in me, mother and child

THE WATER-BABIES, 1915

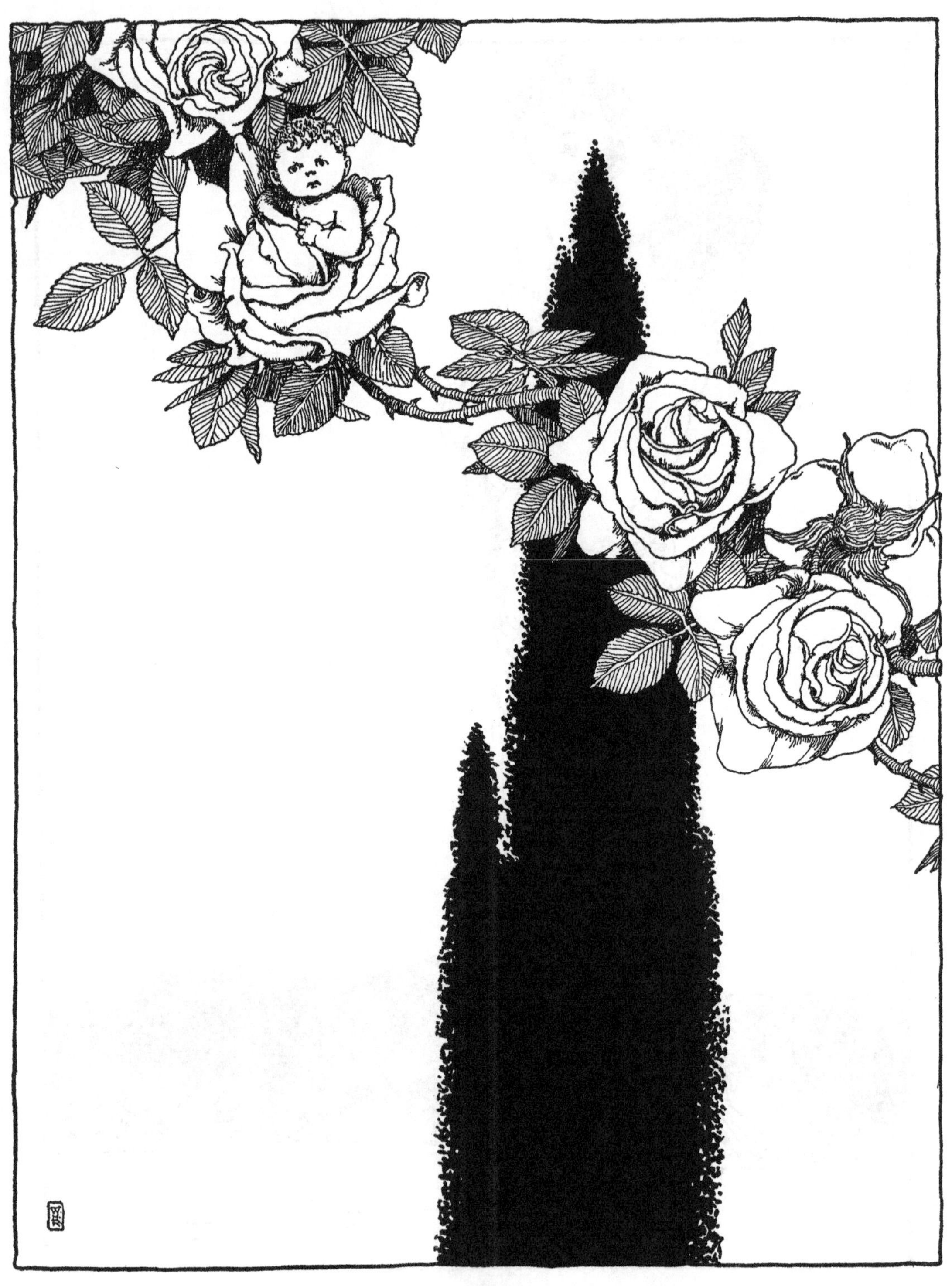

When all the world is young, lad

THE WATER-BABIES, 1915

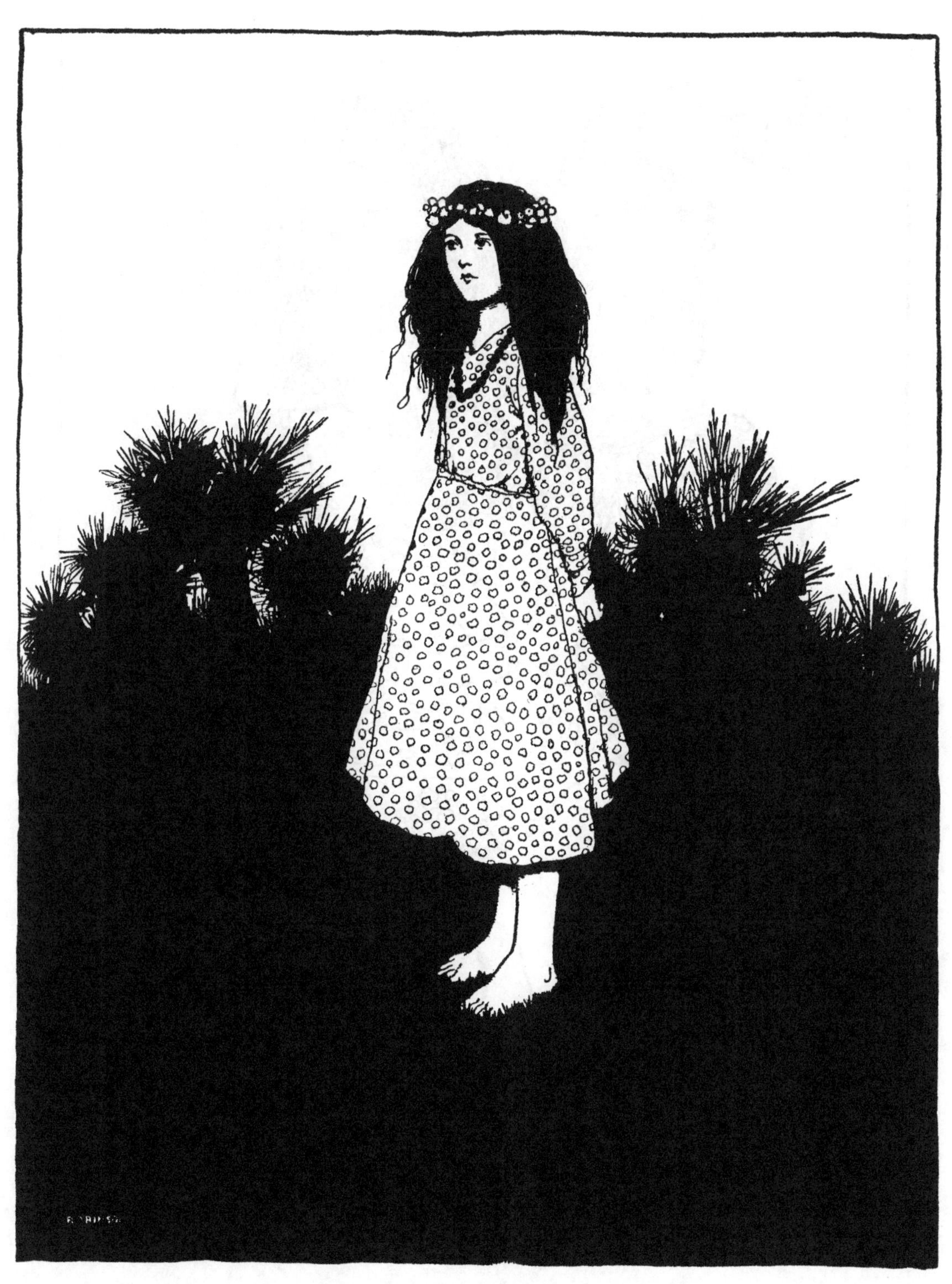

and every lass a queen

THE WATER-BABIES, 1915

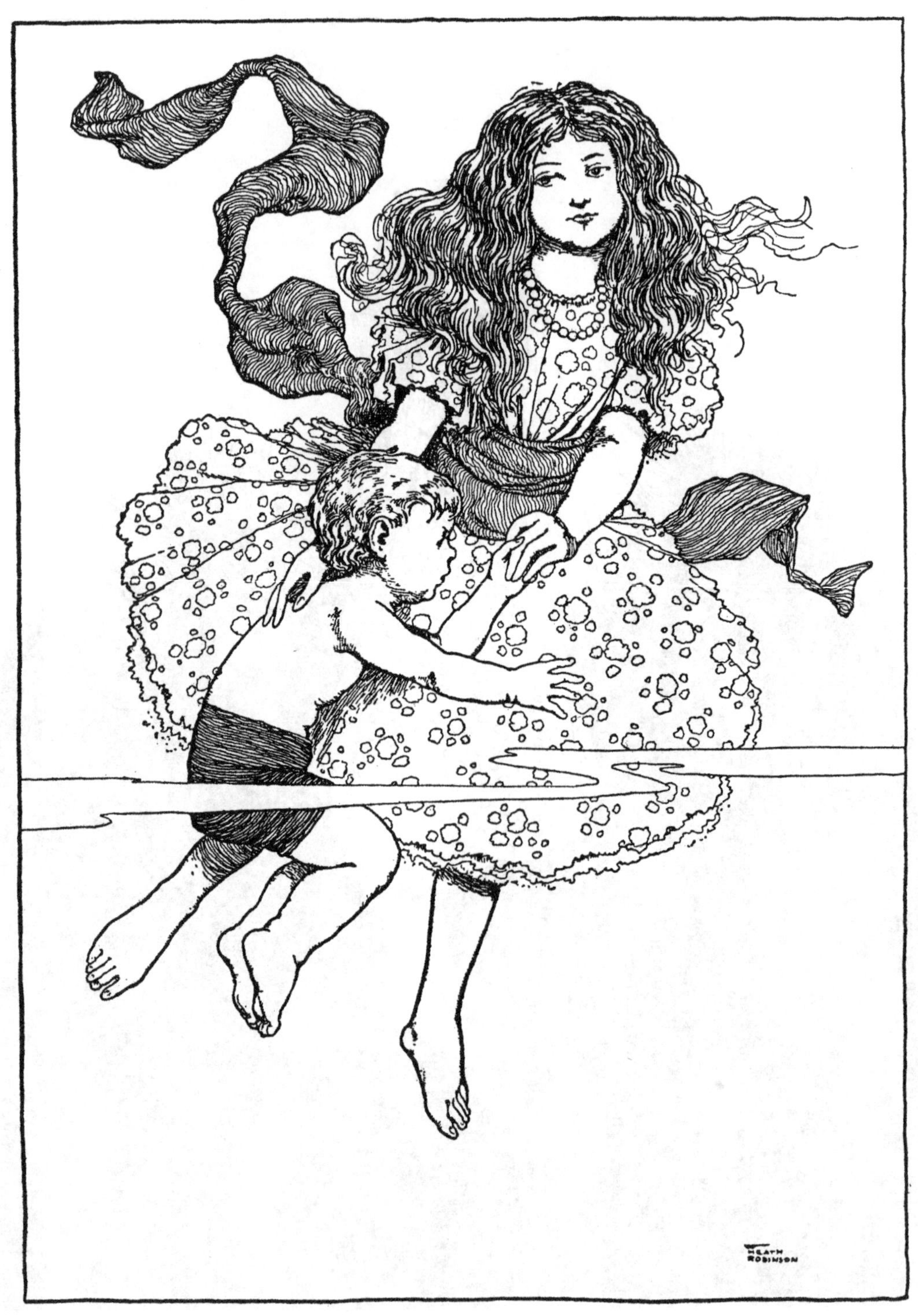

And perhaps he would never have found his way, if the fairies had not guided him.

The Water-Babies, 1915

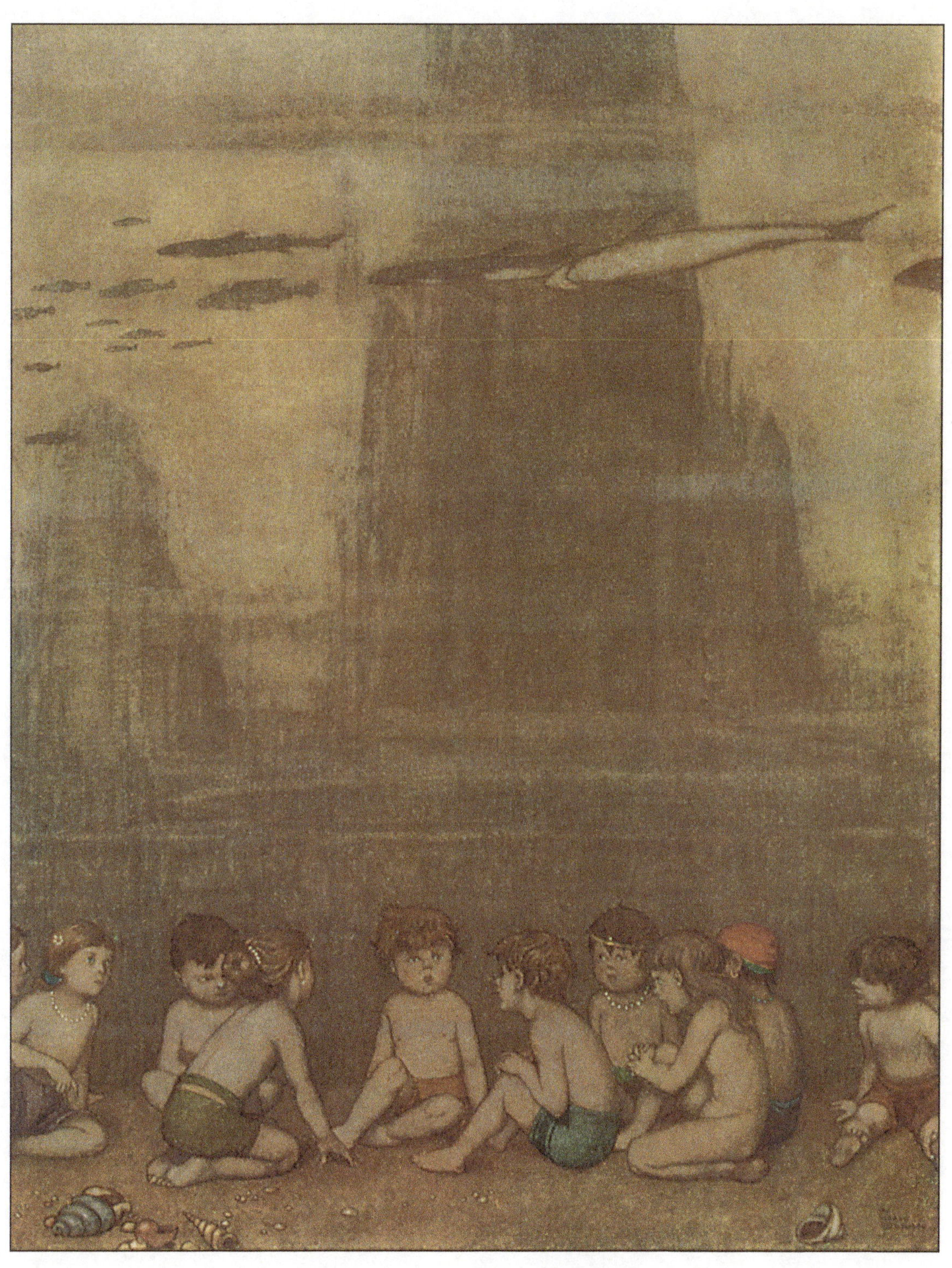

The other children warned him

The Water-Babies, 1915

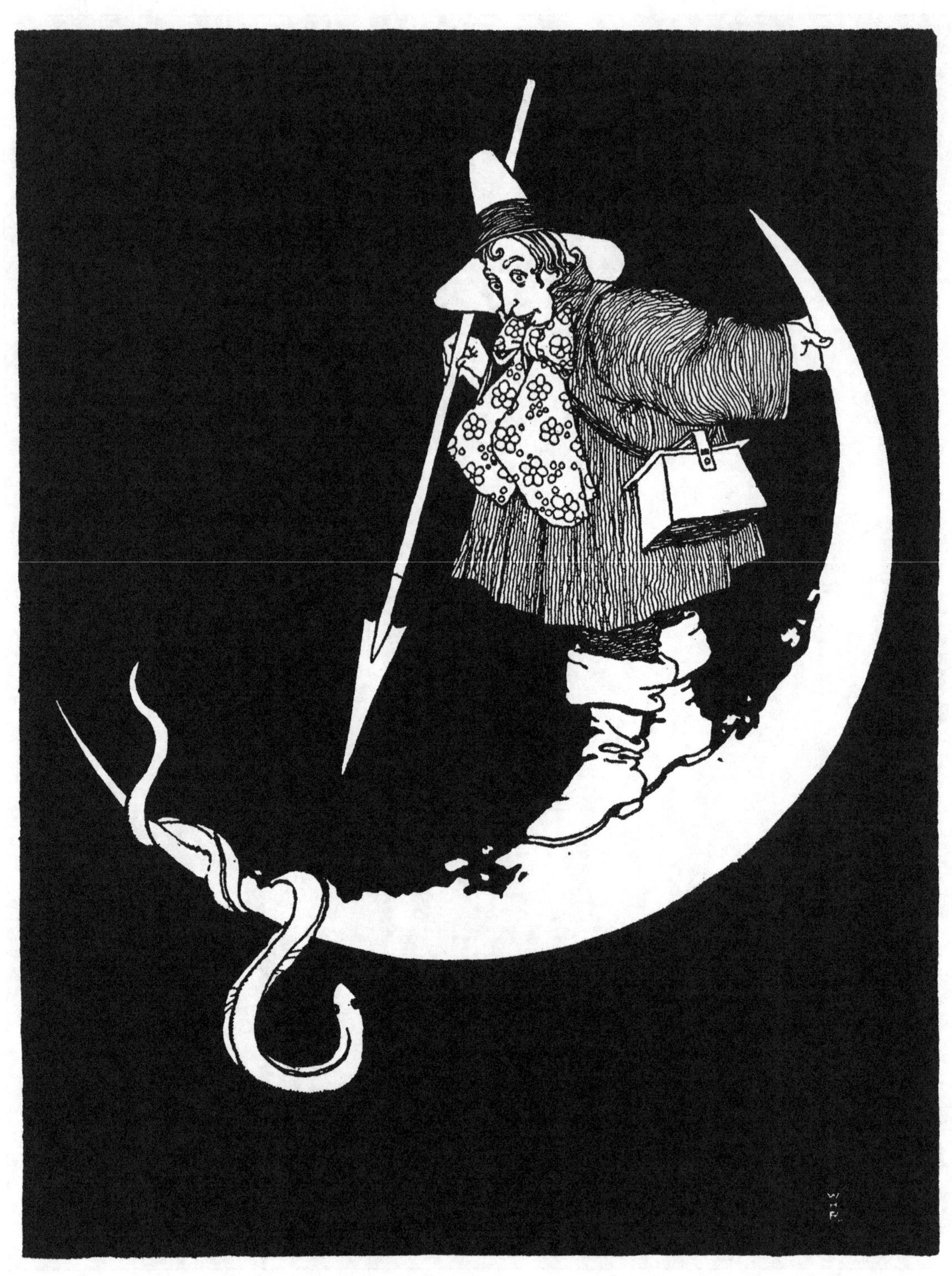

Spearing eels and sneezing

The Water-Babies, 1915

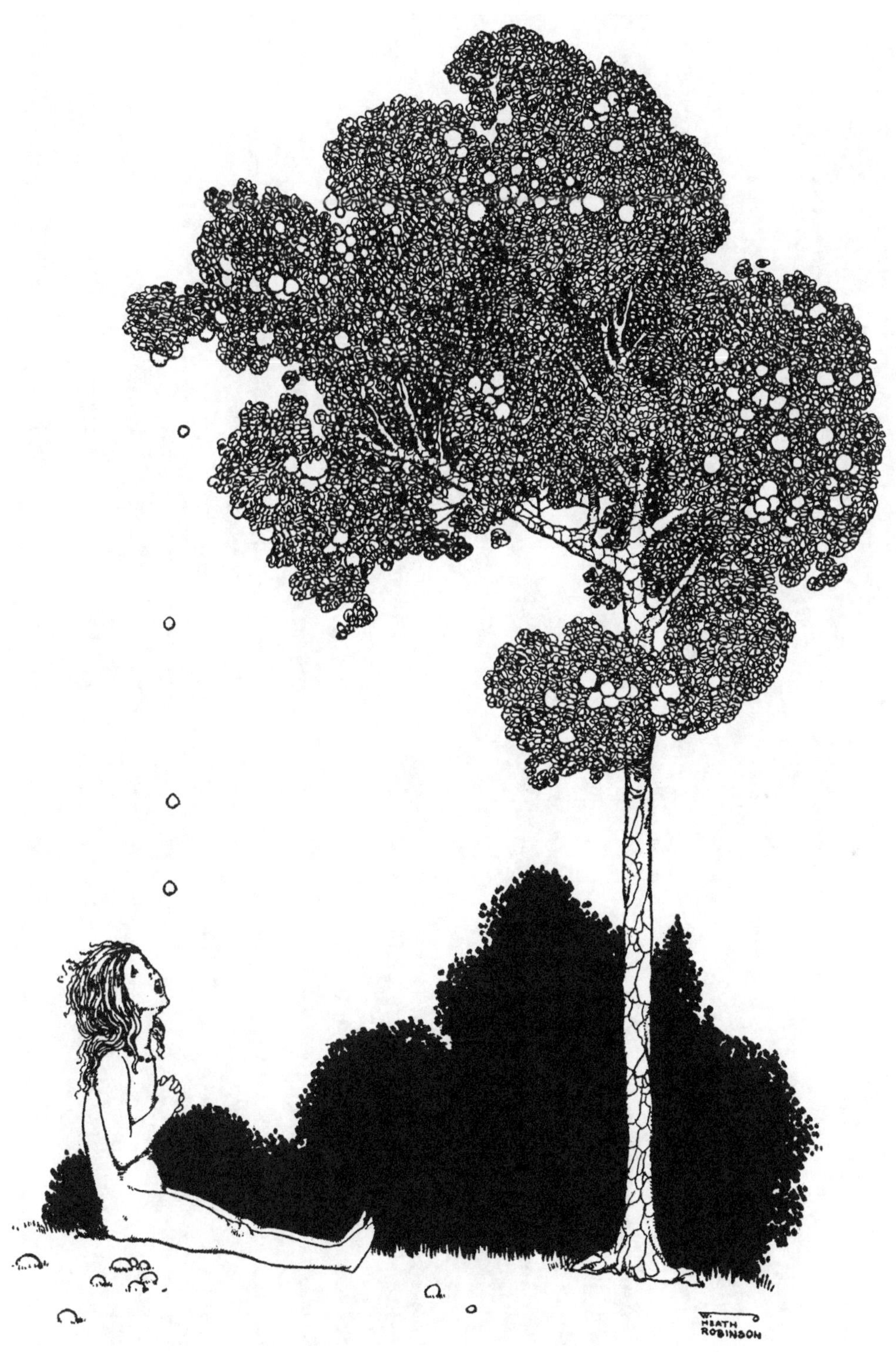

And they sat under a flapdoodle tree

The Water-Babies, 1915

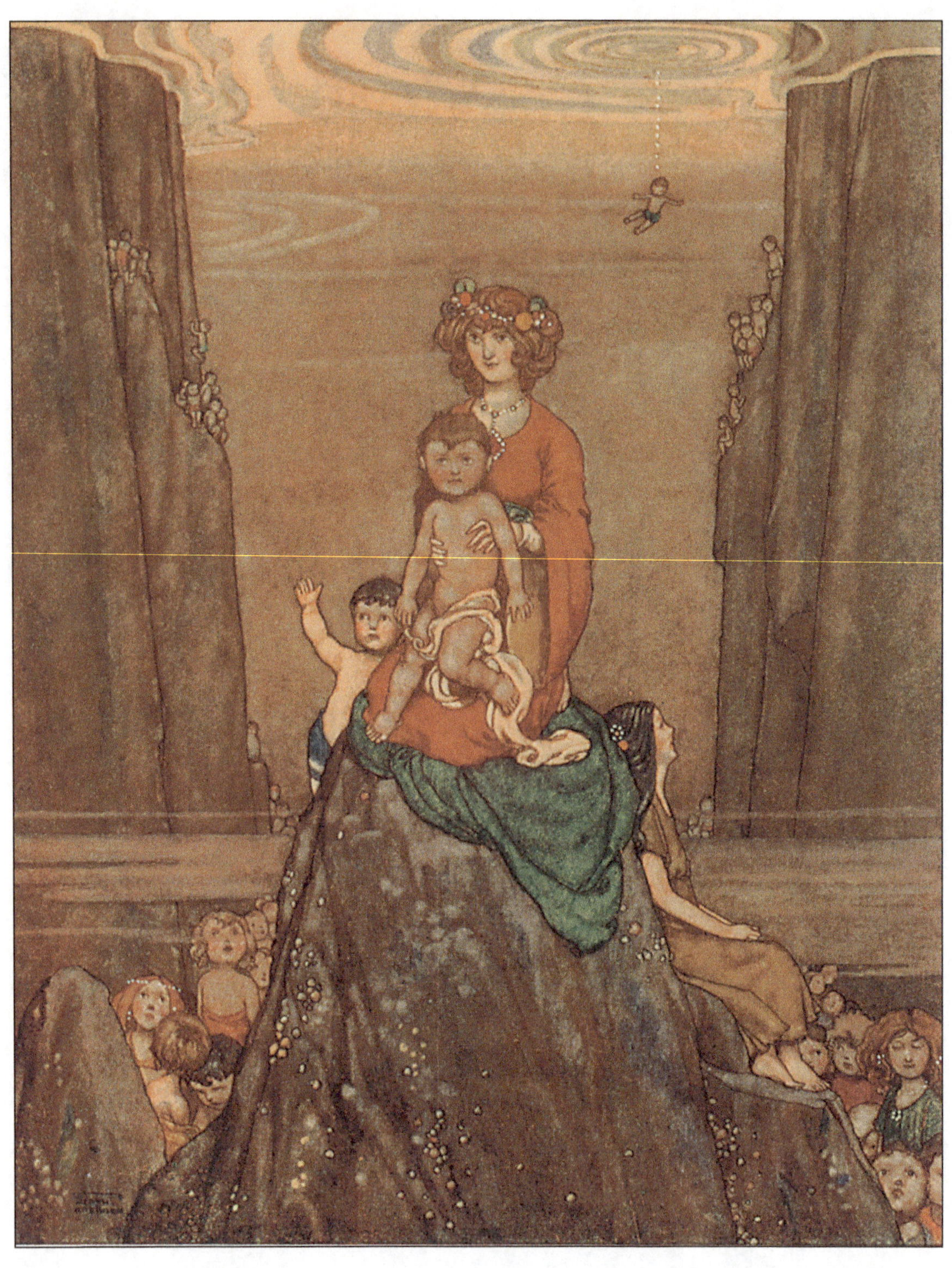

There would be a new water-baby in St. Brandan's Isle

The Water-Babies, 1915

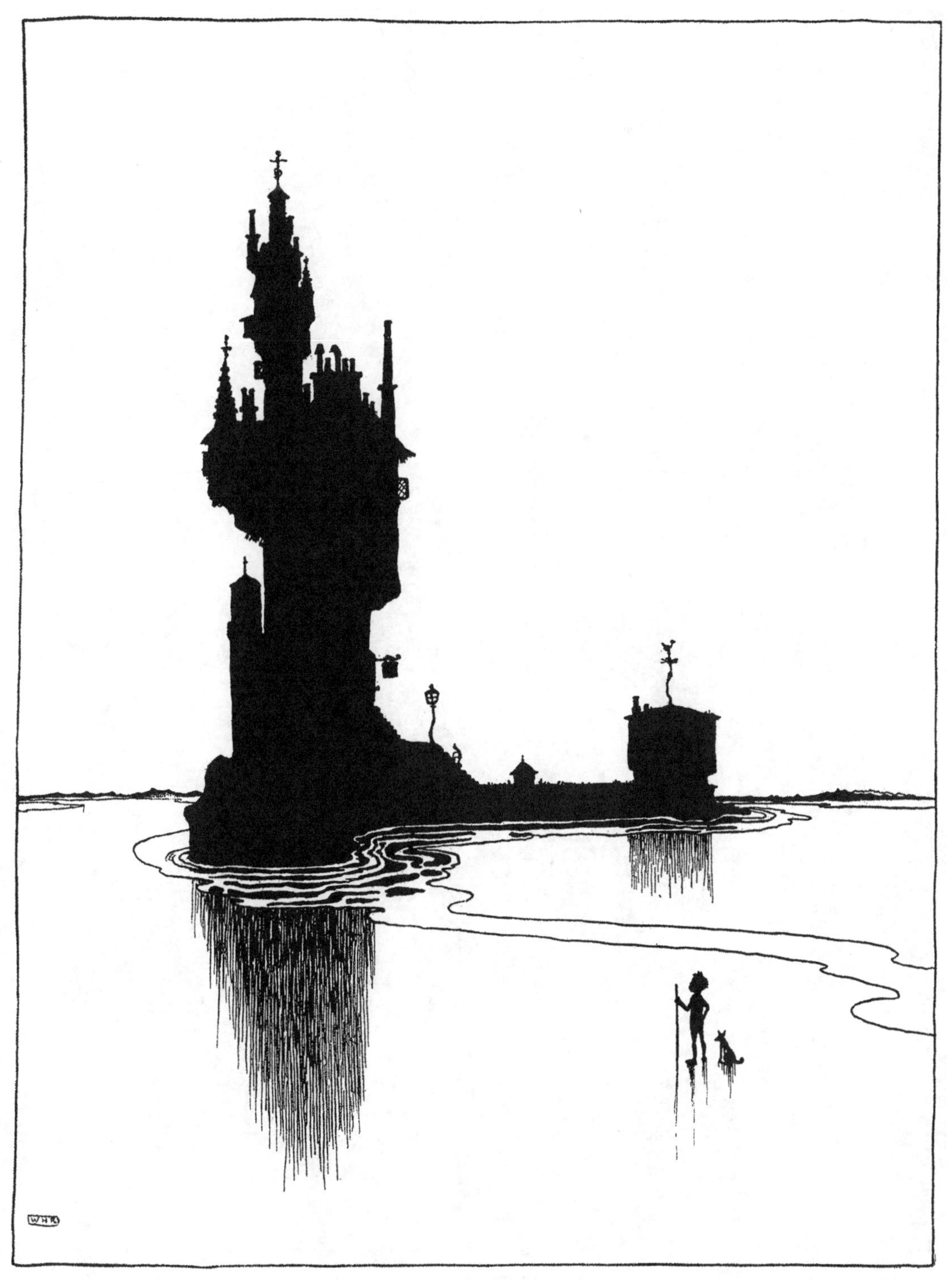

He saw before him a huge building

The Water-Babies, 1915

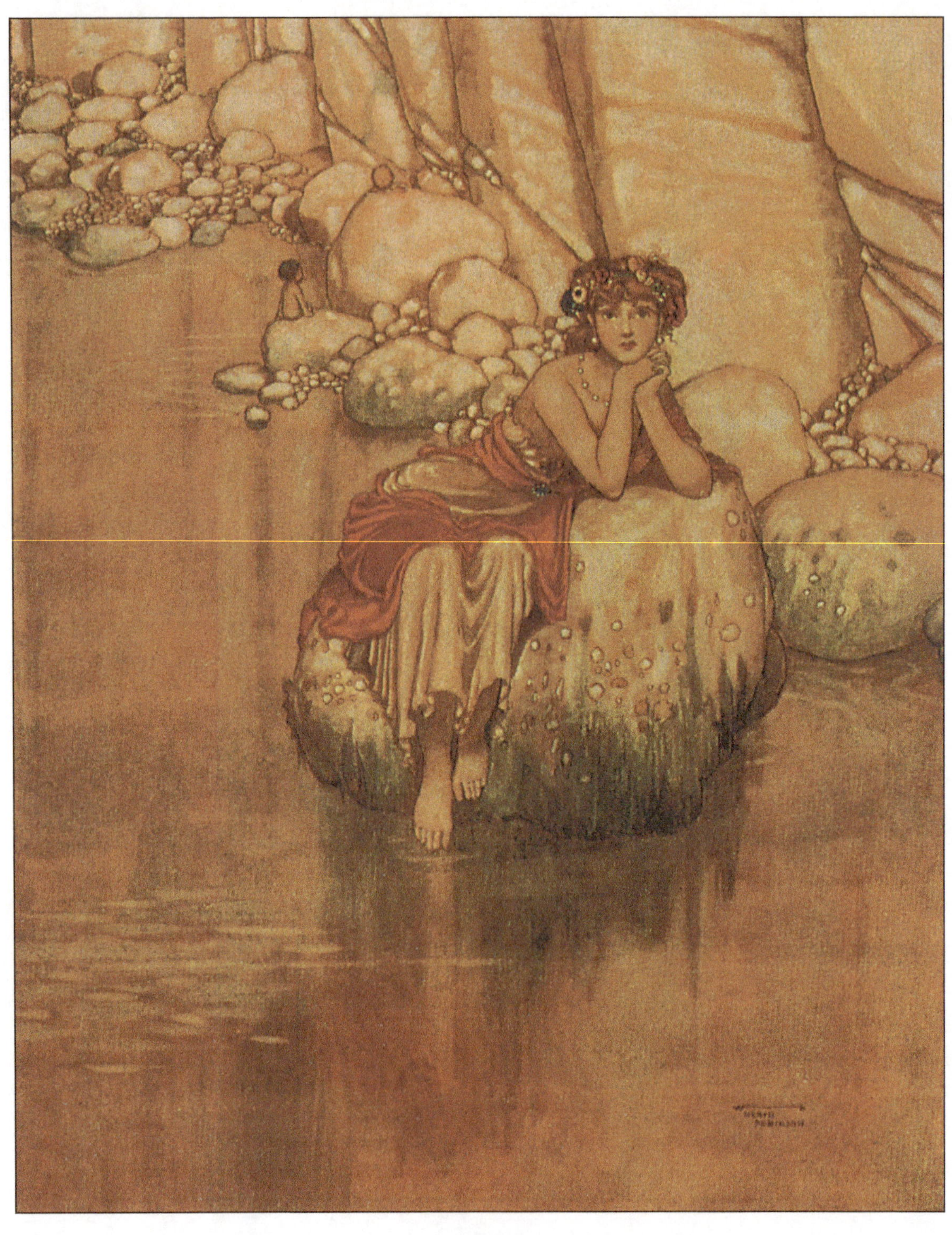

I have been sitting here waiting for you many a hundred years

The Water-Babies, 1915

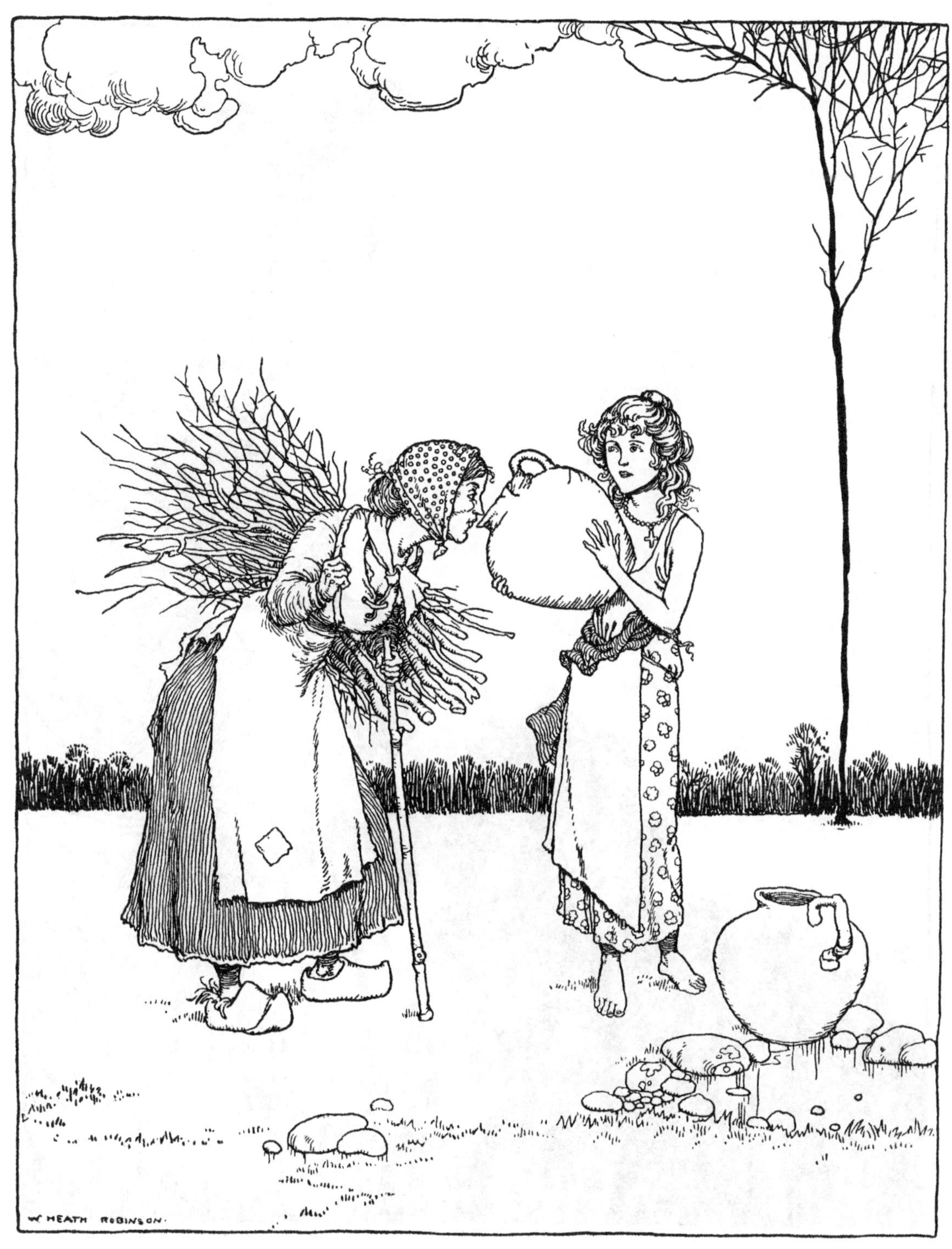

"Lifting up the jug so that she might drink the more easily"

Old-Time Stories, 1921

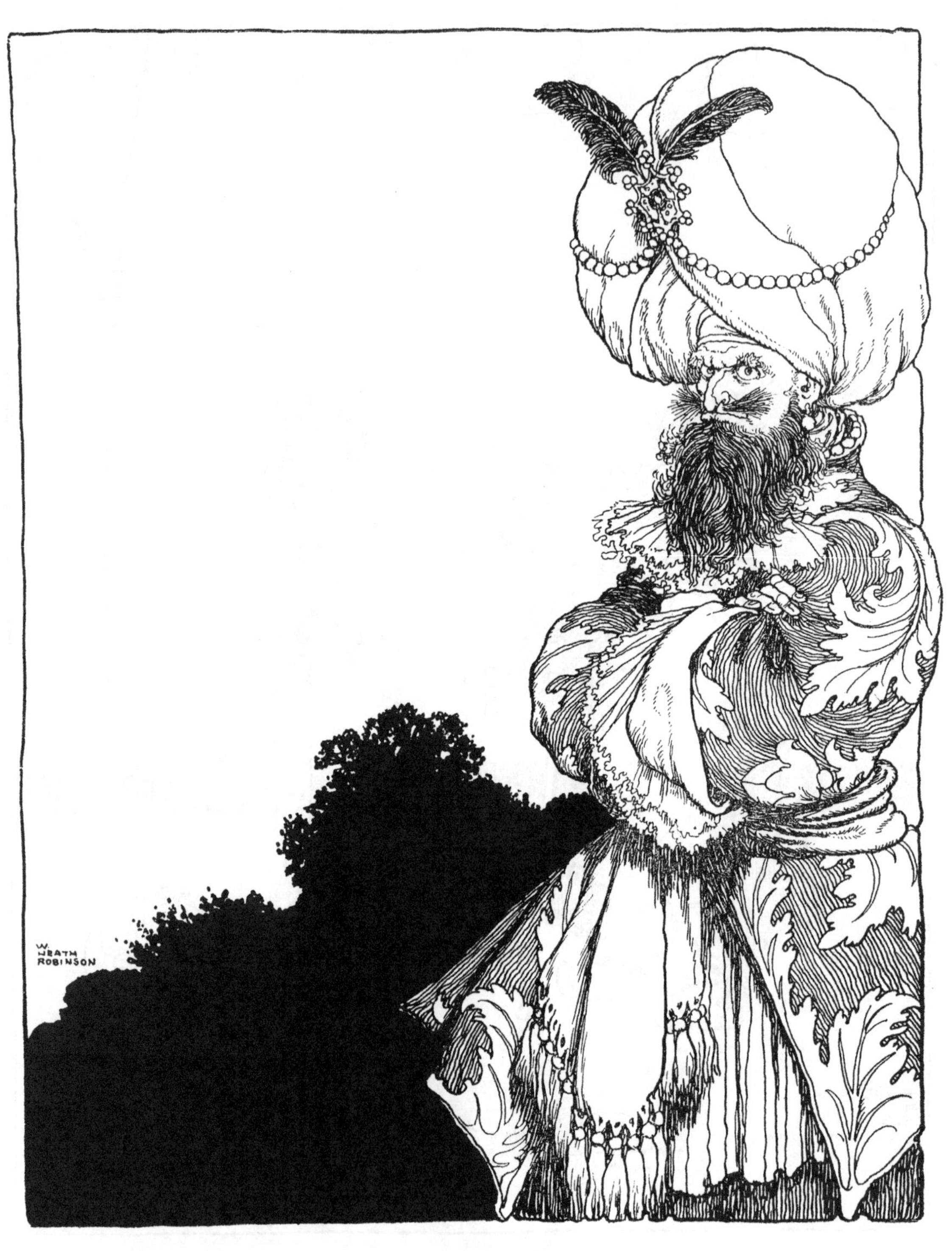

Blue Beard

Old-Time Stories, 1921

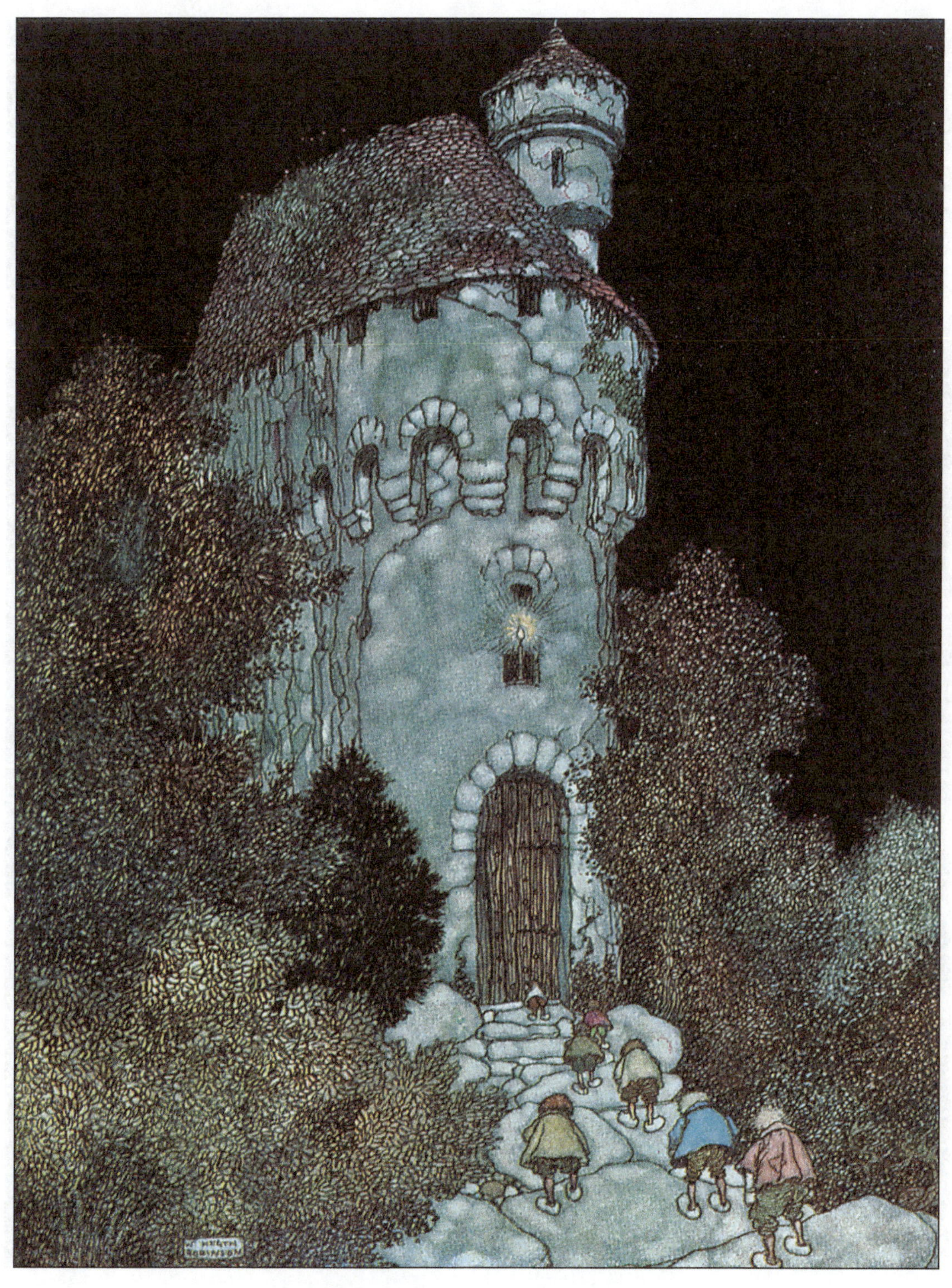

"They reached the house where the light was burning."

OLD-TIME STORIES, 1921

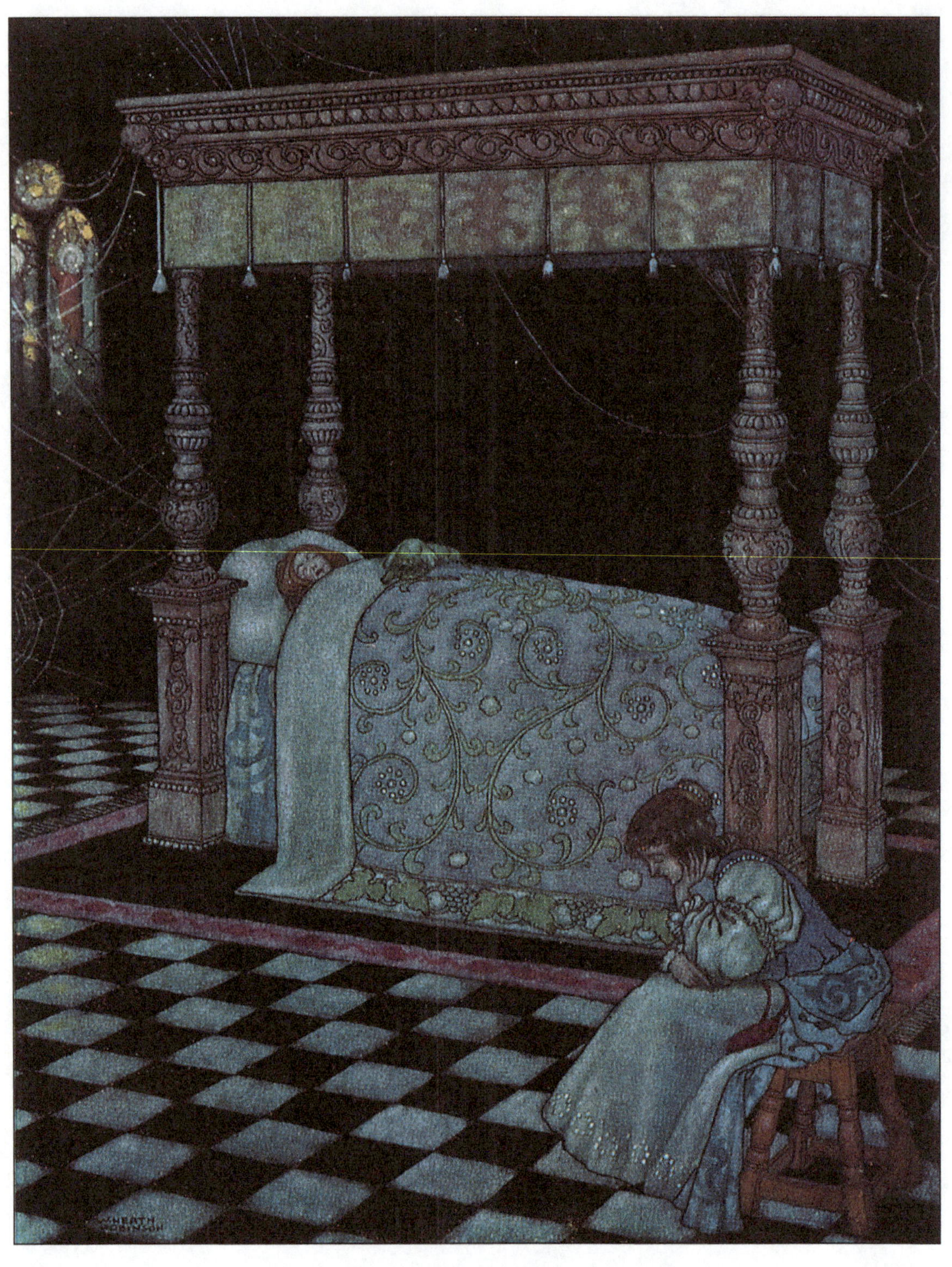

"The most beautiful sight he had ever seen"

Old-Time Stories, 1921

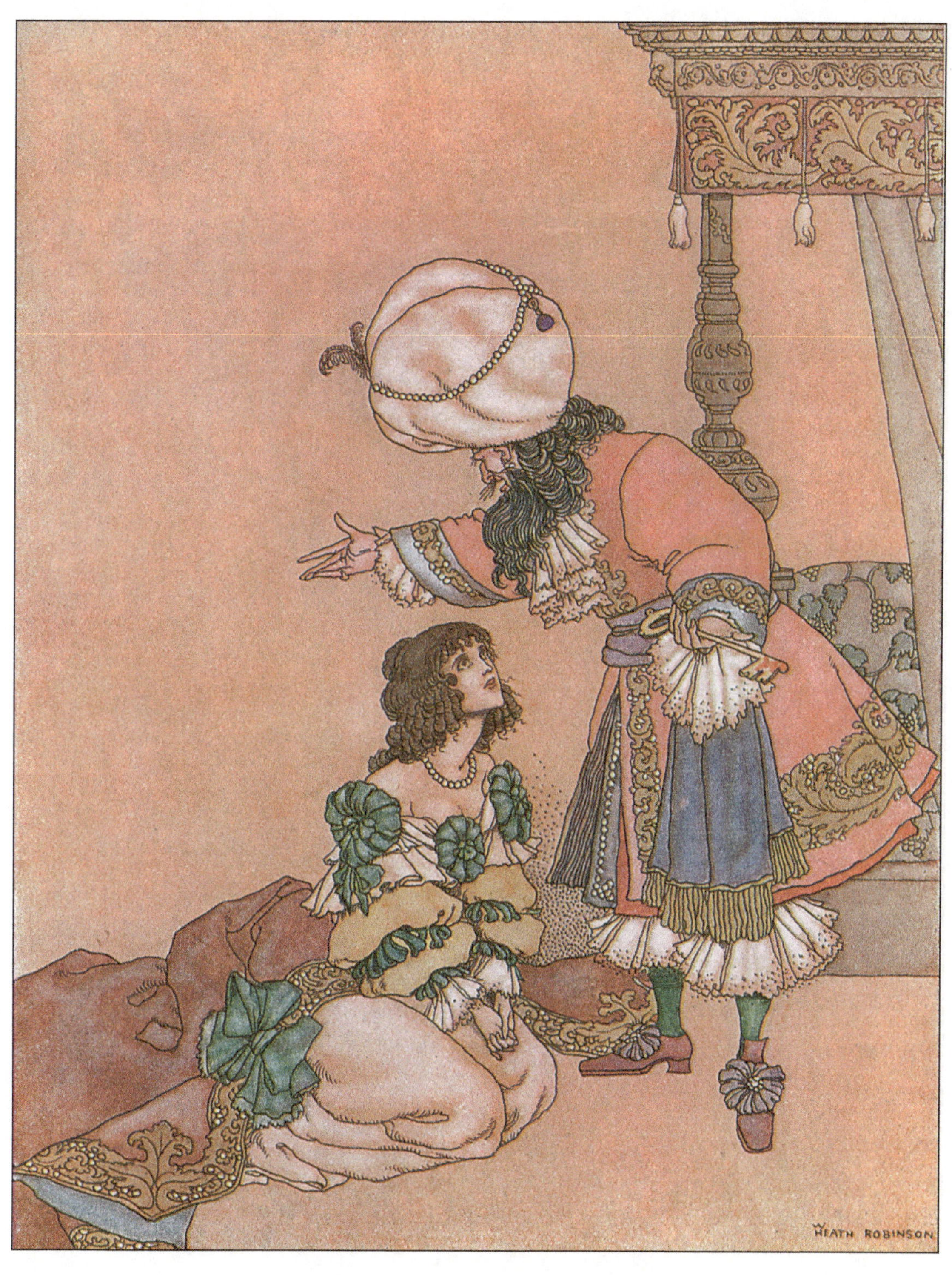

" 'You must die, madam,' he said"

Old-Time Stories, 1921

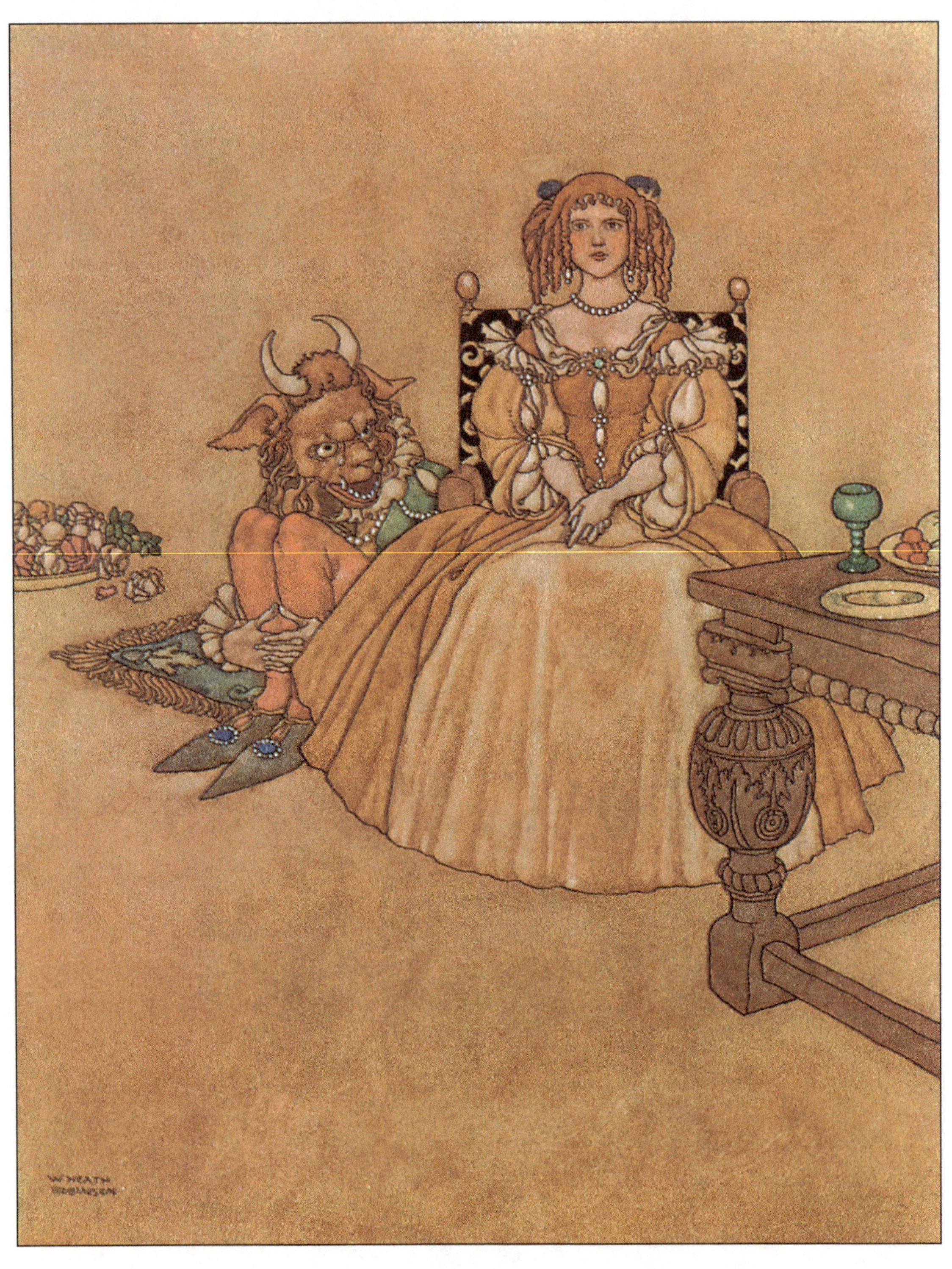

“Every evening the beast paid her a visit.”

OLD-TIME STORIES, 1921

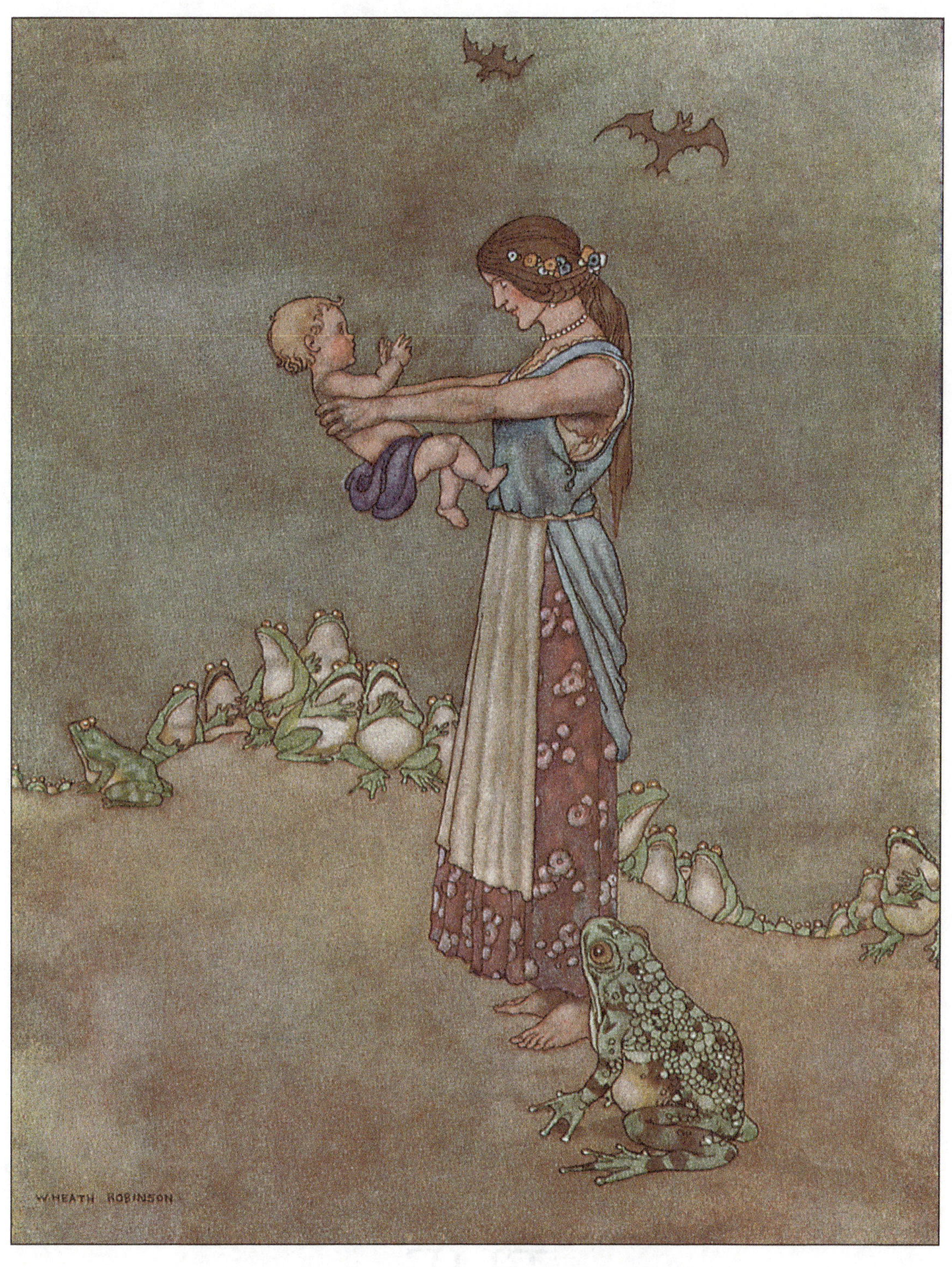

"Could your father but see you, my poor child."

OLD-TIME STORIES, 1921

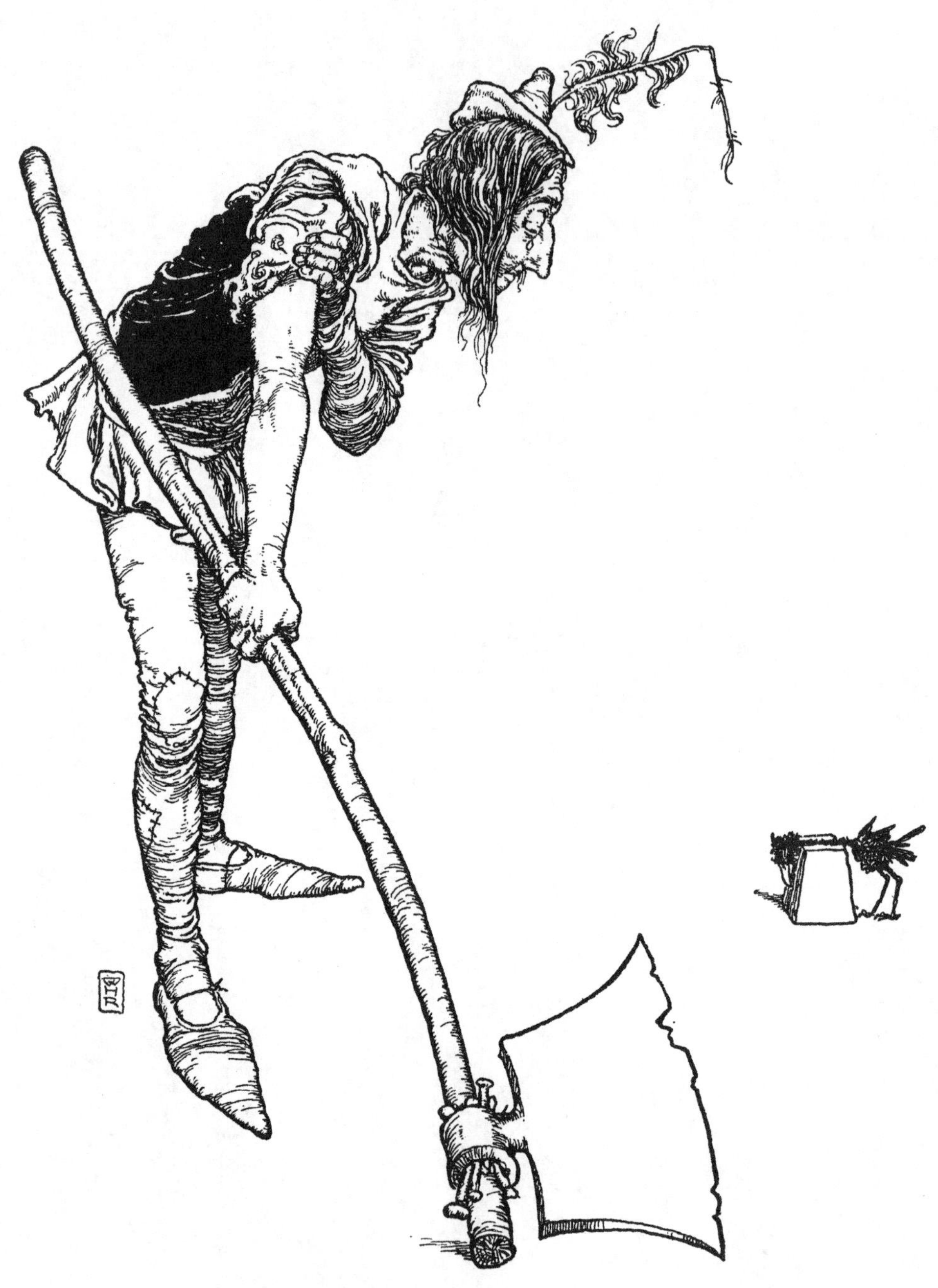

THE
END